MARLBOROUGH COUNTY, SOUTH CAROLINA

MINUTES OF THE COUNTY COURT

1785-1799

and

MINUTES OF THE COURT OF ORDINARY

1791-1821

by

Brent H. Holcomb, C.A.L.S.

Please direct all correspondence and orders to:

www.southernhistoricalpress.com
or
SOUTHERN HISTORICAL PRESS, Inc.
PO BOX 1267
375 West Broad Street
Greenville, SC   29601
southernhistoricalpress@gmail.com

Originally published: Easley, SC. 1981
Copyrighted 1981 by:
The Rev. Silas Emmett Lucas, Jr.
Easley, SC
ISBN #0-89308-298-8
All rights Reserved.
Printed in the United States of America

INTRODUCTION

This volume is one of a series of the South Carolina Minutes of the County Court. The abstracts of Marlborough (now Marlboro) County Court Minutes in this publication were made from microfilm copies of the original court minutes (S. C. Archives microfilm C258 and C566). These court minutes are not always in chronological order. The reason for this order is not clear. However, for easy use, a guide reference is placed on each page in the upper left corner.

Marlborough County was one of three counties (the other two being Darlington and Chesterfield) formed in Cheraws District in 1785. The county court was set up to record deeds, try small cases, take bastardy bonds, oversee the building and upkeep of roads, and other duties. In 1787, this court was also made a court of ordinary (present-day probate court). All such records were kept in one volume until 1791, when the court of ordinary commenced a separate volume. This volume goes through the year 1821, and for the sake of completeness, the entire volume has been abstracted and included here. In 1800, as with other counties, Marlborough County was made Marlborough District. This designation continued until the year 1868.

Prior to 1787, the probates were recorded at the seat of Cheraws District (Greeneville). Apparently, these early records (1781-1787) was lost in the Darlington Court House fire, ca. 1806. Before 1781, such records are within Charleston or Colonial South Carolina records. Two series of publications will make searching those records simpler: the four volumes of Abstracts of the Wills of South Carolina by Mrs. Caroline Moore and three volumes of Probate Records of South Carolina by Brent H. Holcomb (published by Southern Historical Press). Other records pertaining to Marlborough County can be found in Some South Carolina County Records Volume 1 (Southern Historical Press) and in Saint David's Parish, South Carolina, Minutes of the Vestry 1768-1832 Parish Register 1819-1924 (also Southern Historical Press).

Brent H. Holcomb, C. A. L. S.
Columbia, South Carolina
February 27, 1982

South Carolina   )
Marlborough County)
    At a County Court begun to be holden at Garners Bluff on Pee Dee
River for Said County on the first Monday in December agreeable to an
act of Assembly passed the 17th March 1785--It being the first court
held in the Said County.
    Present   Claudius Pegues, Geo. Hicks, Morgan Brown, Tristram Thomas,
Claudius Pegues Junr, Moses Pearson, Thomas Evans, Esquires.

The Commission of the Justices aforesaid being ordered to be read and
Recorded, the following officers were duly elected viz:
    John Wilson, clerk--sworn into office
    John Andrew, sheriff
    Thomas Lide, coroner.

Ordered that the Jury list be made out and drawn for the next court.
Ordered that the Court be adjourned till Tomorrow morning 10 oclock.

The Court met Tuesday according to adjournment. Ordered the following
persons be appointed Constables for the ensuing Year--
Aaron Knight, Nicholas Darby, John Deir, James Hodges, Daniel Cotingam,
John Evans, Wm Cherry, Jessee Johns.

Ordered that the following Persons be appointed overseers of the roads
for the ensuing Year---
James Gilespie from the State line to the forks of the road above Fills
Creek, and that all the hands above the creek except such as work on the
new ferry Road are under his direction for that wk.

Ordered that Claudius Pegues Junr & Jno Wilson be commissioners to lay
off the new Road from Lide's ferry to the State Line agreeable to an act
of Assembly and that Carney Wright be overseer for Said Road the Hands
he has to work are Colo Thomas Lide's, Faulkners, Blantons, Smiths,
Edens's, his own &c.

Nicholas Darby be overseer from the forks of the road above Fills Creek
to Colo Hicks's branch and the usual Hands to work under him (all except
Colo Thomas Lide's).

James Hodges be overseer from Hicks's Branch to Capt Pledgers Grist Mill
and the usual Hands between said places do work thereon.

Ordered that a road be opened from Kolbs ferry to barns bridge agreeable
to an act of Assembly Thomas Evans Esquire, Jon David and Thos Ammons
be commissioners to Superentend the same.

Daniel Welch be overseer from the ferry aforesaid to where it crosses the
main road, that the Hands of Kolbs Estate and Jessee Wilds do work under
his direction and also all the Hands above the creek road and what is in-
side of the marshes below Mrs. Jones's and up to Crooked Creek &c.

Ordered that James Smart be overseer from Kolb's ferry to where it falls
into the Road near Capt Cogdells and that all the Hands Below that and
the River except those that have been ordered on the other roads do work
under him.

Ordered that Mackey McNat be overseer from Pledgers Grist Mill to the
Causeway branch all the hands below Mrs. Jones's outside of the marsh
with all the Hands, three miles back from said Road do work under him.

Ordered that William Evans be overseer from the Causeway branch (the upper side) to the upperside of three Creeks with all the Hands that usually work on Said Road

Ordered that Wm Whitfield be overseer from the upper side of the three creeks to the five mile post with the Usual Hands.

Ordered that Thomas Conn be overseer from Browns Mill to Brockingtons ferry and to Colo Bentons ferry taking the Hands that formerly worked thereon.

Ordered that John Whitington be overseer from the five mile post to the District Line with the usual Hands.

Ordered that Wm Councell be appointed overseer of the road from the Beaver Dam near Mrs. Irby's crossing D. Robertson's Saw Mill and to ex- tend the Said Road to the new road to the most convinent way taking all the Hands within two miles bound---of Crooked Creek Bridge.

Ordered that Capt Danl Sparks be overseer of the Road from Barns Bridge to main road with all the Hands adjacent not ordered on other Roads.

Ordered that the Clerk do Issue Orders to the overseers appointed.

Ordered that the clerk make out a certificate that John Andrews Esquire was duly Elected Sheriff of the County.

Aaron Knight and James Hodges came into Court and were sworn Constables.

Ordered that Morgan Brown and Claudius Pegues Junr Esquires be appointed to inspect the Clerks office.

Ordered that the clerk administer the oath to the Sheriff which was done.

Ordered that the clerk do enter into Bond with good and sufficient Securities for the true performance of his duty--which was done accor- dingly and the Bond ordered to be recorded.

Ordered that the Publick Buildings be erected on two acres of Ground given by Tristram Thomas Esqr. within a quarter of a Mile of his dwelling House and that Geo Hicks, Morgan Brown, Thomas Evans and Tristram Thomas are requested to draw a plan of the Public Buildings and contract with an undertaker.

A Deed of Conveyance from John Brown to John Husband of 90 acres was proved by John Speed Esq; and ordered to be recorded. Also one ditto of 110 acres from said Brown to John Wilson and was ordered to be recorded.

A Deed of Partition from Mary Gordon to Wm Gordon of 200 acres of land was proved by the oath of Morgan Brown Esqr and John Husbands and was ordered to be recorded.

A Deed of Partition from Wm Gordon to Mary Gordon of 100 acres of land was proved by the oath of Morgan Brown and John Husbands and ordered to be recorded.

Ordered that Court do adjourn untill Court in Course.

March term. The Court met according to adjournment. Ordered that the Jury be Drawn, which was done accordingly. Present Claudius Pegues Senr, Geo. Hicks, Morgan Brown, Claud. Pegues Junr., Moses Pearson.

Ordered that the Sheriff commission be read in open court, which was done and ordered to be recorded.

Ordered that the Grand Jurors be Drawn-- Jurors Names Viz.

Daniel Sparks, Daniel Walsh, James Gilespie, Thomas Vining, George
Cherry, Wm Councel, Mackey McNatt, Emanuel Cox, Margness Corgill, Wil-
liam Furnis, Jesse Bethea, Joseph Ellison, John Pledger, Wm Evans, Wm
Thomas. Ordered that the Grand Jury be Sworn.

Ordered that the Petit Jurors be Empaneld. Petit Jurors Names Present,
viz: Gully Moore, Kader Keaton, Samuel Chalker, Robert Purnal, James
Due, Thos Ammonds, Thos Huckaboy, Joel McNatt, John Hillson, John Lee,
James Spears, John Whittington, John Beasley, Hubard Stephens, Short
Long, Light Townshend, John Askew, Wm Cherry, Carney Wright, Robert
Blair, Geo Trawick, Benj. David, Ambrose Forster, and Wm Gordon.
Absent Jethro Moore, Timothy Darby, Joseph Townshend, Lewis Blalock.

Ordered that Doctor Nathan Leavenworth be required and is hereby authorised to prefer Several bills of Indictment as may be necessary at this
or any Court in the County, untill there can be an attorney procured.

Ordered that a certificate which produced in Court by Claudius Pegues
Junr Setting forth that John Coulson had taken the oath of Aligeance
and became a citizen, be Recorded.

A Deed of Conveyance from Hubard Stephens and James Gilispie for 50 acres
of land was proved in open Court by Wm Gordon and James Due, and ordered
to be recorded.

A Deed of Conveyance from Will Reid to Hubard Stephens for 50 acres of
land was proved in open Court by Claudius Pegues Junr and ordered to be
recorded.

William Gordon appeared in Open Court and acknowledged a deed of conveyance from himself to Morgan Brown Esquire of 200 acres of land, and
ordered to be recorded.

Ordered that Court do adjourn till tomorrow morning 10 Oclock.

The Court met according to adjournment. Justices present Claudius
Pegues Senr, Geo Hicks, Morgan Brown, Moses Pearson, Tristram Thomas,
Esqrs. Ordered that the Grand Jury be called.

Presentments of the Grand Jury.

We present as a grievance Luke Prior for keeping and lately having kept
a disorderly house at or near Cashaway ferry--and for damages done a
certain old Lewis by the said Pryors and others.

We present as a Grievance Wm Hardwick for living in adultery with Elizth
Rolo.

We present Rebecca McCormick for having lately a bastard child. Ordered
that the presentment of Rebecca McCormick for having a bastard child be
prefered to Maj. Thomas to bind her over.

We present Margaret Cotingham for lately having a bastard child.

We present the aforesaid Luke Pryor for lately having made Several blas-
phemous Expressions on the Sabath day at the House of Mr. Simion Woodruff.

Ordered that the County Attorney prefer a Bill of Indictment against
Luke Pryor for blasphemy agreeable to a presentment...he be held to
bail for his appearance at the next Court.

We present Welcome Hodges for neglecting his duty as Constable in not
returning a warrant to the proper officer which was Granted against a
certain Able Lewis by Capt Thomas Evans and for the said Hodges having
Suffered the said Lewis to be abused whilst in his Custody.

Ordered that the County Attorney prefer a bill of Indictment against

March term 1786
<u>March term 1786</u>

Welcome Hodges....

We present as a Grievance that the Laws against drunkenness and Profhain
cursing and Swearing more Strickly executed by those in Authority for
the want whereof we apprehend the morals are much corrupted.

And we do return our thanks to the Honorable Bench for there Judicious
charge given to this Jury at the opening of the Session and do request
that the Same be printed in the Public papers.
1 March 1786.

Ordered that the Sheriff take Luke Pryor into Custody or hold him to
Bail for his appearance at the next Court to be held for this County.
And that the County Atty do prefer bills of Indictment against him for
the several Crimes....

Ordered that the County Attorney prefer a bill of Indictment against
Wm Hardwick for the crime mentioned in the presentments....

Ordered that the Overseers of the Roads appointed last Court continue
untill next March court.

Ordered that Wm Legett and Jesse Bethea be additional commissioners on
the Roads from Kolbs ferry to Barns's Bridge.

Ordered that the Court do adjourn till Court in Course.

Monday 5 Day of June 1786. The Court met according to adjournment.
Magistrates Present Claudius Pegues, Geo Hicks, Morgan Brown, Tristm
Thomas, Claudius Pegues Jur., Thomas Evans.

Ordered that all the Recognizances (except Wm Bennets and Rebecca Mc-
Cormicks)be continued over until next Court.

Ordered that on the return of a writ non est Inventus Colo. Geo Hicks
vs Jerimiah Clark there be an attachment Issued against the property
of Said Clerk.

Ordered that James Moore be appointed a deputy Sheriff and approved off
by the Court and the oath was administered to him accordingly.

Ordered that Wm Bennet do pay into the Hands of the Church Wardens for
St. Davids Parish or to Rebecca McCormick the sum of nine shillings, and
four pence & quarter for the maintinance of a bastard child which the
said Bennet had by the said Rebecca McCormick and that he give security
to keep the child from being chargable to the Parish.

September 4th Court met according to adjournment. Magistrates Present
Geo Hicks, Tristram Thomas, Moses Pearson, Thos Evans.

Ordered that the Jury be Drawn for the next Court.
Ordered that the present Jury be empanneld and Sworn.

Joshua David appeared in Open Court and acknowledged a deed of Conveyance
for 100 acres to Tristram Thomas and ordered to be recorded.

A Deed of Conveyance from Thomas Bingham to Philip Pledger was produced
in Court for 100 acres of land provin before Claudius Pegues Esquire
the 5 day of November 1774 which deed was ordered to be recorded.

Geo Hicks appeared in open court and acknolwedged release for 50 acres
of Land, to Drury Robertson, and ordered to be Recorded.

A Deed of Conveyance from Philip Pledger to Jesse Vining for 100 acres
of land was proved in Court by Joseph Pledger and Wm Pledger and ordered
to be recorded.

Geo Hicks at the same time acknowledged one other tract of land to the said Drury Robertson for 100 acres and ordered to be recorded.

Edward Feagin produced a deed of Conveyance proved the 25th July 1778 before Abl Kolb Esqr by Aaron Daniel from Mathew Whitfild to said Feagin for 250 acres of land which was ordered to be recorded.

Philemon Thomas came into open Court and acknowledged a deed of conveyance to Aaron Knight for 209 acres of land and ordered to be Recorded.

Ordered that Demsy Goodwin and Sarah Barringtine be and are sentenced to pay each ℔ 5 proc. money by tomorrow 10 Oclock being both convicted of Bastardy and that the said Goodwin do pay $2 quarterly to said Sarah to maintain the said Bastard child and give security to the Clerk of the County....

Thomas Harringdine appeared in open Court and acknoledged a deed of conveyance of 250 acres of land to James Cook and ordered to be recorded.

A Deed of Conveyance from Burgess Williams to Thos. Harringdine for 75 acres of Land was proved by Joshua David and Wm Hodges and ordered to be recorded.

Philemon Thomas appeared in open Court and executed & acknowledged a deed of conveyance for 150 acres of land to Wm Thomas. the same was ordered to be recorded.

Danl Sparks appeared in open court and executed a deed to Alexr Beverly of 50 acres of land and acknowledged the same and ordered to be recorded.

Geo: Trawick appeared in Open Court and acknowledged a deed of conveyance for 150 acres of land to Wm Townshend son of John Townshend and ordered the same to be recorded.

And at the same time one other tract of 100 acres to Benj Townshend and ordered to be recorded

James McNat was found Guilty of Stealing a Stear from Aaron Pearson, by the Grand Jury and was acquited by the Petit Jury which was recorded.

Welcom Hodges and Josiah David appeared in Open Court and proved a deed from Joseph Gains to James Stubbs for 250 acres of land and ordered to be recorded.

Ordered, Geo Hicks having by attachment obtain a Judgment against Jerimiah Clark for ℔ 40 0 8 old South cur'y and ℔ 33 12/ Like money with cost of Suit which was ordered to be recorded.

Ordered that the Court do adjourn untill tomorrow 10 Oclock.

Tuesday 5 Day Sept 1786. Court met according to adjournment. Magistrates present Geo Hicks, Trist. Thomas, Moses Pearson, Thomas Evans, Esqr.

Mackey McNat appeared in Open Court and produced a lease and release from Wm Auston to him for 250 acres of Land which was ordered to be Recorded.

A Petition and Summons Darby Smith Hart against Edward Smith was called over, the parties not being ready for tryal, Ordered the same be continued over untill next court.

Wm Barringtine being Bound over for Hog Stealing the Grand Jury found No Bill against him.

James McNatt being indicted over for Stealing a Cow Hide the Grand Jury found a Bill. The Petit Jury found him Guilty. Ordered, James McNatt between the hours of two and five Oclock receive 25 lashes on his bare back well laid on.

Ordered that Abbegal Pouncey, and Ann David and Ann Terril be Bound over
by the County Attorney to appear at the next court to answer for Bastardy.
and Wm Bodyford for adultry be bound over Likewise.

Ordered that Carney Wright have a didimus Directed to two Magistrates
in the State of Georgia to obtain a Title of land from Rob Reed a resident
of that state at Present and that the Clerk do the same.

Ordered that Silas Pearce pay to Edward Jackson the sum of Ł 5 sterling
ti being money from Pearse to Peter Butler obtained by attachment against
said Butler in the Hand of Said Silas Pearce.

Trist. Thomas appeared in Open Court and acknowledged a deed of Conveyance
to Isam Hodges for 80 acres of land and ordered to be recorded.

Joseph and John Pledger acknowledged a Conveyance of land to Trist Thomas
which was ordered to be recorded.

Trist Thomas acknowledged a deed from him to Joseph Pledger for ___ acres
and ordered to be recorded.

Ordered that James McNat being found guilty of Stealing one Slaughter hide
have 25 lashes on the bare back well laid on and that the Sheriff do put
the same in execution at five Oclock this day.

Ordered that a Goal be Built by the Commissioners with all Dispatch on the
Ground laid off for the use of the Court House for said County with two
rooms 10 feet Square & do pitch inclosed by 2 walls of Loggs with a vacan-
cy of 6 inches filled in with loon timber.

Ordered that Court do adjourn untill Court in Course.

Court met according to adjournment. Monday 4 Dec. 1786. Ordered that
the Jury be drawn for the next Court. Majestrates Present Geo Hicks,
Morgan Brown, Trist. Thomas, Thomas Evans, Moses Pearson, Esquires.

Jury was called and Sworn to business.

A Deed of Conveyance from Samuel Wise to Edward Crosland and was produced
in Court of 300 acres of land & was ordered to be recorded.

Thomas Quick produced a deed of 125 acres from James Hicks to   Quick
which was ordered to be recorded.

Ordered that a Bill of Sale from Saraar. McTyre and Robt McTyre to Samuel
Brown for a negroe wench be recorded in the Clerks Office it being duly
proved in open Court by the oath of Richard Whittington.

A Deed for Jarrot Whittington to Ephraim Whittington for 133 acres was
proved in Court by the oaths of Richd. & Barnet Whittington and ordered
to be recorded.

A Deed from Geo Traywick to Jacob Green of 150 acres was acknowledged in
Open Court and ordered to be recorded.

A Deed from John Stubbs Senr to Daniel Sparks for 150 acres was acknowledged in Open Court and ordered to be recorded.

A Deed from Peter Smith to Mathew Whitfield for 300 acres was produced in
open Court and ordered to be recorded.

W. Faulkner Esqr. appeared in Court and produced his admission to the bar
the Superior Courts of this State. It is therefore ordered that the sd.
W. Faulkner Esqr. be admitted to the bar of this Court...further ordered
that Wm Faulkner Esqr. be appointed County attorney and that he be allowed
Ł 30 to be paid...for every Bill of indictment one Guinea to be paid by
the delinquent.

<u>Dec. term 1786</u>

Ordered that the Court do adjourn til tomorrow 10 Oclock.

Tuesday 5 of Dec 1786. The Court met according to adjournment. Magistrates present Geo Hicks, Tris Thomas, Thos Evans, Moses Pearson, Esqr.

Ordered that Jesse John and Rhoda Townshend being convicted of Bastardy of a Mail child that the aforesaid John pay to said Rhoda 4/8 quarter to maintain the aforesaid child untill it arrive to the age of Ten... aforesaid Jess John and Rhoda Townshend give sufficient bond....

Ordered Mathew Whitfield, Samuel Sparks and John Frazier, recognazances be forfeited and these bonds be immediately prosecuted.

State vs Wm Bodyford for Hog Stealing. Guilty.

Ordered that the court do adjourn till tomorrow morning 10 Oclock.

Wednesday 6 of Dec. 1786. The court met according to adjournment. Magistrates present Geo Hicks, Tris. Thomas, Moses Pearson and Thos Evans.

John Wilson vs Hubard Stephens for plaintiff Ł 11 s 17 d 8.

James Cook appeard in Open Court and acknowledged a deed of 100 acres to Dixon Pearse which was ordered to be recorded.

VINING vs PLEDGER. Ordered that this case continue over untill next court term--the defendant paying the costs that shall be accrued by such continuance.

Thos & Ann Stephens vs Thos Pearce. Jury found for the Plaintiff. A negroe winch Milly with her ofspring with the bed and furniture
                                        Luke Pryor, fm.

Aaron Daniel produced a deed in Court from Thomas Harmon to John Daniel for 100 acres which was ordered to be recorded.

Darby Smith Hart vs Edwd Smith. decree for the Plaintiff Ł 2 3 4 costs.

Aaron Daniel appeared in Court and acknowledged a deed of 20u acres to Jesse Wilds which was ordered to be recor'd.

Jesse Wilds proved two indentures of Winny Scotts by the oaths of James Moore and Geo Wilds which was order'd to be recor'd.

Isam Hodges vs Pnepsilla Chamless and James James. The Jury found for the defendents.

Ordered that the Court do adjourn till tomorrow 10 Oclock.

Thursday 7 Dec. 1786. Court met according to adjournment. Majestrates Present Geo Hicks, M. Brown, Trist. Thomas, Esquires.

State vs John Frazier. Bag Stealing--larceny. Guilty. Luke Pryor, fm. It is ordered that Frazier be conveyed to an open place in the face of the Court and receive 25 Lashes on the bare back well laid on.

Ordered that Execution be Staid in the Case of the Judgment obtained Pearce vs Stephens and a new tryal next Court.

Ammons vs Frazier Attachment. Frazier confesses Judgment Ł 10 10 with costs.

Wade vs Cook Attachment. Confess Judgment for Ł 15 10 11 with costs.

Burgess Williams vs Abram Cook attachment. Judgment for Plaintiff Ł 10 clk fees pd.

Dec. term 1786

John Walsh vs Jesse Wilds. Ordered that the writ be quashed and the plaintiff non suited.

Thomas Boid vs Isam Hodges. Plaintiff non suited 5/ and costs.

Ordered that the Court do adjourn till the 1st Monday in March next.

Monday March 6th day 1787. Court met according to adjournment. Magistrates Present Trism. Thomas, Thos Evans, Moses Pearson, Esquires.

Grand Jury drawn for June term from No. 2 to 3. Mons. Parker, Richd. Whittington, Geo: Cherry, Wilm. Oats, Josp: Allison, Saml Terrill, Aaron Daniel, Jacob Buckholds, Thos Conn, Jesse Couglass, Joseph Pledger, Wm Pledger, John Pledger, Lewis Conner, Jesse Vining, Thos Dean, Dixon Pearce, Saml Wilds, and Aaron Pearson.

Petit Jury drawn from 1 to 4. Wm Gordon, Jonathon John, Barnebass Henaghan, Robt Purnal, John Beasley, James Due, James Spears, Rubin Jinkens, Jesse Baggott, John Hubard, Timothy Darby, John Knight, Darby Smith Hart, Jonah David, Thomas Herringdine, Joshua David, James Bolton, Edwd Jackson, Abner Broach, Luke Pryor, John Stroud, Wm Jordon, John Johnes G. S, Thos Summertine, Jethro Moore, Short Long, Benj Beverley, Jas. Esterling, Charles Cottingham, John Askew.

The Sherriff returns the Grand Jurors as followeth. viz. John Dyer, Wm Whitfield, Thos Harry, Jno Odum, Edward Crossland, Thos. Cochran, Mackey McNatt, Carney Wright, Wm Evans, Wm Furness, Jno Evans, Saml Sparks, Joseph Mason, Silas Pearce.

Ordered that the clerk for the County do receive a Bond from Ann Parker and Simon Parker for L 8 for the use of the County.

John Odum produced a deed from Abram Odum for 50 acres of land which was ord'd to be recorded.

Edward Crossland produced a deed of conveyance from, which he acknowledged to Levy Quick for 300 acres which was ordered to be recorded.

Moses Pearson esqr. produced a mortgage in court from Lewis Blalock for 2 negroes & Horses & c. which was order'd to be recorded.

Mathew Whitfield produced a deed of conveyance from John & Ann Frazier for 200 acres which was order'd to be recor'd.

John Frazier acknowledged a deed for 100 acres to John Carraway Hubard which was ordered to be recorded.

The Sheriff returns the Petit Jury as follows for March term 1787 viz. Light Townsend, Joseph Owens, Thos. Pearce, Jon Hillson, David Steward, Jno Stubbs Junr, Joseph Fuller, Daniel Gerring, Jas. Cook, Shadrack Fuller, James Stubbs and Jno McNatt.

Ordered that the Recognezance of Hubard Stephens and John Steward continue and Stand over until tomorrow 10 Oclock.

Wm Whitfield returnd his warrant of the road and defaulters as follows Moses Murfee 9/4 pd to the clerk.

Wm Evans returned his warrant defaulters 25--warrant renewed and the said Evans contd. the insuing Year.

James Gilispie return'd his warrant the No. of Defaulters as followith

March term 1787

	HANDS	DAYS		HANDS	DAYS
Capt Claus. Pegues	10	2	Edwd Brown	"	1
Thomas Jones self		2	Joseph Red	"	3
Saml Thomas do		3	Wm Ratcliff		2
Tris Thomas Junr do		2	John Jones		1
Philimon Thomas	1	2	Jesse Dixon		1
Joseph Brown		2	John Jones G. Stocker		1
Claudius Pegues Junr.	10	1			

William Councell Returnd his warrant and the defaulters are as followith
Lewis Stubbs 3 days. John Clark 1 day Dixon Pearce 1 hand 1 day

Mackey McNatt return his warrant defaulters none. The same overseer
continued.

James Smart return'd his warrant and defaulters as followith viz.

	HANDS	DAYS		HANDS	DAYS
Genl. McIntosh Esta.	7	4	John Knight		2
Samuel Evans	1	4	Saml Evans		3
Ann Hughs	1	4	Danl Sparks		3
Britt Goodwin		3	Miss Ells. McIntosh	2	3
Saml Wilds		4	Mathew Booth		3
David Dudley		1	Lewis Goodwin		1

James Smart contd. overseer the ensuing Year.

John David overseer in the room of Danl Walsh.

Geo Cherry proved a mortgage from Thos Stephens to said cherry for Sundry
property by the oath of Wm Branham and Isaac Purkins. which was ordered
to be recor'd.

Geo & Benj Hicks vs Wm Nichols Can Defend. confesses Judgt Ł 6 13/6 &
Intrst.

Geo Traywick acknowledged a deed for 50 acres to Mashack Ginn which was
ordered to be recorded.

Geo Traywick acknowledged a deed of 200 acres to James and Lucy Blair
which was ordered to be recorded.

A deed of conveyance from John Daniel to Isaac Purkens was proved by
Isaac Neavil and John Lee, which was order'd to be rec'd.

A deed for 125 acres from Jno Brown to Saml Brown was proved by Moses
Murfee and Isam Stroud and or'd to be recor'd.

A deed for 50 acres from Jno Brown to Samuel Brown was proved by Moses
Murfee and Isam Stroud and ordered to be recorded.

A deed from Jno Frazier to Alex Bodyford for 100 acres was acknowledged
in open court and or'd to be recor'd.

Kader Keaton acknowledged a deed for 200 acres to Jno Terrel which was
ordered to be recorded.

Kader Keaton acknowledged a deed for 200 acres to Jno Terrel which was
ordered to be recorded.

Ordered that Isaac Neavil be allowed to take out Tavern License with
giving bond according to Law.

Ordered that Benj Beverly pay 20/ sterling for disorderly behavour in
the presence of Court.

Ordered that John Stubbs do pay 20/ Stg for disorderly behavour in the
present of Court.

March term 1787

Ordered that Isaac Purkens be permitted to take out Tavern License on
giving bond according to Law.

Abner Broach proved a deed for 100 acres by Wm Nichols and Thomas Pearce
which was ordered to be recor'd.

Ordered that Court do adjourn till Tomorrow 10 Oclock.

Tuesday 6 March 1787. The Court met according to adjournment. Magistrates
present Geo Hicks, Trist Thomas, Moses Pearson, Thos Evans, Clauds.
Pegues, Esquires.

Mr. James Hodges resigned his warrant of the road. Thos Cochran was appointed by the Court in his room.

John Wilson in the room of Carney Wright.

Ordered that Samuel Lowrie Esqr. having produced his admission properly
authenticated as an attorney that he be and is hereby admitted to the
bar of this court as an attorney.

Joshuah David acknowledged a deed for 100 acres to Trist. Thomas which
was ordered to be recorded.

Trist. Thomas acknowledged a deed to Joshua David which was ordered to
be recorded.

Morgan Brown Esqr. appeared in open court and acknowledged a deed to
Doct. Nathan Leavenworth for 640 acres of land which was ordered to be
recorded.

Nathan Leavenworth appeared in open Court and acknowledged a deed to Morgan Brown esqr. of 640 acres which was ordered to be recorded.

A Commission directed to Magr. Trist. Thomas and Thomas Evans, Esquires
authorising them to examine Eliza'th Brown the wife of Morg. Brown Esqr.
touching her consent to a certain deed from sd. brown and Elizabeth to
Doct. Nathan Leavenworth was returned execut'd with her Renunciation of
inheritance and order'd to be recorded.

John Husbands appeared in open court and acknowledged a deed to Morgan
Brown Esqr. for 100 acres which was or'd to be recor'd.

John Wilson appeared in open court and acknowledged a deed to Morgan
Brown for 20 acres for the term of 20 years and or'd to be recor'd.

Thomas Conn has permission to keep a Tavern with giving Bond and complying
with the Law.

Ordered that Thomas Godfrey be appointed coroner in the Room of Thos Lide
who declined serv'g and that the clerk make out a certificate for his
Commission.

Ordered that Jas Freeborn do pay Ŀ 50 to the use of the County one half
and the other half to Dan Walsh the informer for retailing Spiritous
Liquors contrary to Law. and that he continue in the hand of the Sheriff
till he pay the Same. Daniel Walsh appeared in court and released the
Ŀ 25 which he is entitled to.

Anthony Pouncy appeared in open Court and acknowledged a deed for 100 acres
which was ordered to be recorded.

A deed from Anthony Pouncy to Burrel Huggins for 100 acres was proved in
Court and ordered to be recor'd.

Jesse Vining vs Jas Pledger act'g exrs. of P. Pledger deceased. Jury
found for Plaintiff negro Charles or Ŀ 50 stg.

10

Ordered that the court do adjourn untill Tomorrow 10 Oclock.

Wednesday the 7 March 1787. The court met according to adjournment. Magistrates present Morgan Brown, Tris. Thomas, Moses Pearson & Thos Evans, Esquires.

A deed from Luke Pryor to John Waller Pryor was acknowledged in open court for 150 acres and or'd to be recor'd.

A Bond and Mortgage from Isaach Chanery to Pryor and Murpe was proved by Anguish McClain & was ordered to be recorded.

A Bond and Mortgage from Isom Ellis to Pryor and Murphy was proved in court by Frances Kenedy and was ordered to be Recorded.

A lease and release of 150 acres from Jno Brown to Martin Kolb was produced in court and ordered to be recor'd.

A Lease and release from Peter Kolb to Isom Ellis for 150 acres was produced in Court and ordered to be recorded.

In the case Jesse Vining vs Joseph Pledger tryed yesterday Wm Pledger appeared in Court and moved for a new tryal. Ordered that a new tryal be Granted.

Wm Stubbs appeared in open Court and acknowledged a deed for 100 acres of land which was ordered to be recorded.

A bond and mortgage from Bartholomew Whittington was proved in Court by Luke Pryor and ordered to be recorded.

State vs Jno Steward Larceny. True Bill Thos Cochran, fm.

Ordered that the Sheriff do pay to the Court 4 p for neglect of his duty.

Danl Walsh vs Wm Scott attach. Judgt for Plantiff Ḷ 6 1 2 with costs.

Mark Holloway vs David Dudley. Judg Amot. of his note with Int:

State vs Jno Steward Larceny. Not guilty. Jas Cook, fm.

Jacob Abbot vs Wm Jordon. It is ordered by consent of Parties and their attys that a rule of reference be given in this case that Saml Sparks be arbetrator in behalf of the plaintiff and Nicholas Powers in behalf of the Defendant and in case of their disagreement they do call in Mr. Jas. Little as umpire....

Ordered that Court do adjourn till tomorrow 10 Oclock.

Thursday 8 March 1787. The court met according to adjournment. Magistrates Present Geo Hicks, M. Brown, Moses Pearson & Thos Evans, Esqrs.

Ordered that the Sherriff empannell a new Jury to try the Issue between Jesse Vining and Joseph Pledger Exr. of Philip Pledger.
Jesse Vining vs Joseph Pledger detinue. 2d Tryal. Jury found for the Plantiff negro Charles or Ḷ 50 stg. with costs.

Thos Twity vs Drury Robertson of Tenesy. Attatcht. Defendt. Default & Enquiry.

Danl Walsh vs Hugh Dobbins. Attcht. Judgt. by Default.

Etheldred Clary vs Drury Robertson of Tenesy. Judgt. by Default.

Dunca. McRa vs Lewis Cook attcht. agreed.

Jacob Abbot vs Wm Jordon Debt. Referd. to Saml Sparks and Nicholas Powers and in case of their disagreement it is referred to James Lytle.

Danl Walsh vs Thos Pearce   agreed

Mark Holloway vs David Dudley   Judgt. for Plantiff ₺ 6 16 9½ wt. costs.

Geo & Benj Hicks vs Saml Wilds   Pet.   Judgt for Plantiff ₺ 5 0/7 wt.
costs   Clerk fees pd 7/

Mary McDaniel vs Britt Goodwin   Judgt for Plt. in part of his note
₺ 9 13 4   Int. 7 6   Costs.

Geo & Benj Hicks vs Jas Usher.   Def. confesses ₺ 4 3 9 w Costs.

Saml Wilds vs Saml Sparks   Judgt for ₺ 2 15/ st. costs of suit.

Geo & Benj Hicks vs John Jones   Post.   Judgt. by Default ₺ 4 4 0 3/4 Wt.
costs.

Geo & Benj Hicks vs Richd Edens.   Defendt. Confesses Judgt. for ₺ 5 2 10.

Gully Moore vs Wm Cooper Attcht.   agreed.   James Moore pays costs.

John Lisonby vs Joshua Lesonby.   Judgment for Plaintiff in the hands of
Carney Wright ₺ 4 13 2 with costs.

John Pledger appeared in Court and acknowledged a deed to Wm Pledger for
125 acres which was or'd to be recor'd.

A deed of conveyance from Philip Pledger to Jesse Councell for 296 acres
proved by Trist. Thomas, John Pledger and Daniel Walsh and was ordered
to be recorded.

A Deed of conveyance from Mary Gordon to James Due for 75 acres was proved
in Court by Wm Gordon & Joseph Red and was ordered to be recorded.

David Steward produced a lease and release from Mathew Whitfield for 83
acres which was ordered to be recor'd.

A deed from Barnebas Henneghin for 83 acres was produced in court and
ordered to be recorded.

James Johnson vs Lewis Blalock   P. S.   decree for ₺ 7 16 9 with costs.

Jams. Due, Wm Gordon & Mary Gordon vs Henry Hillison.   Agreed the defendant pays costs.   5 witnesses viz   S. Sparks 5 days; Thos Vinig, 3 days;
Isam Hodges, 2 days; Thomas Henry, 2 days, and Phil. Pledger, 1 day.

A deed from Job Broughton and his wife Mary for 200 acres to Thomas
Hickoboy was acknowledged in open court & ordered to be recorded.

Thos Gum vs John Jones   Judg ₺ 2 16 0 with costs.

Geo & Benj Hicks vs Wm Covington Pn. S.   Judg confessed by defend. ₺ 7
13 9 with Int and costs.
Ordered that court do adjourn till tomorrow 10 Oclock.

Friday the 9 of March 1787   Court met according to adjournment. Magistrates present Geo Hicks, Morgan Brown, Thos Evans, Trist. Thomas and
Moses Pearson, Esquires.

Ordered that Wm Jordon be overseer from the North Carolina line down from
said line to the lower part of Wm Thomas's land with all the hands above
Whites Creek.

Ordered that Joseph Mason be overseer from the place where Wm Jordon
stops down to Mrs. Irbys gate with all the hands between the two places

except those that work on the ferry Road & the Est. of Thos. Williams hands and Henry Hills.

Ordered that Drury Robertson be overseer from Mrs. Irbys Gate down to Naked Creek with all the hands between the sd. places encluding Williams Esta. & H Hills and also that He Open and clear the new road from Pledgers Saw Mills to Pledgers ferry.

Ordered that Thoms. Cochran be overseer from Naked Creek down to the new road from Kolbs ferry to Beauty Spot with all the hands below the two creeks Back to the Beauty Spot road.

Ordered that Jno Whittington do continue overseer one other Year in his Dist. and a new warrant be made out for him.

Ordered that Fully Moore be overseer from Ferrington Spring to Fullers Mill on the 3 creeks including all the hands across down to the East line including the Conners & Hagans's except such as have been ordered on other roads also all below the path from Fullers Mill to Swinny Bluff be under him.

Ordered that Thos. Ammonds be overseer from Fullers Mill to the State Line, that all hands in the Beauty Spot not to work on other roads do work under him.

Ordered that Tavern Keepers be allowed the following rates and no more viz.
for a cold Dinner 10 d)
for a holt dioot 14 d) Groff Wt. Each
Breakfast & Supper 1/ Lodging & night 4 d Oats 2d & quart corn and all other grain 3 d and d Stablage & fodder or Pasturage & Hay 6 p night bailing of fodder or Hay 2d   punch brandy 4 p Jill good run or Gin 4 p d Northward rum of Jaffee 2d pd. all   other Spirits 3 d pd.

Isam Hodges vs Thomas Stephens Judg. by Default.

Ordered that the case Stephens vs Coulson be quashed.

Ordered that the case David vs Edrondson be quashed.

Mason vs Branham Quashed

Broach vs Godfrey Quashed at the plaintiffs cost.

Ordered that a Tax be levyed on all the inhabitants of this county as follows that is to say sixpence P head on all negroes and Eightpence P head on all persons liable to pay a pole tax by the tax act of 1786 and also a tax of one eighteenth part as much as the public tax levyed for the Year 1786 on all Lands and other property made taxable by sd. Act to be paid in Specie or the medeum of this state into the hands of the Sheriff with the tax for the year 1786 and by him paid into the hands of Capt. Evans for the use of this County & by him to be applyed as directed by this court.

Ordered that the Salary formerly allowed to Mr. Wm Falconer County Attorney ceases from this time.

Ordered that the court do adjourn untill Court in Course.

June Monday 4th 1787. The Court met according to adjournment. Magistrates present Geo Hicks, Morgan Brown, Trist. Thomas, Moses Pearson & Thomas Evans, Esquires.   Grand Jury from 3 to 2. Petit Jury form 4 to 1.

Ordered that the Clerks Office be kept at the Same place where it has formerly been and that the clerk do Build a house for an office by next Court and remove his office to it as Soon as finished and that the Clerk be permitted to dispose of the Same at any time after his ceasing to be clerk of said county.

Aaron Pearson appeared in open court and acknowledged a deed to John Holcomb for 100 acres which was ordered to be recor'd.

A deed from John Hothorn to Moses Parker for 200 acres was proved in Court and order'd to be recorded.

Ordered that Benj Purkins Esqr. his Licence of an attorney may be recorded in the record of this Court.

Aaron Pearson appeared in Open Court and acknowledged a deed for 100 acres to Jesse John which was orderd to be recorded.

William Powe appeared in Open Court and acknowledged a deed to Will Whitfield for 300 acres which was ordered to be recorded.

Ordered that the Court do adjourn Untill tomorrow 10 Oclock.

Tuesday 5 June 1787. Court met according to adjournment. Magistrates present Geo Hicks, Morg. Brown, Claudius Pegues, Trist. Thomas, Esqrs.

Mathew Whitfield appeared in Open Court and acknowledged a deed to Burgess Feagin for 86 acres which was ordered to be recorded.

A deed from Anthony Pouncey to John Beasley for 100 acres was proved in Open Court by Mathew Whitfield and Aaron Daniel which was ordered to be recorded.

Ordered that Wm Gordon, James Due, Abner Broach & John Husbands each of them be fined 2 Dollars for absinting themselves after being Sworn and charged as Petit Jurors without leave of the Court.

John Pledger appeared in Open Court and acknowledged a deed to Peter Hubard for 200 acres which was ord. to be recor'd.

A Deed from John Brown to Morgan Brown for 100 acres was proved in Open Court by the Oaths of Nathan Leavenworth and Jas. Brown which was ord. to be record.

Carney Wright on oath confessed that he was indebted to John Fitts about ₤ 60 Va. currency upon note of hand when John Wright levyed an attachment in his hand for 75 Dollars against sd. Fitts. And be it ordered that Carney Wright save as much money in his hands out of said note as the said Attachment was levyed for. With cost which $75 he is to pay to sd. John Wright.

Major Thomas & Joseph Pledger proved a Deed from Jno Darby to John Pledger for 100 acres & was ordered to be recorded.

A lease & release from Saml Win to Joseph Pledger for 310 acres was produced in Court and ordered to be recorded.

Thomas Bingham to Jno Pledger a deed for 150 acres was ordered to be recorded.

A deed from Joseph Pledger to John Pledger for 150 acres and was ordered to be recorded.

James P. Wilson vs Danl Walsh. Jury found for the Plaintiff ₤ 6 11 7 wt. cost of Suit.

Danl Walsh vs Hugh Dobbins attacht. Jury Sworn, we find for the Plaintiff ₤ 21 16 10 without Interest.

Ordered that Edwd Smith do pay into the Hands of Danl Walsh the sum of ₤ 21 16 10. which he has acknowledged he was due to Hugh Dobbens provided he does owe the above Sum to said Dobbens.
Orderd that the court do adjourn untill tomorrow 10 OClock.

14

Wednesday 6 June 1787. The Court met according to adjournment. Magistrates present Geo Hicks, Tristram Thomas, Claudius Pegues Junr & Thomas Evans, Esquires.

A deed from John Husbands to John Wilson for 110 acres was acknowledged in open Court by Jo. Husbands which was ordered to be recorded.

Ordered that the following persons be appointed to serve as constables for the insuing Year.
Viz. Jacob Abbot in the room of Aaron Knight
      Will Fields   Thos Ammonds
      John Dyer   Simon Cherry
      James Hodges   Richd. Whittington

Ordered that the fines of Wm Gordon, Jas. Due, Abner Broach and John Husbands for their abseting themselves after being Sworn and charges as Petit Jurors without leave of the Court be and is here by remitted on their paying the Clerk his fee.

Mary Jones vs Burgess Williams. Writ quashed Plaintiff non suited wt costs.

Thos Stevens vs Danl Sparks Detinue P. Summons. Decree L 3 5/ with costs suit.

Ordered that an order be Given to the clerk and Sheriff for their annual fees for Extra servies to be paid up to December 1786 by the Treasurer of the County which was done accordingly.

Ordered that the clerk do make out Execution against all Persons that are due in fines to this County up to this date.

Ordered that the Court do adjourn untill Court in Course.

Monday Sept. 3d 1787. Court Met according to adjournment. Geo Hicks, Morgan Brown and Trist. Thomas Esqr.

Petit Jury ordered to be drawn from 4 to No 1. Ordered that the Grand Jury drawn last court continue next Term.

Benj. Hicks fm., Gully Moore, Geo Strother, James Gillespie, Thos Vining, Jno Husbands, Wm Covington, Benj. Thomas, Danl Sparks, Richd. Brockington, Wilson Hodges, Barnibas Henighan, Thomas Godfrey, Thomas Hammond, Wm Fernice, Edwd Crosland, Thomas Harvey, Drury Robertson.

a bill of sale from Thomas and Ann Stephens to James Moore, for Sundries therein mentioned was proved in open Court by   and ordered to be rec'd.

A deed from Windsor Pearce to Wm Bennet was proved by Abner Broach & James Bennet, which was ordered to be recorded.

Petit Jurors Isham Hodges, James Spears, Alexr Bodyford, John Stubbs, Benj Beverly, James Conner, Jethro Moore, Joel McNatt, Thomas Conner, Junr; John Lee, John Hillson & Geo Traweak.

James Blanton appeared in open court & acknowledged a deed to James Gillespie for 50 acres of land which was ordered to be recorded.

James Gillespie appeared in open court & acknowledged a deed to James Blanton of 50 acres which was ordered to be recorded.

State vs Thos Herringdine Jury Sworn true Bill T A & B
Petit Jury Sworn and arraigned not Guilty.

A bond and mortgage from William Lide to John Wilson & Jas Gillespie was proved in open Court by Joshua Prout which was ordered to be recorded.

A deed from Wilson Hodges to James Hodges for 50 acres was acknowledged
in open court, which was ordered to be recorded.

Geo & Benj Hicks vs Britt: Goodwin   writ
Agreed on Goodwin paying the costs.

A bill of sale from Brittain Goodwin to Ezariah David for Sundries mentioned
therein was proved by Jinkin David which was ordered to be recorded.

Tristram Thomas Esqr. appeared in open Court and acknowledged a bill of
sale to Gully Moore 1 negro woman Juday, 2 negro Boys named Sharper and
Adams which was ordered to be recorded.

Sarah Nevins vs Dan Walsh P. L. decree for the Plantiff Ł 5 12 and
costs. clerks fees 12 6   Sheriff do 3 6 Atty do.

James and Gully Moore appeared in open Court & acknowledged a Bill of
Sale for one negro woman named Milla and her three children to Trist.
Thomas Esqr. which was ordered to be recorded.

Ordered that Court do adjourn untill tomorrow 10 Oclock.

Tuesday 4th Sept 1787. Court met according to adjournment. present Geo
Hicks, Tris. Thomas, Claudius Pegues Junr., Moses Pearson & Morgan Brown.

A deed from Thos Bingham to Geo Strother for 250 acres was proved in open
court by John Husbands and Eliz. Fields which was ordered to be recor'd.

Thomas Coner appeared in open Court and acknowledged a deed to Daniel
Mackintyre for 100 acres which was ordered to be recorded.

State vs Eliza. Morgan. Larceny. upon her arraignment pled not Guilty.
Petit Jury sworn and found the defendant not Guilty.

Ordered that John Stubbs do pay 2 Dollars for absenting himself after
being sworn as a Petit Juror without leave of this court.

Joel Bullard appeared in open court and acknowledged a deed for 200 acres
of land to Quillar Quick which was ordered to be recorded.

Ordered that the case between John Edens plaintiff and John Husband deft.
be continued over untill next Term upon the defendants paying the costs
accruing upon such continuance and that the Clerk do Issue a Dedimus for
said deft. to take the deposition of Andrew Gipson in North Carolina
and also that the Plaintiff be permitted by consent of the Deft. and his
atty. to take the examination of any witnesses and that in case of death
or removal shall be good Evidence.

John Wright vs John Fitts   Atty. Executed in the hands of Carney Wright
who being Summoned and sworn as a Gar. as he declared on oath he owes
Ł 60 Va. currency to said Fitts.   Jury found for Plt. Ł 19 12 with
cost suit.

William McDowel vs Andrew Gibson. Attach executed in the hands of Will
Gordon who being summoned as Garnashe declares that he owes Ł 8 or 9 to
said Gipson. Ordered that said William Gordon do pay to sd. McDowell
Ł 4 s 19 with Ints. from the 1st day of Jan 1786 with cost of suit.

Jethro Moore appeared in open court and acknowledged a mortgage Nathaniel
Saunders for Sundriès, Lands, Toll of Negroes, and Stock and Household
furniture which was ordered to be recorded.

Rich Edens vs Will Covington. P. Summons Decree for the Plaint. Ł 1 3 4
wt. Cost suit.

A deed from Sarah Kolb to Edmond Botsford, Pastor. Able Edwards, John
David and Magness Corgell deacons for the Baptist church in the Walsh

Sept. term 1787

neck & for the use of said church was proved in open Court by the oaths
of James Smart & Geo Hicks Esqr which was ord. to be record.

Ordered that the Court do adjourn untill tomorrow 10 Oclock·.

Wednesday 5 day Sept 1787. Court met according to adjournment. Magistrates
present Geo Hicks & Morgan Brown, Trist. Thomas & Clau Pegues, esqrs.

Lamdon vs Jordon P Sum nonsuited by Default at Plaint. costs.

Snowden vs Hillson attach. Ordered that the deft. be wit. to Special
bail.

A lease and release from Joseph Johnston to Jno Pledger for 200 acres
was proved by Joseph Pledger and Benj Outlaw and Hardy Steward which was
ord. to be record.

Geo. Cherry vs Blalock & Owens. Continued by consent of Parties.

Thos Stephens vs Isam Hodges   agreed.

Ordered that Benj Beverly, John Stubbs and Thomas Conner Junr be and are
hereby fined 2 Dolls each for drunkenness after being sworn as Petit
Jurors.

John Hodges vs Danl Sparks   Slander. The Plaintiff atty moved that the
deft. give Security to the Court for Cost of suit in case of being cost in
sd. suit. Motion granted and Isam Hodges offered and was recd. by the
Court   Jury Sworn and found for the Plaint. Ł 2 0 0.

A deed from Philip Pledger to Joseph Pledger was proved by Mathew Whitfield and Trist. Thomas for 145 acres which was ordered to be recorded.

A deed of gift from Aaron Daniel to Ann Daniel for 1 negro boy named
Peyroe was proved inCt. by the oaths of Mathew Whitfield and Jno Daniel
which was ordered to be recorded.

A deed of gift from Mathew Whitfield to Ann Daniel for 1 negro girl Jinny
was acknowledged in open court by said Whitfield and ordered to be record.

Ordered that Court do adjourn untill tomorrow 10 Oclock.

Thursday Sept. 6, 1787. Court met according to adjournment. Magistrates
present Geo Hicks, Morgan Brown, Trist. Thomas, Claud. Pegues Jr.,
Moses Pearson & Thos Evans esqr.

John Hodges vs Isam Hodges non suited by deft.
John Hodges vs Ann Thomson non suit by deft.
John Hodges vs Joseph Pledger non suit by Deft.
Wilson Hodges vs Twitty. contd over untill next court.
Mason vs Edens P Sums   agreed
Joseph Pledger vs Jno Hodges   attcht. Decree for Plaintiff Ł 4 18 wt
   cost of suit for Plant. Orderd that the goods be sold upon motion
Saml Wilds vs Danl Sparks Suit withdrawn at plantf. cost.
Thomas vs Hodges deft confesses Judgt. for Ł 10 14 8 on condition that a
stay of execution untill the 31st of Jan next at which time he agrees to
pay the whole debt.

Philimon Thomas appeared in Open court and acknowledged a deed to Will
Coward for 132 acres which was ordered to be recorded.

A deed from JohnDavid to Ezariah David for 150 acres was proved by John
Dyer and Joel McNatt which was ordered to be recorded. Also one other
tract by the same wit. from the aforesaid John David to sd. Ezariah David
which was ordered to be recorded.

Ordered that Mr. Joel Winfield be appointed Deputy Clerk was qualified
accordingly.

Sept. term 1787

Ordered that the clerk as his deputy do attend at the office near Majs.
Thomass every Saturday from date untill the 6th of October and after
that day every Thursday and Friday untill Dec. term next attendance to
be given from the Hours of 10 in the forenoon untill 3 in the afternoon.

Ordered that Geo Hicks Esqr. be permitted to sell Spiritous Liquors by
the quart.

Quick vs Gross   attcht.   default & Enquiry.   Lewis Holmes sumd. as Garnashe declares that he owes the said Gross 56 3/4 Gallos. of Northward
Rum. Mr. Holmes says that Gross owes him 3 or 4 Dolls on private Accot.

Ordered that any person who wants or would wish to obtain letters of
admn. do apply to the Clerk of the County for a Citation who is hereby
Ordered to Issue the Same to admonish the kindred and Creditors of
such person to apply at the next Term for said admn.

Ordered that Geo Hicks, Morgan Brown and Claudius Pegues Senr & Junr
Esqrs. are a committe to provide and furnish the Court with forms concerning obtaining letters of admn, etc.

Ordered that the Court do adjourn untill Court in Course.

December the 3rd Court met according to adjournment. Majistrates present Geo Hicks, Morgan Brown, Trism. Thomas & Thomas Evans, Esqr.

Grand Jurours drawn from No 3 to No 2 for next March term. Jurors named
Moses Parker, Tho. Conn,Dixon Pearce, Wm. Councell, Moses Fortt, Jesse
Douglass, Aaron Pearson, Thomas Cochran, Wm Whitfield, Aaron Daniel,
Mackey McNatt, Jesse Vining, Saml Sparks, Wm Edens, Lewis Conner, Wm
Pledger, John Pledger, Carney Wright & Silas Pearce.

Grand Jurors to serve to Dec. term 1787. Ben. Hicks, f. m.; Gully Moore,
James Gilispie, Thomas Vining, John Husbands, William Covington, Ben Thomas,
Daniel Sparks, Richard Brockington, Welcom Hodges, Barnabas Henneghan,
Thomas Ammons, Edw Crossland, Thomas Harry & Drury Robertson.

William Covington appeared in open court & proved an indenture from
Sarah Rogers to Mary Andrews, which was ordered to be recorded.

A mortgage from Thomas Williams to Drury Robertson, Alex Sheras & Wm
Smith for one negro boy Dempsey one do Charity a Girl & one Bey Horse
was proved by Joel Winfield and ordered to be recorded.

A deed from William Gordon to James Gillespie for 200 acres was proved
by Morgan Brown & Joseph Brown and ordered to be recorded.

A bill of Sail from Wm Gordon to James Gillespie for one negro man Stephen,
one boy Peter and one girl Jude was proved by Morgan Brown and Joseph
Brown which was ordered to be recorded.

A bill of sail from Hubart Stevens to James Gillespie for a negro wench
Poll with her 2 children & Pompey was proved by John Wilson which was
ordered to record.

State vs John Beesley Larceny G. I. No Bill,Ben Hicks, f. m.

Levy Gibson vs Jno Windham Debt Ordered that the deft. do give Special
bail Mr. Richd. Brockington, bail.

Wm. Standard vs Jno Windham. Debt Ordered that the defendt. give special
bail   Mr. Richd. Brockington, bail.

James Graves vs Dixon Pearce P. S. debt Decree for Plaintiff Ł 4 5 1
with cost of suit

18

Sept. term 1787

Wm Henry Mills vs Griffin Nunnery Debts Returned N. E. Ordered that an attachment is Issue with this case.

Mark Allen vs Luke Robertson P. S. debt Decree for Pl. Ł 8 17 Proc. with cost of suit.

Thomas Twitty vs Drury Robertson of Tenecy. Inquery Jury sworn. We find for the Plaintiff Ł 26 15 with cost of suit. Luke Pryor, fm. Ordered that a fiere facias do Issue in this case.

Wm Thomas appeared in open court & acknowledged the assignment on the back of a Grant for 29 acres to John Jones which was ordered to be recor'd.

Ordered that Court do adjourn till court in Course.

Tuesday Dec. 4th Court met according to adjournment. Present Morgan Brown, Geo Hicks, Tristram Thomas & Thomas Evans, esquires.

Captn. Daniel Sparks appeared in open court & acknowledged a deed of 125 acres to Stephen McClendall which was ordered to be recorded.

Ordered that Mr. Joseph Freeborn & Coggshell be permited & has approbation of this court to retail Spiritous liquors in the county by the quart, for & during the term of 12 months from this day on his giving sufficient bond.

Isham Hodges appeared & acknowledged a deed to Jno Stubbs for 88 acres which was ordered to be recor'd.

Orderd that Burrill & Green be permitted to retail Spiritous liquors in this County during the term of one year from this day on their giving a sufficient Bond....

Etheldred Clary vs Drury Robertson of Tenecey. Attachment executed. hands of Edw Smith & Danl Walsh. Decree in favor of the Plt. against the garnishees Ł 10 & cost of suit.

Jonathan John appeared & acknowledged a deed for 150 acres to John Wilson, which was ordered to be recorded.

State vs John Cook. Larceny Jury Sworn No Bill Ben Hicks, fm.

Welcom Hodges vs Thomas Twitty. Case. Agreed Plaintiff pay one half the cost & defend. the other half.

Thomas Conner Senr. appeared in open Court & acknowledged a deed for 250 acres which was ordered to be recorded.

Capt. Danl. Sparks appeared in open court & acknowledged a deed to Wm Smith for 125 acres which was ordered to Record.

John Edens vs John Husbands. Case Jury Sworn. We find for the Plaintiff Ł 7 0 9 Stg. with cost of suit. Luke Pryor, fm.

Witnesses attendance in the case of Edens & Husbands, viz: James Blanton, 3 days; Phillip Edens, 4 days.

A deed from Thomas Conner Senr to Isaac Wetherly was acknowledged by sd. Conner for 100 acres and ordered to be recorded.

Robert Lide Esq. came into opencourt & produced a Paper containing the following words, viz. To the Justices of the County Court of Marlborough County this last will and Testament of Thomas Lide is directed that administration may be Granted thereon which paper when opened contain a last will & Testament signed Thos. Lide the due Execution of which was proved by the oath of Morgan Brown & James Blanton.

Ordered that the court adjourn till tomorrow 10 oclock.

<u>Dec. term 1787</u>

Wednesday 5th Dec. Court met according to Adjournment. Majistrates present Geo Hicks, Morgan Brown, Tristram Thomas, Claudius Pegues Junr., Moses Pearson & Thomas Evans, Esquires.

Wm Thomas vs Danl Sparks. P. S. Decree for the Plaintiff Ŀ 5 10 with cost of suit.

State vs John Beasly Larceny. Ordered on motion that the defendant have a copy of his Indictment in this case.

Wm Oats vs Bartholomew Whittington. P. S. Debt Ordered on motion of the Plaintiff that an attachment Issue in this case.

Thomas Ellerbee vs The Exrs. of James Hicks. Capias in debt. Ordered that an Attachment do Issue in this case upon motion.

Daniel Sparks appeared in open court and acknowledged a deed to Pearce Stevens for 100 acres which was Ordered to Record.

Solomon vs Solomon Gross. Attachment. Jury sworn. We say that the acct. is Just & that the rum was worth s 3 d 9 the Gallon. L. Pryor, fm.

John Odham vs Isham Hodges. Trover Jury sworn. We find for the defedt. L. Pryor, fm.

Mason & Taylor vs John Douglass. Agreed.

Edward Jackson vs Robert Allison & Elizabeth Allison his wife. Decree for the plaintiff according to specialty with costs of suit. (Subject to Installment Law.)

Ordered that the Court do adjourn untill tomorrow 9 Oclock.

[N. B. The following are the minutes for the terms of 1790. They appear thus in the original volume. December term 1787 resumes after December term 1790.]

Thursday March the 4th 1790. The court met according to adjournment. Present George Hicks, Morgan, Brown, Tristram Thomas, Drury Robertson and Samuel Brown, Esquires.

Thomas Evans Esquire returned a Dedimus with Bond executed by Edward Smith, admr. of Frederick Smith, with William Pledger, John Dyer, securities, which was approved of by the Court. Ordered that letters of admn. issue to Edward Smith.

Thomas Cochran made application for Licence to retail Liquors. Ordered that Thomas Cochran be permitted to retail Spiritous liquors of his own Distilling by the quart during the term of one year ensuing this Day.

Ordered that Maj. Thomas, William Easterling Esquire, Barnabus Hennagan & Thomas Ammons be commissioners to Lay out a new road from Marlborough Court House to McIntire Mill to cross Little Pee Dee at Swenneys Bluff on said river, and that Barnabus Hennagain be overseer....

Ordered that Moses David & Cornelius Manderville be permitted and shall have the approbation of this court to retail Spritous liquors by the quart during the term of one year ensuing this day.

Carney Wright vs Hubbart Stevens. Ordered by consent that this case be argued on the next course.

Philip Hodges vs John Mayes. Non suit.

Daniel Sparks vs Alex Campbell. Dismissed at plaintiff cost.

James Johnson & others vs John McDaniel & Others. Non suit.

20

March term 1790

Benjamin Hicks vs Moses Knight. Agreed.

Benjamin Hicks vs Alex Campbell. Agreed.

Ordered that the overseers of the high from Wilds Saw Mills to the creek
be continued the ensuing.

Ordered that John Wilson be appointed overseer of the road from Lide Ferry
to the No. Carolina Line--including the river Road from the lower end of
Mrs. Morgans lane to the lower end of Mr. Wilson lane.

Ordered that the following persons be appointed Constable for this County
To wit, Jacob Abbot, William Coward, James Hodges, William Fields, John
Dyer, Jesse Bethea Junr., Jesse Vining, Frances Kennedy

Orderd that Luke Pryor, George Cherry, Joseph Ellison & Thomas Vining &
Jesse Vining be appraisers to the estate of Jno Brown. Ord. that a Dedimus be directed to Moses Pearson Esqr. to qualify the said appraisers.

Ordered that Tristram Thomas, Mackey McNatt, John David, Aaron Daniel &
William Forniss be appointed appraisers to the Estate of Josiah Evans
decd., and that a Dedimus be directed to Morgan Brown Esqr. to qualify
the said appraisers.

Ordered that Richard Stinson be permitted and has the approbation of this
Court to keep a Tavern at Wm Spedger Saw Mills on his giving security...
on that the Court do approve of Mr. Robert Allison as his security....

Ordered that Drury Robertson Esquire be directed to Bind out to such
Persons as he may think proper the following children Nancy Driggers,
Joseph Driggers, Leasy Driggers & James Johnson.

Ordered that the Clerk do keep office at Drury Robertson Esquire untill
next court--as therein ordered: and that all former orders relative to
the same are Declared Void.

Ordered that the clerk provide a book for entering all cases argued in
court that are a particular Kind that involve points of law or Rules
of Court. Also that he provide a Book for Entering all fines.
And provide an appoarance Book for Entering attornies.

William Pledger being Elected Sheriff of this county, made known to the
court that by some accident he could not procure his commission. Ordered
that said William Pledger and Philip Pledger be and is hereby authorised
to act as Deputy Sheriff untill next Court.

Ordered that the County Treasurer do pay to William Pledger Ł 1 s 10 stg.
the balance due him for Executing two criminals. And it is the Decision
of tnis Court that the sheriff is allowed by Law Ł 1 stg. for whipping
any condemned person.

Ordered that the Court do adjourn untill Court in Course. Geo Hicks,
Morgan Brown, Wm Thomas, D. Robertson.

Monday June 7th 1790. the Court met according to adjournment. Present
Tristram Thomas, Thos. Evans, Moses Pearson, Sam Brown, William Easterling,
& Drury Robertson, esqrs.

Whereas Joel Winfield late Clerk of the County of Marlborough has absented
himself from his office as Clerk & has neglected to give the necessary
attendance in line of court. The court are of opionin his office become
vacant. Therefore proceeded to the Election of a Clerk when Drury Robertson Esqr. was duly elected....

Ordered that the court do adjourn untill tomorrow 10 Oclock.

June term 1790

Tuesday June 8th 1790. Court met according to adjournment. Present
Thomas Evans, Moses Pearson, Samuel Brown & William Easterling, esqrs.
Petit Jurors from No 3 to No 1 and 1 to 3;Grand Jurours names

1. William Sister
2. William Council
3. Benj Hicks
4. Welcome Hodges
5. Jas Harris
6. John Dyer
7. John Wilson
8. Wm Leggett
9. John Pledger
10. Henry Hill
11. Benj. Thomas
12. Azariah David
13. Edwd. Smith
14. Rich Brockington
15. Peter Hubbard
16. Edward Crossland
17. James Easterling
18. William Morris
19. Dickson Pearse
20. Jesse Bathea

PETIT JURORS

1. Richard Green
2. Josiah Beesley
3. Jacob Barringtine Sr.
4. Thos Summerlin Jr.
5. Carney Wright
6. James McCarter
7. John LittleJohn
8. Thomas Godfrey
9. William Edens
10. Isaac Summerlin
11. Job Insley
12 John Sutton
13. Lewis Holmes
14. Aley John
15. James Cook
16. Burwell Huggins
17. Thos Huckabe
18. John Lee
19. Barnabas Hennagan
20. Jacob Green
21. William Conner
22. Simon Cherry
23. William Fields
24. Sion Odom
25. Isam Stroud
26. Wm Wilson
27. John McNatt
28. Isaac Perkins
29. Stephen Parker
30. Charles Frazer

The State vs David Lee. Ordered that a rule to show cause why and Information should not be filed vs defendt. for selling rum by the small
measure returnable this day 12 Oclock do Issue. On motion of the county
attorney.

Whereas a dedimus was directed to Morgan Brown Esqr. to qualify the
appraisers of the Estate of Josiah Evans decd which have not been executed,
Ordered that Mackay McNatt, John David, Aaron Daniel, Samuel Terril &
Wm Forness be appointed appraisers to the said Estate and that a dedimus
directed to Tristram Thomas Esqr. to qualify the said appraisers.

Cornelius Rous produced a citation praying the admn. of the estate of
John Rous decd. Ordered that letters of admn. issue....

William Fields appeared and entered into bond with William Pledger and
Philip Pledger securitys for the execution of the admn. of the estate of
Wm Terrill decd...Thomas Godfrey, William Covington, Jno Andrews, Benj.
Hicks & Isam Hodges are appointed appraisers...dedimus directed to
George Hicks Esqr to qualify the said appraisers.

Edward Edwards and Joshua Jones produced a citation praying the admn.
of the estate of Thos Harry decd.... Ordered that Thos Evans, Mackay Mc-
Natt, John Jones James, Enoch Harry & Saml Terril be appointed appraisers...
dedimus directed to Tristram Thomas Esqr. to qualify sd. appraisers.

Ordered that Daniel Sparks is appointed Constable for this County and
that Geo Hicks Esqr. do qualify him as such.

Ellerbe, Wilds & Williams vs The admrs. of Jas Hicks decd. Ordered that
Jas. Moore Esqr. Sheriff of this County do return the money into This
court levied in an Execution in this case or show cause to the contrary
and in default thereof that an attachment Issue.

June term 1790

Survivors of Robt. Collins & Co. vs Wm Ratcliff & Aaron Knight. P. Sum.
Decree for the plaintiff for Amt. of Note & Int. & cost suit.

Ordered that Jesse Brown be appointed constable in the room of Jesse
Bethea Jr. & that Wm Eastering Esqr. do qualify him as such.

Thos Hancock vs John Pledger. Debt. The deft. confessed Judgment according to specailty.

Alexr. Smith vs John Pledger. Debt The deft. confessed Judgment according to specialty.

Survivors of Robt Collins & Co. vs John Pledger & Edward Smith. P. Sums.
Decree for plaintiff for amount of Note & lawful Interest with cost....

Adam Marshall vs Aaron Daniel. P. Sum Decree for the Plaintiff by Confession of the deft. for Ł 9 3 4 with legal interest with cost of suit.

Adam Marshall vs Britton Goodwi.. P. Sum. Decree for the Plaintiff by
confession of the deft. for Ł 5 16 8 with interest and cost of suit.

Adam Marshall vs Jesse Doughlass. Debt. Deft. confessed Judgment according to specialty with cost of suit.

Ordered that Samuel Brown Esqr. be directed to bind out Elizabeth Alvan
an Orphan Girl to such person as he may think proper.

Ordered that Edward Smith do pay to Mary Walsh the sum of s 14 sterling
in merchantable produce at the end of every three months from this date
towards the maintanance of her Bastard child untill otherwise ordered
by Court.

Jesse Jones vs Jesse Wilds. Debt. dismissed at Deft. cost.

James Moore sherriff of Marlborough County appeared and acknowledged a
deed purporting to be a bargain & sale of 50 acres to George Hicks Esqr.
sold by virtue of a writ of fifa--also one other of 100 acres, all of
which were sold by a writ of fi fa and acknowledged in open court

Adam Marshall vs Samuel Terrel. P. Sum. Decree for the amt. of the note
with interest & cost of suit.

Agness Heustiss vs Jesse Wilds. P. Su. Decree for the admt. of the note
with interest & cost of suit.

Richard Whittington & wife vs Samuel Brown. Dismissed at Plaintiff cost.

Mary Wise vs Geo Stanton & wife. Slander. Dismissed at Plaintiff cost.

John Pledger vs John Due. Case. The plea filed by the deft. in this
case appearing to the Court to be Evasive and defection so that legal
Justice cannot be done, on motion of Plffs. Attorney. Ordered that the
deft. do plead a substancial plea, the deft. attorney refusing to plead.
Ordered that Judgement be entered agt. the Deft. by Nihil Decit.

Carney Wright vs Hubbard Stevens. Debt. Judgment for the Plaintiff by
Default.

Admors of Jno Jinkins vs Britton Goodwin & Azariah David. Debt. Dismissed
at Deft. cost.

Thomas Cochran vs Richd Stanton. Issue joined. Ordered on motin of Plts.
attorney the the deft. be ruled to give special bail.

Alexander Smith vs Phillip Pledger. Judgt. confessed by Deft. for amt.
of specialty with interest & costs with stay of execution three months.

23

William Standerd vs John Windham. Contd. untill next term

Adam Marshall vs Edward Smith. Issue joined.

Adam Marshall vs John Andrews & Joel Winfield. Judgt. confed. by John
Andrews for the amt. of the note with lawful intrest & cost with stay
Extn. 3 months.

Adam Marshall vs Alexander Smith Issue Joined.

Malichi Murphey vs Stephen Parker. Alias writ to issue.

Admrs. of John Jenkins vs Azeriah David. Issue joined.

Survivors of Robt Collins & Co. vs Phillip & John Pledger. Issue joined.

The State vs David Lee. A rule having been served on the deft in this
case to show cause why information should not be filed against him for
retailing spirits & not having shown sufficient cause. Ordered that the
rule be made absolute.

William Pledger having been elected Sherriff of this county, made known
to the court that by some accident he could not produce his commission,
Ordered that the said William Pledger & Phillip Pledger is hereby author-
ized to act as deputy Sherriff untill next court.

Ordered that court do adjourn untill first Monday in September next.

Monday Sept. 7th 1790. The court met according to adjournt. Majistrates
present Morgan Brown, Claudius Pegues & Thomas Evans, Esqrs.

Ordered that the Grand and Petit Jurors be called. Mr. Thomas Godfrey
being one of the Petit Jurors made an excuse from giving his attendance
which was granted by the court.

Mr. Eli King made application to the Court for leave to retail Spiritous
Liquors by the quart which was granted accordingly.

Ordered that Court do adjourn for half an hour then to meet at the court
house on the county land.

The Court met according to adjournment. Ordered that the Petit Jury be
drawn from No 1 to 3.

Petit Jurors Names

1	Charles Cottingham	4	Charles Barringtine
2	Edward Traywick	5	Thos Sealy
3	William Smith	6	Luke Pryor

7	William Stubbs	19	Lawson Clayter
8	Enoch Harry	20	Daniel Cottingham
9	Thos Hodges	21	Dill Cottingham
10	Robert Pirnal	22	Mathw Murphey
11	James Bolton	23	William Ratcliff
12	Thos Herringdine	24	Solomon Lissenby
13	Wm Gainer	25	William Jordan
14	Richd Perdue	26	John Edens
15	Jacob Abbott	27	Richd Whittington
16	John Daniel	28	John Clarke
17	Wm Hickmon	29	Shadrach Easterling
18	Jesse Askew	30	Lewis Stubbs

The Petit Jurors to draw next term from No 1 to 2 & Grand Jurors from
3 to 4.

The following persons appeared and was sworn on the Grand Jury, John
Willson, Benjamin Hicks, William Lester, William Council, Welcom Hodges,
William Leggett, Henry Hill, Azariah David, Peter Hubbard, Edwd Crossland,

24

Sept. term 1790

James Easterling, Dickson Pearce & Jesse Bethea.

The State vs Zerababel Stafford. Assault & Battery. G. Jury sworn true Bill. Jn Wilson, fm.

Ordered that Benjamin Thomas be permitted to keep a Tavern at the Court House, and his giving bond & complying with the requesits....

The State vs David Lee. Assault and Battery. Grand Jury sworn. True bill Jn Wilson, fm.

The State vs Zerababel Stafford. Assault & Battery. Jury sworn Guilty. Carney Wright, fm.

The State vs David Lee. Assault Jury Sworn. Guilty Carney Wright, fm.

Tristram Thomas Esqr. returned to this court a dedimus directed to him to qualify the appraisers to appraise the estate of Josiah Evans duly executed. John Jones James returned at same time the warrant of appraisement of the above estate...letters testamentary do issue....

Tristram Thomas Esqr. returned a dedimus directed to him to qualify the appraisers of the estate of Thomas Harry decd duly executed. Edward Edwards returned at same time warrant of appraisement. Ordered that letters testamentary do issue to the administrators of said estate.

John Pledger vs Peter Hubbard. Debt Dismissed at Plaintiffs cost.

Wm Standard vs John Windham. Debts Dismissed at Defendants costs.

Nathan Leavenworth vs John Pledger. P. Sums. Debt. Judgment for plaintiff for ballance of note & Interest.

John Murdock vs Andrew Davis. Case Dismissed at Deft. costs.

Sarah Jenkins daughter of John Jenkins decd. made application to the court to choose a Guardian. Moses Brown & Tristram Thomas Esq. were appointed by this Court to examine her privately touching her free choice....she voluntarily chose Azariah David.

Ordered that court do adjourn untill tomorrow ten Oclock.

Tuesday Sept. the 7th 1790. Court met according to adjournment. Present George Hicks, Morgan Brown, Thomas Evans, William Easterling, William Thomas, Moses Pearson and Claudius Pegues, Esquires.

John Andrews vs Claudius Pegues. P. Sums. Services set aside at Plaintiffs cost for Irregularity.

The State vs Thomas Waters. for stealing a rifle gun. G. Jury Sworn. A true bill. Jno Wilson, Fm.

The State vs David Growter. Assault & Battery. G. Jury sworn. A true bill. John Wilson, Fm.

The State vs David Growter. Assault Battery. Pleaded not Guilty. Jury sworn. Guilty Carney Wright, Fm. Ordered that David Growter be fined ₺ 1 sterling.

Peter Smith vs William Frazer. Damage Discontinued.

Exors of Jno Mitchell vs Mathew Whitfield. Sums. Debt. Continued at defts. cost.

Marlborough County) 1st The Grand Jury present as a very great Grievance
September Term   )   that there is no established weight nor measure
in our county and we do humbly pray that the Worshipful Court will Im-

mediately take the same into their consideration.

2nd   We do present Peter Butler living in adultery with Sarah HedgeCock
and being married to two women at the Same time, both living at this
time, Call on Dickson Pearse, William Council & Sarah Cargill.

Admors of John Jenkins vs Azariah David. Capea Case Prom. & Assumpt.
Jury sworn   we find for the pltff ₺ 7 18 11 sterling and cost of suit.
Carney Wright, Fm.

Mr. Benj. Hicks appeared and acknowledged a deed to Charles Barringtine
for 100 acres which was ordered to be recorded.

Thos Cochran vs Richard Stenson. Damage. Welcome Hodges special bail
came into court and delivered up the deft. & bail discharged.

John Murdock vs D. & C. Manderville. Capias Debt. Judgment confessed
by deft. Amt. of Specialty & cost of suit.

Honbl Thos Waties vs Wm & Mary Gordon. Debt Judgment confessed by deft.
for ₺ 7 16 5 & cost of suit with stay of execution three months.

John Chesnut vs John Pledger. Debt. Defendt. confessed Judgment according to specialty.

Thos. G. Scott vs Smith & Cannon. Debt. Dismissed at Deft. cost.

Joseph Kershaw vs Robert Allison & wife. Debts. Jury sworn. We find
for the plft. with one shilling damage & cost of suit. Carney Wright, fm.

Finlay Christie & Co. vs Aaron Daniel P Sums. Plantiff Judgment for
amount of specialty and cost of suit.

Adam Marshall vs Edward Smith. Debt. Dft. confessed Judgment for amt.
of specialty and cost suit.

Survivors of Robt Collins & Co. vs Phillip and John Pledger. Judgment
confessed by Phillip Pledger for amt. of specialty and cost of suit.
John Pledger having confessed the same last court.

Adam Marshall vs Samuel Evans. Debt Judgment for Plaintiff by default
for amount of specialty & cost of suit.

Adam Marshall vs Alexander Smith. Debt Dismissed at Defts. Cost.

Thomas Cockran vs Richard Stinson. Damage Robert Allison appeared in
open court and acknowledged himself special for the defendts.

Benjamin Wright appeared in court and proved hi acct. for attendance as
a witness in the suit John Murdock vs David and Cornelius Manderville
₺ 1 s 5 d 9.

The state vs Zerobabel Stafford. The court fined the deft. ₺ 5 sterling
payable next term by giving good free hold security, if not to remain in
Gaol until Paid.

The State vs David Lee. The Court fined the deft. the sum of ₺ 8 sterling
payable next term by giving good free hold security, if not to remain in
Gaol untill paid.

Sarah James appeared in open court and entered into bond with Saml Terril
and Britton Goodwin, securities for the due admn. of the estate of William
James decd.

Ordered that the court adjourn until tomorrow 10 Oclock.

Wednesday September 8th 1790. Court met according to adjournment. Majistrates present   Moses Pearson & Samuel Brown, Esqrs.

Ordered that John David, Enoch Harry, Edward Terril, Mackey McNatt, & Azariah David be appraisers on the estate of William James decd, and a dedimus issued to Thomas Evans Esquire to qualify the said appraisers.

Thomas Cockran vs Richd Stinson. Case in assumt. Jury sworn. We find for the plaintiff Ł 10 5 4 sterling with cost of suit. Carney Wright, fm.

Malachi Murphey vs Stephen Parker. Specialty. Judgment by Default.

John Cogdell & Co. vs Thomas Godfrey. Debts Judgment by default.

Survivors of Robt Collins & Co. vs Peter & Edward Smith. Judgment confessed by Plaintiff for amt. of specialty & cost of suit.

Philemon Hodges vs Peter Smith Jr. Case Judgment by default.

Isham Hodges vs Saml Sparks. Debt Issue joined.

Benj Moore vs David Growter. Slander. The defendant demurs to the declaration to be argued next court by order

John Pledger vs John Due. Case Agreed.

Philimon Thomas vs Wm Coward. Debt The deft demurs to the Declaration ordered to be argued next court.

Philimon Hodges vs Peter Smith Jr. Case Judgment by default. writ of inquiry ordered to be executed next court.

Alexander Smith vs David Cannon. Attachment Continued.

Philimon Thomas vs Exors of Wm. Hardwick. Debts. Put on docket by consent of Deft. without service. Pleading to be made up next court by consent.

James Hodges appeared and made application to the court for leave to join Rachel Hodges, his wife, late the widow Kolb, in the joint admn. of the estate of Josiah Kolb deceased, which was granted....

Ordered that Bennett Easterling be appointd constable for this County, and that William Easterling Esqr. do qualify him as such.

Nathaniel Cogshell vs John McPherson. Attach. Decree for Plaintiff for Ł 7 s 10 & cost suit. Ordered that the property attchd be sold to satisfy the debt & cost.

William Covington & William Falconer. Jury Sworn. We find for the Plaintiff Ł 14 sterling with costs. C. Wright, fm.

Elizabeth Doughlas daughter of Nathaniel Doughlas decd. made application to choose a guardian....she chose Thomas Evans Esqr.

Ordered that George Cherry, Joseph Ellison, John Windham, Thomas Williams, and Richard Brockington be appointed appraisers to the estate of Elizabeth Stroud decd, and a dedimus directed to Samuel Brown Esquire to qualify them.

Ordered that Robert Allison, John Pledger, Joshua David, James Due & Isham Hodges be appointed appraisers to the estate of Josiah Kolb decd. and a dedimus directed to Thomas Evans Esqr. to qualify them....

The Court approved of John Jones James and Mackay McNatt as security, for Thomas Evans conduct respecting the guardianship of Eliz. Doughlas.

Ordered that the court adjourn untill tomorrow 10 Oclock.

Thursday September 9th 1790. Court met according to adjournment. Majistrates present Moses Pearson, Thomas Evans, Saml Brown, Morgan Brown, Wm Easterling, Tristram Thomas.

Whereas it is necessary to this county for the purpose of defraying the Expence of building a court house--Ordered that a tax be levied on all the Taxable property within this county in the following manner (to wit) one half of the publick tax for the year 1789 to be paid at any time on or before the 1st of Feb. 1791 in good merchantable corn, pork, or Indigo, prices to be assertained at next December term.

Ordered that Benj. Thomas, receitps givin in the following words. Received the   day of   M. For the building the Court house of Marlborough County. Shall be received in payment of the above tax by the Sherriff of this County.

Ordered that the afsd. Benjamin Thomas receipts given in the manner above mention be received in payment of all fines arrearages of Taxes now due to this County.

Mr. Robert Allison brought into this court a statement of the amt. of Joseph Pledger decd. executor of the estate of Phillip Pledger, against the estate of the said Phillip Pledger decd for moneys paid. Ordered that it be filed in the clerks office a farther consideration of the court.

Isham Hodges and Welcome Hodges made information this Court that they were likely to suffer as securitys for Solomon Lisenby admr. of the estate of James Reid decd and prayed relief thereupon. Ordered that Enoch Harry be appointed admr. to said estate, and that Solomon Lisenby do deliver up to him all the property of the said James Reid decd....

Ordered that Messrs. Drury Robertson and Joel Winfield be permited to retail spirituous liquors by the small measure within this county.

John Bridges made application to this court to be relieved from his securityship for the admn. of the estate of John Hubbard decd. Ordered that Sarah Hubbard admx. of said decd shall not make away or dispose of any part of said estate without consent of said John Bridges.

Ordered that Moses Pearson Esqr. be directed to bind out to suitable persons the following poor who are likely to become chargeable to the Court. children for the term of time prescribed by law (vizt). Darkes Hindley, Judah Hindley, Selah Hindley, Dicey Hindley & Tempe Owens.

William Coward constable of this county produced an affidavit wherein he makes oath that Zerobabel Stafford on 7 Sept inst. was put into his custody by the sherriff who made his Escape without his consent. Ordered that an escape warrent do issue.

Ordered that Thomas Hodges be appointd constable in the room of William Coward and that Drury Robertson Esquire do qualify him as such.

Drury Robertson Esqr. Clerk of this court resined his office....Joel Winfield was duly elected clerk of Marlborough in the room of Mr. Robertson who was duly qualified.

Ordered that William and Philip Pledger do act as Deputy Sheriffs untill next court.

Ordered that Court do adjourn untill Court in Course.

Monday December 6th 1790. Court met according to adjournment. Majistrates Present. George Hicks,Tristram Thomas, Thomas Evans. Esqr.

Mr. Drury Robertson produced to this court a commission of his appointment

Dec. term 1790

as Deputy Clerk of this county which was read and ordered to be recorded.

Mr. William Pledger produced to this court his commission as sheriff...
ordered to be recorded.

Ordered that the Grand Jurors be drawn from No 3 to 4 and Petit Jurors
from No 1 to 2.

Grand Jurors Names

1	Jacob Green	7	William Edens
2	Stephen Parker	8	Josiah Beesley
3	Sion Odom	9	James McCartee
4	Alcy John	10	John Little John
5	John Lee	11	Isaac Summerlin
6	Barnabas Hennagan	12	Job Insley
13	Richard Green	17	Lewis Holmes
14	William Branham	18	Charles Frazer
15	Wm Conner	19	Thos Summerlin Jr.
16	John Sutton	20	Burwell Huggins

Petit Jurors Names

1	Jonathan Cottingham	16	Lauchlan Currie
2	Benjamin David	17	William Murray
3	James Spears	18	Samuel Sparks
4	Daniel Herring	19	John Huse
5	John Teague	20	Mackay McNatt
6	Thomas Cockran	21	Demsey Watson
7	Aaron Snoden	22	Geo Smith
8	James Waters	23	Isaiah Watkins
9	Normon McLoud	24	Samuel Evans
10	Stephen McLendon	25	William Coward
11	David Growter	26	John Evans Jr.
12	Benj Parish	27	James Conner Jr.
13	Alexander Beaverly	28	Richd. Edens
14	Jonathan John	29	William Covington
15	James Falkner	30	Benj. Outlaw

Ordered that the Grand Jurors be called.

William Gordon and Elizabeth his wife appeared and acknowledged a deed to
their Right Titel & claim to a certain tract formerly the property of
Francis Gillespie decd. to James Gillespie which was ordered to be recorded. at the same time Tristram Thomas & Thos Evans examined the sd.
Elizabeth respecting her right of Dower....

Philimon Thomas vs William Coward. Debt on bond. Judgment for the
plaintiff for debt & cost & s 1 damage.

Philimon Hodges vs Peter Smith Jr. Writ of Enquiry. We find for the Pltf.
Ь 9 5 8 with Int. from 1st June 1786 & cost of suit.

Mr. Robert Campbell appeared & Proved the last will & testament of
Robert Blair decd, by oath of Jonathan John...at the same time was qualified as an exr. Ordered that Magnis Cargill, Jonathan John, Jethro
Moses, Thomas Vining & Wm Evans be appraisers of sd. estate,and that a
dedimus directed to Thomas Evans esqr. to qualify the sd. appraisers.

Ordered that the court do adjourn untill tomorrow 10 Oclock.

Tuesday December 7th 1790. Court met according to adjournment. Majistrates present Tristram Thomas, Thomas Evans, William Thomas, Esqrs.

Ordered that proclamation be made at the door for all those that are
Bound in recognizance to appear either to answer or prosecute. Thos
Waters & Esther Stafford do not appear, ordered that their recognizance
be forfieted and that a Scire Facias do Issue.

Dec. term 1790

Exors of John Mitchell vs Mathew Whirfield. Sums. Debt. Continued.

Thos Pearse vs Thos Stevens Discontinued upon the Plaintiff paying costs.

Alexander Smith vs David Cannon Attachmt. Jury Sworn. We find for the
plaintiff L 28 6 2 & cost of suit. Enoch Harry, fm. Ordered that the
property attached be sold to satisfy debt & cost on motion of the pltff.

James Moore, formerly sherriff, appeared and acknowledged a deed to
Gulley Moore for 400 acres which was ordered to be recorded.

Whereas a Schedule of debts said to be due to the estate of James Reid
decd of which Solomon Lisenby was admr. to said estate, the amt of which
is L 59 16 6 appears to be in depreciated currency of this state agreeable to the respective dates.

Isham Hodges vs Samuel Sparks. Debt Jury Sworn. We find for the Plaintiff with s 1 damage & cost of suit.

The Grand Jurors presentments. 1st We present as a great grievance that
the Majistrates are not Furnished with copies of the Laws of the State
and recommend that the Legislature cause to be purchased a number sufficient & to be distributed agreeable to the Act of Assembly....
2nd We present also that no provision is made for paying Jurors for
their attendance on the Court of Sessions and that an Attorney General
is not appointed in Each District to conduct the business of the court
since the courts are now Independent of one another.
3rd We recommend that the line of Division between Georgetown and Cheraw
District be runout agreeable to the Original Intention of the Legislature
by continueing the same from the Easterly line of Williams Burg Township
untill it arrive at the North Carolina Line--and we Request that a copy
of our presentments be laid before Each branch of the Legislature & our
representatives instructed to endeavour to procure Laws for Remedying
the Grievance above present.

Ordered that the Clerk do make out a fair copy of the above presentments
and transmit a copy to Each branch of the Legislature....

Benjamin Moore vs David Growter. Demurer, The court are of opinion the
Declaration is good and that the plaintiff have Judgment of the Demurrer.

Isham Hodges vs Thos Downer. Issue Joined.

Ordered that a commission be directed to George Hicks, Tristram Thomas
Esqrs. authorizing them to take the examination of Mrs. Elizabeth Brown
wife of Morgan Brown Esqr. touching her renunciation of dower respecting
certain deeds to William Thomas....

Philip Pledger is appointed Deputy Sherriff of this county....

Ordered that those persons assessd by the County for Building a Court
house do pay their assessmt. to Mr. Benj. Thomas in Produce at the following prices (viz) corn @ 1/4 P Bar Pork at 14/   Indigo prime Cooper 4/
P lb.

Welcome Hodges vs Saml Underwood. Attcht. Judgment by Default. Ordered
that the property attached be sold to satisfy debt & cost.

Ordered that court do adjourn untill next in course.

[Two blank pages occur here. The following few entries are in a different
 handwriting than either of the 1787 or 1790 minutes. It is not certain
 to which court term they belong. Then the minutes for December term
 resume where they left off, see page 19 of this volume.]

Rachel Blackford vs Lewis Stubbs. P. Summons Decree for the Plaintiff.
L 1 1 9 and cost of suit.

December term 1787

A deed of conveyance from Thomas Bingham to Philip Pledger for 200 acres was proved by Joseph Pledger & John Pledger and ordered to be recorded.

Arnold Calvin vs William Councill. Pr. Sum. Decree for the Plaint. ₺ 4 9 5 & cost of suit.

Snoden vs Hillson. Attachment. Ordered that the dedimus be admited by consent of the plaintiff & the suit continued over untill next court.

Tristram Thomas appeared & acknowledged a deed of conveyance to the Justices of the County Court of Marlborough for the use of the County 2 acres of land for Court house & goal which was ordered to be recorded.

Ordered that Court do adjourn till tomorrow 10 Oclock.

Thursday 6 Dec. 1787. Court met according to adjournment. Present Geo. Hicks, Morgan Brown, Tristram Thomas & Moses Pearson, Esquires.

Isaac Nevill vs Sampson Shoemake. Ordered that a Dedimus do Issue for Buen Mixon in the State of Georgia in behalf of the Plaintiff in this case.

Charles Booth vs James Wise. Case. Suit withdrawn at the Plaintiff cost.

Ordered that Morgan Brown Esqr. be appointed to have a Seal made for the use of this County with such motto & representation as he may think proper & that he call upon the County Treasurer for two Guineas to be expended about the same who is desired to take his rect. for sd. money.

Ordered that a Dedimus do Issue from this Court for the Examination of Aaron Turner, Thos Hall, Nathan Clerk & in the case of Isham Hodges vs Peter Heazans.

State vs John Fuller, Larceny. Jury sworn. We find the Prisoner Guilty of tresspass. Luke Pryor fm.

Ordered that John Fuller be fined ₺ 5 sterling for the use of the County, and that he do give bond & good security....

Robert Lide & Duncan McRa applied for letters of Admn. of all and singular the goods & chattles of Thomas Lide decd. with his will annexed... dedimus directed to Morgan Brown to qualify sd. admrs.

Joseph Pledger actg. exr. of P. Pledger. vs Danl Sparks & Samuel Sparks. Case. Judgment by default against the defendants.

The Court proceeded to elect a Sheriff and Mr. James Moore was chosen.

Ordered that the County treasury do pay to Tristm. Thomas Esqr. all the County tax that is been paid for last year.

Ordered that Majr. Thomas Thomas Evans (sic) Esquires be appointed to inspect the clerks office to make report next Court.

Ordered that the Court do adjourn till Court in course.

Monday March 3rd 1788. The court met according to adjournment. Present Trist. Thomas, Thomas Evans, Samuel Brown. Ordered that the Court do adjourn till tomorrow 10 Oclock.

Tuesday March 4th. The Court met according to adjournment. Present Geo. Hicks, Trist. Thomas, Thomas Evans, Saml Brown, Esquires.

Petit Jury No 2 to 1. Grand Jury called & Adjourned to tomorrow 10 Oclock.

Morgan Brown produced to the court a seal with the following emblem (viz) a cask of Indigo, two ears of corn, two half Bushels and a pair of balances

with the words (Marlborough County Court Seal) in capital letters round
the same. Ordered that the above seal be considered as the Court seal
of this county and that the Clerk do sffix the same in future to all
writs and other process issuing out of his office. Ordered that the
County treasury do pay Morgan Brown Ł 2 s 8 d 6 being the amount of Mr.
Thomas Abernethie acct. for making the above mentioned seal.

A deed from James Beasely to Daniel Silivan for 100 acres was acknowledged
and ordered to be recorded.

Luke Pryor appeared & acknowledged a deed to Geo Cherry for 100 acres
which was ordered to be recorded.

James Beasely appeared & acknowledged a deed to Sinah Beasely for 125
acres which was ordered to be recorded.

William Council appeared & acknowledged a deed to Daniel Sparks for 100
acres which was ordered to be recorded.

Burrel Whittington & Garret Whittingham appeared and proved a mortgage
from Thos. Williams to Prior & Murphey for two negroes Luke & cato which
was ordered to be recorded.

Ordered that Messrs Cornish & Clark be permitted & has the approbation
of this court to retail spirituous liquors by the quart during the term
of one year ensuing this day.

Ordered that Lewis Holmes be permitted & has the approbation of this court
to retail spirituous liquors by the quart during the term of one year...

Isham Hodges appeared & acknowledged a deed to Wm Stubbs for 400 acres
which was ordered to be recorded.

Orderd that Mandevel & Murdock be permitted to keep a tavern at Cashaway
Ferry on Pee Dee river....

On motion and cause shown Ordered that the Exrs. in the case of Thomas
Twitty vs the garneshees of Drury Robertson to wit Edward Smith & Daniel
Walsh be set aside and all proceeding thereon hereafter stayed....

On motion made, Ordered that the Execution in the case Wm Thomas vs Daniel
Sparks the exn. be stayed and all proceeding thereon.

Ordered that the court do adjourn till tomorrow ł0 Oclock.

Wednesday March ye 5th. The court met according to adjournment. Majistrates present George Hicks, Tristram Thomas, Thomas Evans & Samuel
Brown.

Ordered that the Grand Jury be called which was done accordingly.
Names of the Grand Jurors which appeared
1 Thomas Cochran fm   7 Jesse Vining
2 Dickson Pearce   8 Samuel Sparks
3 William Councell   9 Lewis Conner
4 William Whitfield   10 William Pledger
5 Aaron Daniel   11 John Pledger
6 Mackay McKnatt   12 Silas Pearce
                    13 Carney Wright

James Moore appeared & produced his commission for sheriff of this county...

Daniel Sparks appeared and acknowledged a mortgage for sundry diferent
tracts of land & negroes which mentioned, to Drury Robertson which was
ordered to be recorded. He also at the same time acknowledged to the
afsd. Drury Robertson one other mortgage for a waggon gear & four horses,
which was ordered to be recorded.

March term 1788

At a County Court began and held on first monday in March 1788. On motion
of Daniel Walsh by Sam Lourie his atty the execution, Doctor Wilson vs
Danl Walsh which issued from this court for a sum over Ⱡ 5 is quashed.
The Sheriff of Darlington County to whom said execution was directed and
who has levied on the property of said Walsh to wit and negro negro wench
by virtue thereof is directed to give up said property to said Walsh and
return said writ to the office from whence it issued.

Snowden vs Hillson. Attachmt. The opinion of the court is Snowden pay
the cost.

Ordered that James Stubbs be fined in the sum of 4/8 for neglect of duty
after being empanaled a Petit Juror.

Wm Standard vs John Windham. Debt On motion of the plt atty the case
be continued over, Ordered by the court.

Ordered that Wm Robertson be permitted to retail spiritous liquors by the
quart for one year.

Thos Ellerbee vs Amrs. of J. Hicks. Attcht. Judgment for the Plaintiffs
& that the property attcht be sold on motion.

Isaac Nevill vs Sampson Shoemake. Trover. Jury Sworn. We find for the
Plt Ⱡ 32 10 0 & cost of suit. James Boulton, fm.

Geo Cherry vs Blalock & Owens. Debt. continued.

Ordered that the Court do adjourn till tomorrow 10 Oclock.

Thursday March 6th. The court met according to adjournment. Majistrates
present Geo Hicks, Trist. Thomas, Claudius Pegues Jur., Thos Evans,
& Saml Brown Esqrs.

Ordered that Stephen Parker be permitted to keep tavern at Parkers ferry
on Pee Dee River for one year....

Ordered that the fine of 4/8 which was inflicted on James Stubbs be remited.

State vs Benjamin Arnold. Misdemeanor. True Bill. Ordered that a
bench warrant do Issue vs Benjamin Arnold.

Joseph Pledger actg. Exr. of Philip Pledger vs Danl Sparks & Saml Sparks.
Case Jury Sworn. Jurors Names James Boulton, fm., John Daniel, Az'ah
David, George Traywick, Thomas Huckabee, Joel McNatt, Jas Spears, James
Conner, Isaac Perkins, James Stubbs, Joseph Fuller, Jn Hubbart & returned
the verdict Find for Pltff. Ⱡ 22 3 3 with cost of suit.

John Stubbs appeared & acknowledged a deed for 88 acres to Jacob Darby
which was ordered to be recorded.

Wm Henry Mills vs Griffen Nunnery. Judgt. Attachmt. returned N. L. &
Judgt by Default. Ordered that an alias do issue in this case.

Benjamin James exr. of Cary Van dd. vs John Stevens. Trover. Jury sworn.
the same jury as the last tryal. We find for pltff. Ⱡ 14 16 3½ with cost
suit.

Jesse Vining vs Jos Pledger actg. exr. of Philip Pledger. Continued till
next court.

John Fraizer appeared & acknowledged a deed for 50 acres to John Bridges
which was ordered to be recorded.

Ordered that the Court do adjourn till tomorrow 10 Oclock.

Fryday March 7th. The Court according to adjournment. Present George

Hicks, Morgan Brown, Trism Thomas, Claudius Pegues Jur. & Thomas Evans.

The Court approves of Mr. William Pledger as Under Sheriff for the County.

Thoas Evans vs Isham Hodges. Appeal from a majistrate Judgments affirmed for ₤ 1 12 8 with cost.

Thomas Harringdine vs Burgess Williams. Malicious Prosecution. Continued over.

Ordered that the mode of obtaining a Dedimus for the Examination of a witness issuing out of this Court shall in future be as follows (vizt.)
   The party applying shall make oath before some Justices of the peace of the disability of witness or absence out of the State and give ten days notice to the opposite party before what Justices he intend to make application and also ten days notice of the time and place of his examining the witness.

Isham Hodges vs Peter Heagan. Trover The plantiff non suited 5/ cost of suit.

Isham Hodges vs Wm Branham. P Sums. Judgement by Default for Debt & cost.

Wm Hodges vs Benm. Outlaw, PS Agreed.

Wm Barringtine vs Ann tompson Extx. of Enuch Tompson. P Summons Non suit.

Benj. James exr. of Cary Van vs John Stevens new trial granted.

Solo. Lisonby vs Wm Covington. P Sums. continued.

Francis Griffin vs Lewis Blalock. Ordered that a Judicial Attachment do issue in this case.

Aley John vs Saml Sparks Decree for the plaintiff ₤ 10 & cost of suit.

Thomas Bingham vs Admrs. of Jas Hicks. Attacht. Decree for plaintiff ₤ 3 7 5 & cost of suit.

James Howard appeared and produced by petition to the court an affidavit that Jno Stubbs had lately bit off the ear of him the petitioner....

A lease and release from Richd James to John Hodges for 256 acres was proved by the oath of Joseph Jones before Hugh Gibes Esqr. which was ordered to be recorded.

Alex Swinton vs Pryor & Murphey. Debt Non suit 5/ cost of suit.

Ordered that the court do adjourn till tomorrow 10 Oclock.

Saturday March 8th The court met according to adjournment. Majistrates present George Hicks, Morgan Brown, Tristm. Thomas, Claudius Pegues & Thomas Evans, William Easterling, Esquires.

Benjamin Williams appeared in open court and was qualified as a constable.

Ordered that an execution do issue vs the security of Lundman in the case of Lundman vs Jordan for cost.

A deed from Welcome Hodges to Thomas Cochran for 150 acres was proved by George Harris, before Geo. Hicks Esqr. which was ordered to be recorded.

Ordered that George Hicks, Morgan Brown, Tristram Thomas & Thomas Evans be appointed commissioners to agree with a workman to build a Court House on the[land] laid out for that purpose of such Dementions as they may proper.

March term 1788

Benjamin Arnold vs Dickson Pearce. Dismiss'd at Plaintiff cost.

Dickson Pearse vs David Dudley. Decree for the pltff. Ŀ 8 0 0 & cost of suit.

James Stubbs vs Tymothy Darby. Agreed at Deft. Cost.

Ordered that the present sheriff do cite Mr. John Andrews to appear at next June term in order to settle with the court.

Ordered that the Clerks office be kept at Mr. Wm. Pledger's till next term.

Ordered that the Court do adjourn till court in course.

Monday June the 2nd 1788, the Court met according to adjournment. Majistrates present Geo Hicks, Trist. Thomas & Sam Brown Esqrs.
Grand Jurors drawn from No 3 to No 2. Petit Jurors drawn from No 4 to No 1.

Ordered that Tristram Thomas & Thomas Evans Esqrs. do make out a Grand & Petit Jurors List & return the same to next court and that the sheriff do provide a Jury box.

Ordered that the Grand Jurors be calld. which was done accordingly. Thos Cochran, rm, Dickson Pearce, Wm Council, Wm Whitfield, Aaron Daniel, Mackey McNatt, Saml Sparks, Silas Pearse, Carney Wright, Moses Fort, Moses Parker, Jesse Vining.

Benj. Hicks Jr. vs Thos Dean. Agreed at Plaintiffs cost.

Ordered that the Petit Jury be called to serve this term. Joseph Cosneham, William Conner, Edward Roe, George Cherry, Wm Covington, William Morris, Thos Summerlin, James Waters, Willm Farnace, Barnabas Hennagin, Dill. Cottingham, Richard Brockington, Drury Robertson & Lewis Stubbs.

Elihu H. Bay vs Jethro Moore. Pet Sums. A decree for the Plaintiff Ŀ 3 10 8 & cost of suit.

Duncan McRa & Co vs Isham Hodge. P. Summs. A Decree for the plaintiff Ŀ 7 9 2 & cost of suit.

A deed from Robert Reed to David Cole for 191 acres was proved by James Reed which was ordered to be recorded.

State vs Elizabeth Sanders. Larceny A true Bill Thos Cockran, fm.

Duncan McRa & Co vs Thos Pearse. P. Sums. A decree for the Plaintiff Ŀ 7 15 2 & costs of suit to be pd. agreeable to the installment Law.

A Deed of Gift from Sarah Kirby to Mary Driggers was Proved by Luke Prior which was ordered to be recorded.

State vs Elizabeth Sanders. Larceny A true Bill Thomas Cockram, fm.

Duncan McRa & Co vs Burgess Williams. P. Summs. Decree for the Plaintiff Ŀ 7 1 4 and cost.

Ordered that the sheriff do apply to Moses Fort for the prisoner Elizabeth Sanders. Sir: You will be pleased to Deliver to the Sheriff of Marlborough County, Elizabeth Sanders who you have in Costody in the District Goal. Jno Wilson, Clk.

Edmund Brown vs Samuel Sparks. Writ Debt Agreed at Plaintiff costs.

Pryor & Murphey vs Jesse John Writ Debt agreed at Plaintiff cost.

Archibald Freeman vs Thomas Herringdine. Writ Slander. Withdrawn at Plaintiff costs.

Josiah Freeman vs Thos Herringdine. Writ Slander. Withdrawn at Plaintiffs cost.

State vs Elizabeth Sanders. Whereas Mary Falkner is a material & necessary evidence to be produced & examined upon behalf of the state in this case, it is therefore Ordered that the said Mary Falkner do appear tomorrow by 10 Oclock in the forenoon & that the sheriff do serve sd. Mary Falkner with a copy of this order.

Prior & Murphey vs Wm Whitfield. Writ Debt Agreed at defts. cost.

Thos Dickson vs Samuel Evans. P Sums. Debt A decree for the Plaintiff Ł 5 5 10 with cost of suit 18/11 of which to be immediately paid the remainder agreeable to the installmt. law.

Exors of John Mitchel vs Daniel Sparks. P S Decree for the Plaintiff Ł 5 15 7½ & cost suit.

Ordered that a dedimus be directed to Saml Brown Esqr. to qualify the appraisers to appraise the estate of Charles Kirby decd.

Ordered that William Cherry be appointed as Constable....

Ordered that the court do adjourn till tomorrow 10 Oclock.

Tuesday June 3rd 1788. Court met according to adjournment. Present Geo Hicks, William Thomas, Tristram Thomas, Thomas Evans, Saml Brown, Esqrs.

STATE OF SOUTH CAROLINA) A capias as in breach of covenants.
& COUNTY   ) To the sheriff of sd. County Greeting
We command you that you take the body of A. B. if to be found within your County and him safely keep so that you have his body before the Justices of our County Court of D aforesd upon the   in   next to answer to CG of a Plea of Breach of Certain Covenants to the Damage of the said AB   Pounds sterling & so forth and have then & there This writ   Witness   Do
The above form is approvd of by me   Adamus Burke
19 April 1788   A true copy

(Also is given the form to arrest a person for a plea of tresspass....)

Geo Cherry vs Blalock & Owens. Debt Plaintiff non suited

Whereas John Elixis Dibbley have produced his Licence as an Attorney to this Bar, be admitted to the same.

James exor of Cary Van vs John Stevens. Trover. Agreed at Defendants cost.

State vs Eliz Sanders. Larceny Jury sworn. Guilty. George Cherry, foreman. Ordered that Elizabeth Sanders be taken by the sheriff to some convenient place in the court yard, and there to receive twenty five lashes on the back. After tryal the Prisoner appeared in open Court & made oath that she had not wherewith to pay the cost of the Prosecution.

Danl Walsh appeard in open court & acknowledged a deed to gift to Silas Pearse for one dark bay mare which was ordered to be recorded.

James Falkner vs James Reed. Agreed Plaintiff pay the sheriff fee & the defendant the Clerks.

Thos Dickson vs Saml Evans. P. S. Debt (stricken)

Jno Lide vs Richd Purdue. Slander. Agreed at the defendants cost.

Wed. 4th June 1788. Court met according to adjournment. Present Tristram Thomas, Thomas Evans and Moses Pearson, Esquires.

James Gillespie appeared and acknowledged a deed fo 200 acres to Edwd Crossland which was ordered to be recorded.

Exs. of Jones vs Killingsworth. Attcht. Ordered that the returning officer give up the property so by him attached to the defendt, upon deft. giving bond.

David Lee vs Griffin Nunnery. Attacht. Ordered that the property in the Schedule mentioned, so much as shall satisfy a Debt of L 8 4 0 & cost be sold by the sheriff.

William Powe appeared in open Court and acknowledged a deed of lease & release to Francis Bridges for 150 acres which was ordered to be recorded.

Jesse Vining vs Joseph Pledger actg. Exr. of Philip Pledger. Writ case Jury Sworn. non suit s 5 and cost of suit.

Jno Kimbrough vs Joseph Mason P S Dismissed

Jno Kimbrough vs Cooper Clark P. Summons Dismissed

Jno Kimbrough vs Jno Lisonby Dismissed

Jno Kimbrough vs Jno Firhitts Dismissed

Jno Kimbrough vs Morgan Brown Dismissed

Joshua Lucas vs the exr of Jno Mitchell. P Summons Decreed for the Plaintiff L 6 s 7 d 1 sterling with interest from March 1784 and cost of suit.

John Davis vs Exors of Philip Pledger. Case. The plaintiff this case agreed to withdraw his suit at his own cost.

Thomas Herringdine vs Burgess Williams. Malicious Prosecution. Jury Sworn. The verdict to be returned tomorrow by 10 Oclock if by that time agreed.

Ordered that the Court do adjourn till tomorrow 10 Oclock.

Thursday June 5th 1788. Court met according to adjournment. Present George Hicks, Tristram Thomas, Thomas Evans & Sam Brown, Esquires.

Thomas Herringdine vs Burgess Williams. A decree for the plaintiff L 9 s 13 d 2 3/4 stg. and cost of suit.

The exors. of Charles A. Stewart vs Daniel Sparks. Debt. We find for Plaintiff L 29 13 3 old currency with lawfull interest and cost of suit.

Ordered that a dedimus be directed to Thomas Evans to qualify the admr. and appraisers of Estate of Joseph Downs decd.

Ordered that a dedimus be directed to Thomas Evans Esqr. to qualify the admrs. and appraisers of the estate of David Luke decd.

Ordered that a dedimus be directed to Thos Evans Esqr. to qualify the admrs. and appraisers of the estate of Amr(?) Hughs deceasd.

Solomon Lisonby vs William Covington. P. Summons Case, agreed at plaintiffs cost.

John Beasely vs Mackey McNatt. Malicious Prosecution. non suit s 5 and cost of suit.

Exors of John Mitchell vs Franics Kenedy. Debt. nonsuit s 5 and costs

June term 1788

John Andrews vs Stephen Parker. Debt Withdrawn at plaintiff costs.

Ordered that the court do adjourn till tomorrow nine Oclock.

Friday the 6th day June 1788. The court met according to adjournment.
Present George Hicks, Tristram Thomas and Thomas Evans, Esquires.

Bartholomew Whittington vs Jarrett Whittington. Agreed at plaintiff costs.

William Whitfield vs Mathew Murphey. tresspass Judgement by default,
and writ of enquiry.

Francis Griffin vs Lewis Blalock. Judgement by Default.

Clerk vs James Moore & Isam Hodges. Agreed at Defendant cost.

Wm Henry Mills vs Griffin Nunnery. Judg. Attachment. Alias to issue.

Mehetibel Lide vs Isham Hodges. Decree for the plaintiff Ł 8 s 19 d 9
3/4 stg. and cost of suit.

Isham Hodges vs John Wilson. Damage. Continued till next court.

Pryor and Murphey vs Joseph Owens. P Summons   agreed at Defendant cost.

Ordered a new Tryal be granted in the suit tryed yesterday in the case
of Exrs. of Charles Augustus Steward vs Daniel Sparks.

Henry Easterling vs Burrel & Green. Debt agreed at Defendants cost.

Ordered that George Hicks Esqr. is appointed to settled with Mr. John
Andrews late sheriff on account of his collections of the County tax....

Ordered that the clerks office be kept where it is at present till next
term.

Ordered that the County Treasurer to pay to Moses Fortt the sum of Ł 1
s 2 for maintaining Eliz Sanders in Goal 15 days.

Wm Oats vs Bartho. Whittington. Judg. att. agreed at Plaintiff cost.

Ordered that court adjourn untill court in course.

Monday. Sept. 1st of 1788. The court met according to adjournment. Present George Hicks, Tristram Thomas, William Thomas, Thos Evans, William
Easterling & Saml Brown, esqrs.

The state vs Elias Braner. Larceny. Jury sworn we find the prisoner
not guilty. Jesse Baggett, foreman.

Daniel Sparks appeared in open court and acknowledged a deed to Josiah
Evans for 500 acres which was orderd to be recorded.

The State vs Cornelious Manderville. The prisoner being brought into
court and arraigned and pleded not Guilty. Jury sworn we find the deft.
Guilty of Assault & Battery. Ordered that Cornelious Manderville be fined
1/p sterling.

The State vs John George. The prisoner being brought into court and arraigned pleded not guilty. Jury sworn we find the prisoner Guilty.

William Thomas vs Carney Wright. P. Summs Debt the deft. appeared and
confessed judgment for Ł 6 s 4 d 8 sterling with interest and cost of suit.

Wm Ratcliff vs John Wright Jr. Alexander Smith and Carney Wright appeared
and acknowledged themselves special bail in the above suit.

Sept. term 1788

Freeborn and Coggeshall vs Stephen Parker. The defendant confessed Judgment for Ⱡ 105 s 5 d 3 with interested from 26th dec. last and stay of execution untill November next.

Drury Robertson vs Edward Smith. Debt. Judgment by nihim dicit and that execution do issue according to specialty.

Ordered that George Cherry be permitted to keep a tavern during the term of one year....

Wm Ratcliff vs John Wright Jr. The court pospones the further consideration of this case untill the second day of next Court.

Ordered that a dedimus do issue to take the examination of Michael Alls in North Carolina in this suit. Wm Ratcliff vs John Wright.

Drury Robertson appear and was qualified as a majistrate for this county.

Ordered that the Court do adjourn untill tomorrow 10 Oclock.

[N. B. The minutes here are again out of sequence. The following
begins with June term 1789. The minutes for September term 1788 resume
a few pages on.]

Thursday June the 3rd. The court met according to adjournment. Magistrates present Tristram Thomas, Morgan Brown, and Thomas Evans, esqr.

Exrs. of Ely Kershaw vs Burgess Williams. The defendant appeared and confessed judgment according to specialty with stay of execution three months.

Ordered that Moses Murphey Junr be appointed constable for this county and that Samuel Brown Esqr. be directed to qualify him.

Admrs. of Charles A. Steward vs William Shepherd. Attachments. Jury sworn, we find for the deft. with cost of suit. Jesse Baggett, foreman. On motion of the plaintiff attorney, ordered that an appeal be granted in this case.

Ordered that Thomas Allison be appointed overseer of the Road from Brown Mills to Cassaway Ferry.

Moses Knight vs Andrew Gibson. Attach. Jury sworn. We find for the plf. Ⱡ 103 north currency with interest from the date due May 4th 1778. whereupon the deft. appealed.

Ordered that the Court do adjourn untill tomorrow 10 Oclock.

Thursday June 4th 1789. The court met according to adjournment. Magistrates present George Hicks, Tristram Thomas, and Thomas Evans, Esqrs.

Jonathan Wright vs William Posey. Jury sworn, we find for the pltf. Ⱡ 1 damage with cost of suit. Jesse Baggett, foreman.

The State vs John George. New Trial Grant. Ordered that the deft. do give security for his appearance at next court.

Ordered that Thomas Clinton be fined Ⱡ 3 sterling for a breach of the peace made in court....

Richard Perdue vs Mary Falkner. Slander. We find for the plaintiff s 1 damage.

Isham Hodges vs Thomas Stevens contd.

Gully Moore vs Thos Stevens continued.

June term 1789

Whereas a new trial was granted in the case Isham Hodges vs Peter Heagan
on the plaintiff paying all costs, which he has neglected to do--it is
therefore ordered that Judgement be entered up agt. the sd. Plaintiff
for cost.

Jacob Abbott vs Andrew Gibson.   Agreed at the plaintiff cost.

David Growter vs Benj. Outlaw.   Agreed at the Defendants cost.

Francis Griffin vs Thos Williams.   Ordered that a Judicial attachmt do
issue in this case.

Moses Knight vs Andrew Gibson.   Attachment, ordered that a new trial
be granted in this case.

Ordered that the clerk do attend at the place where the Court is last
held on the last day in every week and that he be allowed to move his
office to any secure place where he may think proper in this County.

Ordered that the Court do adjourn untill Court in Course at Pledger
Saw Mill.

Monday Sept. 7th 1789.   The court met at Wm Pledgers Saw Mill according
to adjournment.   Present   George Hicks, Tristram Thomas, Thomas Evans,
& Moses Pearson,Esqrs.   Ordered that the petit Jurors de drawn from
No 3 to No 1.

Ordered that the Grand Jurors be called.   Joseph Brown, Samuel Terrel,
Joel McNatt, George Cherry, Moses Parker, James Due, William Furnace,
Thomas Vining, Jesse Brown, Gully Moore, Jesse John, James McGee, Aaron
Danie:., Francis Kennedy, Edward Feagan, Joiathon Marine & Jesse Wilds.
Defaults Jesse Stevens, Charles McRa, and Josiah Evans.

Geo & Ben Hicks vs Wm Fields.   P Sums.   The Defendant appeared and
confessed Judgement for Ł 5 s 3 d 3 sterling with interest   from 5 May
1785.

Tymothy Darby vs Wm Fields.   P. Sums.   The defendant appeared in open
Court and confessed Judgment for Ł 8 sterling with interest from 15 Dec
1787.

William Griffin vs Wm Fields.   P Sums.   Decree for the plaintiff.   Ł 3
s 10 sterling with cost of suit.

Moses Pearson Esqr. returned a dedimus with Bonds executed by Simon
Cherry admr. of Wm Cherry and George Cherry and Francis Kennedy, securities,
which was approved of by the court...letters testamentary do issue....

Ordered that Sterling Brewer now a prisoner in Cheraw Goal be brought to
Court tomorrow by 12 Oclock by the Sheriff.

Ordered that a dedimus be directed to Samuel Brown Esquire to qualify the
admrs. of the estate of William Watkins decd....

Mason & Taylor vs William Covington.   The deft. appeared in open court
and confessed judgement according to specialty.

Ordered on motion in the case of Henry Wm Herrington vs Wm Powncey and
Stephen Parker that the defts. go five special bail.

Thomas Evans Esqr. returned a dedimus with bonds executed by Wm Evans
and Jesse Douglass admrs. of Enoch Luke decd.   Jonathan John & James Hodges,
securities.

Thomas Evans Esqr. returned a dedimus with bonds executed by John McPherson admr. of Murdock McPherson & Jesse Hodges & Dickson Pearce, securities.

Wm Ratcliff vs John Wright. Attacht. Non suit 5/ & cost of suit.

Ordered that the court do adjourn till tomorrow 10 Oclock.

Tuesday September 8th 1789. Court met according to adjournment. Present George Hicks, Tristram Thomas, Thomas Evans and Samuel Brown, Esquires.

Jacob Abbott vs Andrew Gibson. P Summons. Dismissed at the plaintiff costs.

The State vs Samuel Evers. Inditement Larceny. G. Jurors Sworn. True Bill. George Cherry, foreman. Ordered that Samuel Evers be taken in custody of the Sheriff.

Alexander Campbell & Co. vs Edward C. Debruhl. P Sums. Ordered that the Defendant be ruled to special bail in this case.

The State vs Sterling Brewer. G. Jurors Sworn. A True Bill.

The State vs Samuel Evers. Larceny. Petit Jury Sworn. Guilty. Thos Cochran, forman.

The State vs John George. Inditement for assault & battery. Grand Jurors sworn. A true bill. Ordered that Samuel Evers be taken into some convenient place within this court yard and there receive by the sheriff fifteen stripes on the bare back well laid on.

John George was called in open and pleaded Guilty in the state vs himself. Ordered that the said John George be fined L 5 sterling. And that he do remain in the custody of the sheriff untill he give sufficient security for the payment of the same, by next December court.

Presentment of the Grand Jurors. We present as a Great Grievance That the officers of Justice in the County are not respectively furnished at the public Expense with a copy of the laws of every Session of the Assembly as soon as they can be printed. For it is impossible that people can certainly obey or officers execute laws which they cannot know.

Ordered that this presentment be laid before the Legislature....

Ordered that the Court do adjourn till tomorrow 10 Oclock.

Wednesday September the 9th day 1789. The court met according to adjournment & Present. Morgan Brown, Tristram Thomas, Thomas Evans, and Drury Robertson Esquires.

Moses Knight vs Andrew Gibson. Continued.

Alexander Campbell & Co. vs William Evans. The Defendant appeared in open court and confessed Judgment for L 23 s 17 d 8 sterling with interest from 1st day of January last.

William Robertson vs Daniel Sparks. The deft. appeared & confessed Judgment for L 57 s 1 d 7½ with interest.

Enoch Evans Junr vs Samuel Sparks. The deft. appeared in open court and confessed judgement for L 24 s 11 d 2 sterling with interest.

Edward Jackson vs Downer & Powers. P Sums. Dismissed at the Deft. cost.

Finley Christie & Co. vs Samuel Ferrell. Judgement confessed for L 7 s 11 d 7¼ interest to this date L 2 s 5 d 3 3/4 sterling to be pd. agreeable to the installments (to wit) one fifth of the principal and one fifth of the interest at each installment.

Bartholomew Whittington vs Francis Kennedy. P Sums. Debt Decree for the plaintiff L 6 s 2 & interest with cost of suit.

41

Exors of Charles Mason vs William Furniss. Petition & Summons. Contd.

James Johnson vs Simeon Woodruff. Debt N. E. ordered that a Gudecial (sic) do issue in this case.

John Cogdell & Co vs Edward Smith. Debt. Ordered that the deft. be ruled to special in this case.

Alexander Campbell & Co vs Edward c. Debruhl. P Sums. Case the Deft. in this case moved that this trial be by a Jury. It was ordered that a Jury be sworn...We find for the Plaintiff ₺ 1 s 12 d 7 sterling.

The state vs Sterling Brewer. Larceny Petit Jury Sworn Guilty Thos Cochran, forman. Ordered that the sheriff do take sd. Sterling Brewer to some convenient place within this Court Yard and there receive 15 lashes on the bare back well laid on..the afsd. Sterling Brewer sworn that he was not able to pay the cost of his prosecution.

George Cogdell vs David Dudley. Ordered that the aforesaid process be dismissed at plaintiff cost.

The survivors of Collins & Co vs Daniel Sparks. Debt Jury sworn We find for the plaintifss ₺ 32 s 19 d 6, subject to the installments law.

Mr. John Ward appeared and proved his attendance as a witness in the above suit which amts. to ₺ 2 s 2 d 10 sterling.

Ordered that James Hodges do sell at publick sale in the court yard a certain horse taken up by Jesse Bathea.

Ordered that the Court do adjourn till tomorrow Ten Oclock.

Thursday September 10th 1769. The court met according to adjournment. Present George Hicks, Tristram Thomas & Moses Pearson, Thomas Evans and Samuel Brown, esquires.

Ordered that a dedimus be directed to George Hicks and Drury Robertson esqrs. to examine Martha Sparks, wife of Daniel Sparks, touching her consent to a certain deed from sd. Daniel to Josiah Evans....

Ordered that William Driggers be bound as an apprentice to Michael Mason be Maj. Tristram Thomas to lear the art and mistery of a Blacksmith untill he is 21 years of age....

Mr. Patrick Danelly appeared and proved his attendance as a witness in the suit Alexander Campbell & Co. agt William Evans which amounts to s 11 d 6 sterling.

James Johnson & others vs John McDaniel & others. Debt Ordered that the declarations in this case be consoladated.

Mason & Taylor vs Carney Wright. Agreed

John Cogdell & Co vs John Jones. Debt Ordered that the Deft. do give special bail in this case.

Federick Folk & Co vs Joseph Brown. Debt. Ordered that the Deft. do give special bail in this case.

William Furniss vs Stephen Parker Debt. Ordered that the Deft. be ruled to special bail in this case.

John Cogdell & Co vs James James Senr. Debt. Ordered that the Deft. be ruled to special bail in this case.

Ordered that the county Treasurer do pay to William Pledger deputy sheriff ₺ 4 s 18 d 8 sterling the full amount of the expences for maintaining Sterling Brewer in Goal 87 days.

Joseph Booth vs Dickson Pearce & Daniel Sparks. Debt. Ordered that the Deft. do give special Bail in this case.

Joel Winfield vs Richard Stinson. Withdrawn.

Samuel Sparks vs Willis Williamson. Debt. The defendant appeared in open Court and confessed Judgment in this case according to Specialty.

John Cogdell & Co. vs Philip James. Debt. Ordered that the deft. do give special bail in this case.

William Bevel vs Jesse Wilds. Agreed at the plaintiff.

Exrs. of Chs Mason vs Wm Branham. Agreed at the plaintiffs cost.

Daniel Sparks vs Benj Arrandall. Appeal. Continued over till next court

Ordered that the County Treasurer do pay to James Moore sheriff of this county ₤ 1 s 9 d 6 sterling for all fees in two prosecutions the state against Elizabeth Sanders and the state agt. Sterling Brewer.

Ordered that the County Treasurer do pay to Mr. Benjamin Thomas s 10 d 8 sterling for putting & detaining Sterling Brewer in this County Goal six days.

Ordered that Mr. Falconers receipt be good to the sheriff for Capt. Taylors county tax.

Exors of Charles Augustus Steward vs Daniel Sparks. Debt ordered that the payment be depreciated.

Ordered that the county Treasurer do pay to Joel Winfield s 16 for his fees in the case the state vs Sterling Brewer.

Ordered that James Hodges do sell at publick sale in this Court Yard a certain cow taken up by the Reverend Peter Bainbridge.

The State vs John George. Larceny. Ordered that the Recognizance in this case be continued over.

Ordered that the Court do adjourn untill the first Monday in December next. Then to meet at Pledger Saw Mills.

Monday December 7th 1789. Court met according to adjournment. Present George Hicks, Tristram Thomas, Drury Robertson and Samuel Brown.

Grand Jurors drawn from No 4 to 2 Petit Jurors 3 to 1.

Ordered that Samuel Brown eqr. is appointed to bind over Davin Mandeville, Cornelias Mendeville, Wm. Hickmon & Wm Hutson to appear to the next Court and in evidence in the case the state vs John George Unless they do appear before the adjournment of this Term.

Jesse Goins appeared and made oath that he was not able to attend as a G Juror last court and was excused.

Wm Evans vs Stevens & Pouncey. The deft. appeared and confessed Judgment for ₤ 8 s 1 d 3 sterling with interest from Jan. last.

Joseph Brown & wife vs James Due. Agreed.

John Cogdell & Co vs John Jones. Jury sworn we find for the plaintiff s 1 damage with cost of suit. Luke Pryor.

William Forniss vs Stephen Parker. On motion of the Defts. attorney ordered that leave be granted in this case of the defts. to withdraw his plea. Confessed Judgement according to Specialty....

Dec. term 1789

Alexander Campbell & Co vs John Pledger. On motion the defts. atty
ordered that Leave be granted in this case for the deft. to withdraw
his please. and confess Judgement according to specialty....

John Cogdell & Co vs James James. Jury sworn. We find for the plaintiff
s 4 damages with cost of suit....

John Cogdell & Co vs Philip James. Jury sworn. We find for the plaintiff one shilling damages and cost of suit.

Moses Knight vs Andrew Gibson   agreed.

Smith E. Mitchell & Co. vs Vining & Evans. Jury sworn we find for the
plaintiffs with one shilling damages and costs of suit.

Benjamin Outlaw vs David Growter. Agreed at Plaintiffs

William Coward vs Willis & Wm Hodges. Agreed at plaintiff cost.

Samuel Brown returned a dedimus with bonds executed by Isiah Watkins
and Elizabeth Watkins with Luke Pryor and George Cherry, securities....
letters testamentary do issue.

James Gordon vs Luke Pryor. The deft. appeared and confessed Judgment.

Ordered that William Easterling Esqr. be appointed to bind Peardy Tray
a poor orphan Lad to David Stewart and his complying with the requisets....
and giving the lad twelve months schooling.

Ordered that the court do adjourn untill tomorrow Ten Oclock.

Tuesday Dec. 8th 1789. Court met according to adjournment. Present
George Hicks, Tristram Thomas, William Easterling, Samuel Brown and
William Thomas, Esquires.

Gulley Moore vs Thomas Stevens. The deft. appeared in open court &
confessed judgment for ₺ 20 and cost of suit.

Thomas Stevens vs Isham & James Hodges. Jury sworn. Names of the Jurors:
Luke Pryor, Jacob Darbey, Dill Cottingham, Enoch Harry, Daniel Cottingham,
David Lee, Thos Herringdine, Benjamin Outlaw, Mathew Murphy, John Evans
Junr., James Gillespie, Demsey Walton. We find for plaintiff s 10 and
costs of suit.

The commissioners appointed to let out the public building made the
following report. To the Worshipfull the Justices of the County Court of
Marlborough County--The first report of the Commissioners appointed to
let the County buildings and draw plans of the same--is submited: Your
Commissioners have let the building of a Goal of the following Demintions
Viz, Seventy four feet long & wide enough to contain two rooms Ten feet
in the clear each and eight feet pitch.
    The building was let to the lowerst bidder for ₺ 70. Majr. Tristram
Thomas became the undertaker and has finished the work agreeable to
contract which has been received by your Commissioners & th Keys herewith
presented to the Court.
    Your Commissioners therefore recommend that the County Treasurer
be directed to make a settlement with the undertaker and pay him for his
service agreeable to our Contract with him and the order of Court for
raining the last County Tax.
    Ordered that the Keys be Delivered up to the sheriff of this County.

Henry William Harrington vs Wm Pownsey & Stephen Parker. Wm Pownsey appeared and confessed Judgement for ₺ 119 s 16 d 8 sterling with interest
from January last with stay of Execution 2 months.

Jesse Evans vs Danl Sparks & Silas Pearce. Judgment confessed according
to specialty & cost.

Dec. term 1789

William Ratliff vs John Wright. Dismissed.

Exor of Mason vs Wm Furnall. Continued.

Ephraim Rigdon vs Andrew Gibson Non suit.

Hubbard Stevens vs John Coulson Agreed

Joseph Boothe vs Dickson Pearce. On motion of the defts. attorney, ordered that leave be granted for the defts. to withdraw his pleas and confess judgment for the amount of specialty & cost.

Daniel Sparks vs Benjamin Arrandell. Appeal Judgment affirmed with cost of suit. Samuel Sparks attendance 5 days 12/0

The court proceeding in the election of a Sheriff and Mr. William Pledger was unanimously elected.

The court proceeding in the election of a coroner and Mr. John Wilson was unanimously elected.

Ordered that the court do adjourn untill tomorrow Ten Oclock.

Wednesday Dec. the 9th 1789. The court met according to adjournment. Present George Hicks, Thomas Evans, William Easterling, Morgan Brown and Drury Robertson, Esquires.

Ordered that a dedimus be directed to Thomas Evans Esqr. to qualify Edward Smith admr. of the estate of Fredrick Smith and appraisers to appraise sd. estate.

Finley Christie vs Daniel Sparks. Agreed.

Alexander Campbell & Co. vs Aaron Snoden. Jury sworn. We find for the plaintiff ₤ 33 2/2 and cost of suit.

Richard Stinson vs John Due. Sam Sparks attendance 6 days 15/ continued at plaintiff cost.

Mason & Taylor vs Jess Doughlass. continued.

John Cogdell & Co vs Edward Smith. Jury sworn, we find for plaintiffs ₤ 13 17/3 and cost of suit. Subject to Installments.

Drury Robertson vs Peter Bainbridge. Jury sworn. We find for the plaintiff and one shilling damages and cost of suit.

Peter Smith vs Wm Fraizer. Issue Joind.

John Doughty vs Carney Wright. Issue Joind.

Luvesey Faircloath vs John Jorge. Issue Joind.

Henry Easterling vs Aaron Pearson. Issue Joind.

Wm Stubs vs James Wise. Issue Joind.

Outlaw & Smith vs D & S Sparks. Issue Joind.

Thos G. Scott vs Nathanil Cogshall. Issue Joind.

Dill Cottingham appeared and proved his attendance as a witness in the suit Thos Stevens vs Isham & James Hodges which amounts to s 13 d 6 stg.

Benjamin Hicks vs Alexander Campbell The defendant pleaded in abatement to the writ. ordered that the decision be posponed untill next Term.

45

Dec. term 1789

Isham Stroud appeared and proved the last will and testament of Elizabeth Stroud the due execution of which was proved by Isaiah Watkins.
Ordered that a dedimus be directed to Samuel Brown Esq. to qualify the appraisers....

Drury Robertson vs Peter Bainbridge. Ordered that an appeal be granted in this case as the deft. complying with the requisets required by law.

Ordered that a dedimus be directed to Morgan Brown and William Thomas Esqr. to take the examination of Sarah Hicks wife of Col. Hicks touching her consent concerning a deed from sd. George Hicks to Drury Robertson...

George Hicks and Drury Robertson made their return and dedimus directed to them to take the examination of Martha Sparks touching her consent to a deed from Daniel Sparks to Josiah Evans....

Ordered that the Court do adjourn untill court in course.

Monday March the first day 1790. The court met according to adjournment. Present George Hicks, Morgan Brown, Thomas Evans & Wm Easterling, Esqrs.

Ordered that the petit Jury be drawn from No 3 to 1 for next June term. Ordered that the Grand Jury be called which was done.

Thomas Evans Esqr. returned a recognizance from Elias Hillson to the Justices of this County, continued over till next term.

Duncan McRa & Co vs Dickson Pearce. P Summons The deft. confessed judgement Ŀ 4 s 16 d 5 stg. with lawfull interested from 4 June 1786. Subject to the Installment law.

Finley McCaskell vs Robert Gray. P. S. Ordered that a Judicial Attachment be granted in this case.

Exors of Charles Mason vs William Forniss. P. S. Agreed at the defts. cost.

William Powe appeared and acknowledged a deed to Thomas Stevens for 400 acres which was ordered to be recorded.

Daniel Brown Esqr. wishing to be allowed the liberty of pleading at this bar...so ordered.

William Pegues appeared and proved the last will and testament of Claudius Pegues Esqr. decd, the execution of which was proved by William Powe and Daniel Hicks.

Ordered that the court adjourn till tomorrow nine Oclock.

Tuesday March 2nd 1790. The court met according to adjournment. Present George Hicks, Morgan Brown, Tristram Thomas.

Isham Hodges vs Thos Stevens. Attatchment Dismissed at Plaintiff cost.

Peter Smith vs Wm Frazer Continued.

Henry Esterling vs Aron Pearson Judgment confessed according to special.

Thomas G. Scott vs Nathaniel Coggshall. Agreed at the defts. costs.

John Jones James appeared and proved the will of Josiah Evans Esquire deceased. The execution of which was proved by Enoch Harry.

Lucres Faircloth vs John George. Jury Sworn. We find for the pltff. Ŀ 20 sterling with cost of suit. Benj. David, foreman.

March term 1790

Ordered that Jacob Abbott constable be fined 2/6 for neglect of his duty.

Phillip Hodges vs John Mayes. John Lide bail for deft....
Ordered that the sehriff do take John Mayes into his custody untill be
given special bail in the above case.

Carney Wright vs Hubbart Stevens. Jacob Abbott bail for deft. in this
case appeared & delivered the deft. Hubbart Stevens. Ordered that the
sheriff take sd. Hubbart Stevens into his custody untill he give special
bail in the above case.

Jonathan John appeared and acknowledged himself special bail in the
above case.

William Stubbs vs James Wise. Slander. Jury Sworn we find for the
pltff. Ь 2 s 5 sterling with cost of suit.

Sarah Allison vs David Dudley. Decree for the pltff. according to specialty with costs of suit.

The court approves of Aaron Daniel and Magness Cargill as securities for
Samuel Brown esqr. for admn. of his fathers John Brown's estate.

Ordered that the court do adjourn untill tomorrow 9 Oclock.

Wednesday March the 3rd 1790. Court met according to adournment. Present
Morgan Brown, Tristram Thomas, Samuel Brown, Esquires.

Richard Stinson vs John Due. Jury Sworn. Ordered that the court do adjourn for 15 minutes then to meet in the house of Mr. Richard Stinson.

The court met according to adjournment.

John Wilson appeared and proved a mortgage from James Due to James Blanton for one negroe wench and child which was ordered to be recorded.

Majr. Tristram Thomas exr. of Philip Pledger decd. returned an acct. of
the receipts and expenditures...but cannot make a conclusive settlement
for want of a return of the papers relative to sd. estate which were in
possession of Joseph Pledger Esqr. deceased.

Ordered that the admx. of Joseph Pledger deced. return to the next court
all papers & accounts relative to Philip Pledgers estate....

Samuel Brown Esqr. appeared and entered into bond with Aaron Daniel &
Magness Cargill licenters for the due extn. of the admn. of John Browns
estate....

Exors of John Mitchell vs Mathew Whitfield. Continued.

John Wilson vs James Reed. Withdrawn at the plaintiffs cost.

Benjamin Arrandell vs Daniel Sparks. Discontinued at the Plaintiff.

Sarah James vs Francis Brown admx. of Thos Ayer. Agreed at Defendants
cost.

Josiah Audabesh vs Daniel Sparks. Judgement confessed according to
specialty with stay of execution three months with cost of suit.

The Jury in the case Richard Stinson vs John Due returned following...
We find for deft. Benj. David, foreman.

Frederick Felts & Co vs Joseph Brown. Dismissed at the plaintiffs cost.

Robert Allison appeared and made application for joint admn. with his
wife Elizabeth Allison admx. to the estate of Joseph Pledger decd....

March term 1790

William Covington prefered a petition to this court setting forth that
William Falconer practising attorney is justly indebted to him for Ł 20
sterling. Ordered that sd. William Falconer do answer to the above...

Alexander Outlaw & Alexander Smith vs Daniel Sparks & Samuel Sparks.
Jury Sworn. We find for the pltf. s 1 damage with cost of suit.

William Thomas vs John Wright & Carney Wright. Case. Carney Wright
appeared and confessed judgment for Ł 12 s 14 d 7 sterling and cost of
suit on stay of executn. untill the first of Jan. next.

Claudius Pegues, William Pegues, and James Gillespie appeared in court
and proved the will of William Hardick deceased. The execn. was proved
by Moris & Nathl Knight. Ordered that the sd. executors be qualified, and
a dedimus be issued to Claudius Pegues Senr Esqr. to qualify.

Ordered that the court adjourn till tomorrow 10 oclock.

[N. B. the succeeding days of March term and following terms will be
  found on pp. 19ff.]

Tuesday September the second 1788. The court met according to adjournment
Present Morgan Brown, Tristram Thomas, Samuel Brown, Esqrs. Orderd
that the Grand Jurors be called.

Luke Pryor	1	Samuel Terrel	7
John Evans Jun	2	Edmund Brown	8
Joshua Ammons	3	Demsey Watson	9
Shad Easterling	4	Thomas Vining	10
Thomas Ammons	5	John Huse	11
William Leggett	6	Jesse Bathea	12

names of the G. Jurors that do not appear Jesse Wilds, John Odam, John
Dyer, John Sutton, Jonathan Marine, Daniel Sparks.

Names of the petit Jurors that appear William Stubbs, Samuel Cox, Alex
Beverly, George Traywick, John Lee, Jonah David, Isham Hodges, John
Hubbard, James Spears, Joel McNatt, James Stubbs, Thomas Hucabe.

Defaulters of the petit jurors.

Thomas Summerlin	1	James Conner	8
Charles Cottingham	2	Aaron Knight	9
Thomas Godfrey	3	Thomas Perase	10
John Hillson	4	John Daniel	11
Wm Cox	5	Jesse Baggett	12
Joseph Mason	6		
Azariah David	7		

Thomas Evans esquire returned a dedimus with bonds executed by John Dyer
and Wm Luke admrs. of David Luke, Enoch Evans Junr & Azariah David, securities. Orderd that letters of admn. do issue to sd. John Dyer and
William Luke.

State vs Robert Clary. T As battery. True Bill Luke Pryor, fm.

State v Elias Brassier. True Bill Luke Pryor, fm. Ordered that a bench
warant do issue in this case.

State vs Richard Evans. Assault & Battery. True Bill. Ordered that a
bench warrent do issue in this case.

Ordered that Samuel Brown Esqr. is appointed to bind Bartholomew Whittington and Mary his wife over to next court to give evidence in the case
the state vs Elias Brasier.

Ordered that a dedimus be directed to Thomas Evans to qualify the admrs.
of the estate of John Frazer decd.

Sept. term 1788

State vs Robert Clary T A & Battery. Jury sworn Guilty. Isham Hodges, foreman. Ordered that afsd. Robert Clary be find Ł 7 sterling....

Ordered that a dedimus be directed to Tristram Thomas Esqr. to qualify the admrs. and appraisers of the estate of Lewis Edward decd.

Richard Perdew vs Mary Falkner. Slander. Dismissed at plaintiff cost.

Duncan McRa & Co vs Quick & Jordan. Solomon Quick appeared in court and confessed Judgment.

Ordered that Samuel Brown, Luke pryor & George Cherry Esqrs. be arbitrators to determine a matter between William Whitfield plaintiff and Mathew Murphey deft. to make return to next court.

John Daniel vs Joel McNatt. Debt. Jury sworn. we find for the plaintiff Ł 8 s 13 d 10 sterling with cost of suit. Isham Hodges, foreman.

Admrs. of Edward Jones vs Wm Killingsworth. Attach. Decree in favor of plaintiff Ł 8 s 1 d 2 with cost of suit. Ordered that the property in this case be returned to the sheriff in order to be sold to satisfy the above decree.

Isham Hodges vs Daniel Sparks. Debt. We find for the plaintiff Ł 14 s 2 d 3 sterling with cost of suit John Odom foreman.

Luke Pryor vs Ben Cox. Judgement confessed according to Specialty on motion. Ordered that the deft. do give security agreeable to the installment law.

Moses Knight vs Andrew Gibson. Attach. Ordered that the deft. do give special bail and that the cause be continued over till next court.

Ordered that Joel Winfield be fined s 4 d 8 for neglect of his Duty.

Ordered that the court do adjourn till tomorrow 9 Oclock.

Wednesday Sept. 3rd 1788. Court met according to adjournment. Present Morgan Brown, Tristram Thomas, Moses Pearson & Thomas Evans, Esquires.

Ordered that James Moore is fined s 4 d 8 for neglect of his Duty.

Finley Christie & Co vs Charles Frazier. P Summons. Decree for the pltff. Ł 5 s 14 d0½ sterling & cost of suit.

Duncan McRa & Co vs Richd & Mary Edens. P Summons. Decree for the plaintiff Ł 5 s 19 d 5 with cost of suit.

Benj Kolb vs Moses Ford & Joshua Lucas. Debt. Moses Ford appeared in Court and confessed Judgt. for Ł 153 s 3 d 1 sterling and cost of suit.

same vs same Moses Ford appeard and confessed judgt. for Ł 259 s 1 d 3 sterling and cost of suit.

Exors. of Charles Anslee Steward vs Daniel Sparks. Debt We find for the plaintiff full sum of note with lawfull interest, and credit on the back of said note Ł 606 s 2 d 6 paid Nov. 6 1778. Isham Hodges, foreman.

Joseph Costneham vs Daniel Welsh. Case Jury sworn we find for the pltff. Ł 28 11 5 sterling with cost of suit.

Guthridge Lyons vs Wm Field. Appeal. The appelle appeared and withdrawed his suit at his own cost.

State vs Light Townsend. Assault & Battery . True Bill. Ordered that a bench warrant do issue.

Sept. term 1788

Finley Christie & Co vs Samuel Terrel. Debt. Decreed that the deft. be ruled to special bail.

David Evans vs Exrs. of Thomas Pearce. Dismissed at plaintiff cost.

Nathaniel Sanders vs Jesse John. Case. Agreed at plaintiff cost.

Nathaniel Sanders vs Joseph Owens. Case. Agreed at plaintiff cost.

William Kennedy vs Robert McTyre. Debt. We find for deft. with cost of suit.

Martha Freeman vs James Conner. Dismissed at plaintiff cost.

Isham Hodges vs Peter Heagin. Trover. Continued at plaintiff cost.

Isham Hodges vs John Wilson Decree for the deft.

Patrick Bagan vs Jethro Moore. Debt. The deft. appeared and confessed judgt. in this case.

Exrs. of Ely Kershaw vs James Due. Decree for the pltff Ł 7 3 6 with interest and cost of suit. To be paid agreeable to the Installment Law.

Tristram Thomas vs Admrs. of Edwd Jones. Judgement by default.

Gideon Sproles(?) vs James McNatt. Nonsuit.

David Dudley vs Ben Arrandell. discontinued.

Ordered that Jesse Vining be appointed constable for this county.

Ordered that Joseph Brown be appointed overseer of the road instead of Joseph Mason with the same hands to work under his directions.

Ordered that Thomas Evans Esqr. be directed to produce his books in court next term in order to inform the court how much money he has recd as Treasurer of this County & how he has disposed of the same.

Ordered that David Lee be permitted to retail spiritous liquors by the Quart within this county for one year insuing this day.

Whereas it is necessary to tax the county for the purpose of defraying the expences of building a Gaol, Ordered that a tax be levyed in the following manner (viz) one fifth part of Public Tax for the year 88 to be paid on or before the 31st of January next good merchantable pork @ 14 shillings P Ct. good indigo of the first qualify @ 4 shillings P pound shall be received in payment if delivered by the above mentioned day to Colonel Hicks or Major Thomas....

Ordered that this court do dismiss that special verdict in the case Exrs of Steward vs Danl Sparks as _____.

Ordered that Edward Smith pay to the County Treasury $6.25 untill other way directed by the court to be paid to Mary Walsh toward the maintainance of her Bastard child.

Daniel Welsh appeared in court and agree to pay the aforesd. Mary Welsh Ł 5 proc. money.

Ordered that a scape Warrant do issue agt. Robert Clary.

Ordered that Jacob Abbot be continued constable for the ensuing year.

Ordered that the court do adjourn till court in course.

Dec. term 1788

Monday December the 1st day 1788. Court met according to adjournment. Present George Hicks, Claudius Pegues, and William Easterling, esqrs.

Ordered that the grand Jurors be drawn to serve next March term 1 to 4. Ordered that the petit Jurors be drawn from 2 to 3.

Ordered that Daniel Sparks be excused for non attendance last Term as a grand juror.

Ordered that all citations issuing from this court be published ten days previous to the Court they are made returnable to & otherwise contd. to the ensuing court.

Ordered that all the Petit & Grand Jurors that were noted as defaulters last term be excused.

Ordered that a dedimus be directed to Thomas Evans Esqr. to quallify the admrs. and appraisers to the estate of Owen Luke decd.

Ordered that Edward Smith do pay to the county treasurer 4/8 sterling & quarterly instead of $6.25 as was directed last court to be paid to Mary Walsh.

The State vs Darby Smithhart. Inditement for Stealing a hog. a true bill. Luke Pryor, fm.

Ordered that James Hodges do shew cause tomorrow why a rule should not be made for him to deliver up certain property said to be Silas Stevens which he retains in his possession.

Edmd. Brown vs Saml Sparks. Debt. Agreed at the Deft. cost.

Alex Smith vs Jesse Wilds. Debt. Continued by the installment.

Ordered that all debts that come under the installment be & continued over untill the 25th March next.

James Wise vs Jno Stubbs. Case Agreed at the Plts. cost.

Joshua Lisonby vs Wm Gordon. Debt. (stricken)

David Evans vs Danl Sparks & Silas Pearce. Debt. Agrd.

Mary Jones vs Sam Sparks & Thos Vinig. Judgemt. confessed according to specialty to be paid agreeable to the installment Law.

Morgan Brown Esqr. appeared and acknowledged a deed to Jacob Abbott for 150 acres which was ordered to be recorded.

Moses Knight vs John Wright. Agreed.

Martha Freeman vs James Conner. Agreed.

Gideon Sowles vs James McNatt. Agreed.

Mr. John Wilson appeared in open court and resined the Clerk office of Marlborough County and Morgan Brown Esqr. be required to give up his bond for his performance of office.

The Court proceeded to elect a Clerk and Joel Winfield was duly appointed Clerk in the room of Mr. Wilson.

Ordered that the Court do adjourn till tomorrow 10 Oclock.

Tuesday Dec. 3rd 1788. Court met according to adjournment. Geo Hicks, Morgan Brown, Trist Thomas, Saml Brown, Esqrs. present.

Benjamin Cox vs Luke Pryor. Discontinued at plaintiff cost.

Duncan McRa vs Wm Shepperd. Attachment ordered that the property attachd. be sold 22d of this inst., if not replevied by that time by the deft....

John Jones vs Andrew Gibson. Trover Jury Sworn. We find for the plaintiff Ł 5 s 16 d 8 sterling with lawful interest from 1 Jan 1781 with cost of suit. Josiah Evans, fm. Witnesses fees Aaron Knight, 1 day; Jacob Abbott 2 days @ 2/6.

The State vs Darby Smithhart. Hog stealing. Guilty Josiah Evans, fm.

Ordered that Edward Smith do give sufficient security to the Clerk of this county to keep a certain Bastard child of Mary Welsh from being chargable to this county....

A caviat being entered in this case of Wm Hardwick decd. On motion, ordered that all proceeding thereon be stayed untill the caveat be determined.

Hugh Asken vs Wm Whitfield. Debt. Judgemt confessed according to Specialty. consideration for rent.

Samuel Brown Esqr. returned a dedimus with bonds executed by William Driggers admor of Charles Kiby; Luke Pryor & William Mixon securities, which was approved of by the court....

Ordered that the court do adjourn till tomorrow 9 Oclock.

Wednesday Dec. 3rd 1788. Court met according to adjournment. Present Morgan Brown, Tristram Thomas, and Thomas Evans, Esquires.

Ordered Darby Smithhart do remain inthe custody of the Sheriff untill the 18th of this instant, and then to receive twenty five lashes on the bare back well laid on. If the sd. Darby Smithhart does not pay unto the sheriff Ł 5 proc. money at or before that day.

Benjm. Arrandell vs Edwd & Jos. Roe. Debt. Agreed.

Joseph Roe vs Benjm. Arrandell. Damage Agreed.

Samuel Sparks vs John Frazer. P. Summons. Trover Decree for the plaintiff Ł 1 s 10 & cost of suit.

Mary F. Debruhl vs John Frazer. P. Sums Debt decree for the plaintiff Ł 8 sterling and interest with cost of suit.

Robert Biggard vs Hubbart Stevens. Agreed.

Ordered that a dedimus be directed to Moses Pearson Esqr. to qualify the admrs. and appraisers to the estate of Charles Kirby decd.

Tristram Thomas Esqr. returned a Dedimus with bonds executed by Solomon Lisonby admor of James Reed; Isham Hodges and Welcome Hodges, security....

Fredrick B. Myers vs John Holcom. Dismissed.

Joel Winfield vs Danl Sparks. Debt Quashed.

Isham Hodges vs Thos Stevens Attachment Ł 32 Thomas Pearce and Daniel Cottingham appeared and acknowledged themselves special bail in this suit for Ł 32 sterling.
Ordered that the returning officer do give up the property by him attachd.

Gully Moore vs Thos Stevens. Writ. Thomas Pearce acknowledged himself special bail in this suit for Ł 20 sterling.

Ordered that the County Treasurer do pay to Mr. John Wilson the sum of ₤ 5 s 11 sterling for his annual fee for the year 1788.

Samuel Sparks appeared and acknowledged a deed to Willis Williamson for 45 acres which was ordered to be recorded.

Ordered that the settlement with the Tresurer of this county be posponed untill next court.

Ordered that the whole of the county tax for the year 1786 be collected immediately.

Ordered that the court do adjourn untill Court in Course.

March March the second. The Court met according to adjournment. Present George Hicks, Tristram Thomas, Moses Pearson and William Thomas, Esquires.

Ordered that the petit be drawn to serve next June term from No 2 to 3
Ordered that the grand Jury be called. Names of the Grand Jury that appear

Jesse Douglas	1	Joshua David	7
Barns. Hennagan	2	George Cherry	8
Edwd. Crossland	3	Isham Hodges	9
Saml Sparks	4	Benj David	10
Peter Hubbard	5	Dickson Pearce	11
John Daniel	6	James Due	12
	William Covington		

Names of the Grand Jury that do not appear

Magness Cargill	1	Silas Pearce	5
Wm Murry	2	James McGee	6
Richd Brockington	3)	were noted as Defaulters for non attendance	
Wm Brockington	4)		

Ordered that the Petit Jury be called. Names of the petit Jurors that appear

James Conner	1	Wm Mixon	11
Wm Beesely	2	Stephen McClendol	12
Burrell Huggins	3	James Stubbs	13
Jas Spears	4	Thos Herringden	14
Lewis Holms	5	Josiah Beesely	15
Thos Hodges	6	David Growter	16
Robt Purnal	7	James Beesely	17
Benj Thomas	8	John Townsend	18
Wm Fields	9	Benj. Hicks	19
Solom. Lisonby	10	Simon Cherry	20

Names of the Petit Jurors that do not appear

Edwd Traywick	1	Jonathan John	6
Mackey Mcnatt	2	Short Long	7
Hardy Steward	3	Josiah Brown	8
Wm Coward	4	Lochran Curry	9
Light Townshend	5	were noted as Defaulters for non attendance.	

Ordered that David Dudley be permitted to retail spiritous liquors by the quart within this county during the term of one year....

Ordered that Thomas Cochran be permitted to retail spiritous liquors for one year....

William Mixon appeared and acknowledged a deed for 150 acres to Samuel Burkett which was ordered to be recorded.

Ordered that a dedimus be directed to Thomas Evans Esquire to qualify the admx. and appraisers to the estate of Joseph Pledger decd.

Ordered that a dedimus be directed to Thomas Evans Esqr. to qualify the admrs. and appraisers to the estate of John Hubbard decd.

March term 1789

Ordered that the Court do adjourn till tomorrow ten Oclock.

Tuesday March 3rd 1789. The court met according to adjournment. Present George Hicks, Tristram Thomas, Moses Pearson and William Easterling, Esquires.

Ordered that the court do adjourn untill a half past Eleven Oclock to the meeting house above naked creek.

The Court met according to adjournment. (Same justices present)

Jacob Abbott vs John Wright & John Arler. Debt Jury sworn. We find for the plaintiff one shilling damage with cost of suit. Benj. Hicks, fm.

Ordered that Jonathan Wright do give sec'y for in the case J. Wright vs Wm Powsey.

James Due appeared in open court and acknowledged himself security in the above case for cost.

David Dudley vs Benj Arrandell. Continued at pffs. cost.

Richard Perdue vs Mary Falkner. Continued at Defendants cost.

In Sept. last it was ordered that the case Wm Whitfield vs Mathew Murfee should be referred to arbitration...Sept. 5th 1788, we adjudge that Mathew Murfee do pay to Wm Whitfield $3.50 by 1st Monday in Dec. next, with cost of suit. Luke Pryor, George Cherry, Saml Brown.

Jonathan Wright vs Wm Posey. Contd. at pltff costs. Ordered that the deft. give special bail.

Isham Hodges vs Peter Reagan. We find for deft. with cost of suit.

Ordered that the Court do adjourn untill tomorrow Ten Oclock.

Wednesday March the 4th 1789. The court met according to: adjournment. Present George Hicks, Trist. Thomas, Moses Pearson & William Esterling, Esquires.

Isham Hodges vs John Due. Damage Jury sworn. We find for deft. with cost of suit.

On motion, court proceeded inthe determination of the caviat entered Dec. term by John Coulson against the last will and testament of William Hardick decd...court ordered that letters testamentary do issue to the exrs.

Ordered that William Pouncy be permitted to retail spiritous liquors by the quart at Wm Stephen Parkers ferry during one year....

Ordered that Benjamin Hicks & Joel Winfield be permitted to retail spiritous liquors by the quart for one year.

Benj. Arrandell vs Aaron Snoden. Agreed at Deft. cost.

Mathew Whitfield appeared and acknowledged a deed to Benjm Beverly for 84 acres which was ordered to be recorded

Ordered that Messrs. Holms & Coggeshell be permitted to retail spiritous liquors for one year.

Aaron Snoden vs Joel McNatt. Non suit Deft. & cost of suit.

Ordered that Stephen Knight be permitted to retail spiritous liquors by the quart for one year.

March term 1789

Isham Hodges vs Peter Heagans. Ordered that a new trial be granted upon the Plaintiff paying all cost accrued to this Period.

Samuel Smith vs Hubbart Stevens. Non suit.

Robt McTyre vs Thos Williams. Agreed at the Plaintiff costs.

Ordered that David C. Mandeville be permitted to retail spiritous liquors by the quart for one year, at Casuary Ferry on Pee Dee

Ordered that Edward Smith be permitted to keep a tavern within this county for one year.

David Lee acknowledged himself special bail in the suit Wm Whitfield vs Jesse John & Joseph Owens.

Ordered that John McIntosh be permitted to keep a tavern at Kolbs Ferry for one year....

Ordered that George Hicks & Tristram Thomas Esq. be appointed to inspect the Clerks office.

Samuel Sparks vs Daniel Sparks. Discontinued.

Ordered that the court do adjourn untill court in course at Wm Pledger Saw Mill.

Monday the first June 1789. Court met according to adjournment.
Present George Hicks, Tristram Thomas, William Thomas.

Thomas Evans Esqr. returned a dedimus with bonds executed by Elizabeth Pledger, admx. of Joseph Pledger; Tristram Thomas and George Hicks, securities.

Henry Easterling vs Aaron Pearson. Debts. Agreed at Plaintiff cost.

David Evans vs Exrs. of Thomas Pearce. P Summons Decree for the defent.

David Dudley & wife vs Benjamin Arrandell. Assault. Agreed at the plaintiff cost with stay of execution until next court.

Hubbart Stevens vs John Coulson. Non suit.

Ordered that Jesse Bethea Junior be appointed constable in the room of Thomas Ammons.

William Whitfield vs Joseph Owens & Jesse John. Debt. Agreed at the plaintiff cost.

Duncan McRa & Co vs Jesse Bethea. P Summons Debt Agreed at Plffs cost.

David Growter vs Elisha Farless. Agreed at the Defendants cost.

In the case of granting letters of admn. on the estate of Murdock Mc-Fearson, John Murdock having taken out a citation and caviat being entered by John McPherson upon the hearing of which the sd. John Murdock deminish his right & claim...Ordered that a dedimus directed to Thomas Evans Esqr. to qualify John McPharson admr. of Est. of Murdoch McPharson, and the appraisers to said estate.

Ordered that William Evans, Thomas Ammons and John _____ are appointed overseers of the poor for one year....

James Reed vs Richd Perdew. Jury sworn. We find s 5 sterling damages and cost of suit for the plaintiff.

Ordered that the court do adjourn untill tomorrow 10 Oclock.

June term 1789

Tuesday June ye 2nd 1789. The Court met according to adjournment.
Present Tristram Thomas, Thomas Evans and William Easterling.

Ordered that a dedimus to Moses Pearson Esquire to qualify Simon Cherry
as admr. to the estate of William Cherry decd, also the appraisers to
appraise the sd. estate. Thomas Evans Esqr. returned a dedimus with
bonds executed by Moses Fort and Enoch Evans; John Daniel and Samuel
Evans, securities....

Ordered that the sheriff do bring Elias Brasier in court.

Ordered that a dedimus be directed to Thomas Evans Esqr. to qualify
Jesse Douglass and William Evans admors to the estate of Enoch Luke
decd....

John Murdock vs Wm Gordon & Jas. Due. Debt. Agreed at plaintiff cost.

Alexander Smith vs Jesse Wilds. Debt. Jury sworn. We find for the
plaintiff s 1 damage with cost of suit.

Joshua Lisonby vs William Gordon. Debt Jury Sworn we find for the
plaintiff one shilling damage wtih cost of suit.

The state vs John George. Inditement for stealing a bridle. G. Jury
sworn A True Bill   Wm Covington, foreman.

The State vs Cornelious Manderville. Assault. G. Jury A True Bill.

[N. B. The minutes are again out of sequence. The next entry begins
 with March term 1791. The first two pages are badly mutilated, and
 the W. P. A. copy is used to fill in gaps.]

At a County Court of Pleas and Sessions began and held for the County
of Marlborough at the Court House of Said County on 7th March 1791.
Being the first court held under the new Constitution. Before the Honble.
Morgan Brown Esquire...

The Commissions for Morgan Brown, William Thomas and Tristram Thomas
as Judges of the County court are recorded, all dated 19 Feb 1791.

The sheriff, Clerk and county attorney took the oath prescribed by the
constitution.
Jacob Abbott, William Coward, Thomas Hodges, James Hodges, Jesse Brown,
John Dyer, Thomas Ammons,Jesse Vining, Francis Kennedy, Barnebus
Hennagin & Isaac Perkins were appointed constables. Wm Coward, Thos
Hodges, Jesse Brown, John Dyer, Thomas Ammons, Francis Kennedy and
Barnebus Hennagin attended in court and took the oath....

Ordered that the Grand Jury be drawn to serve next Sept. term from No 1
to no. 3.

1. Simon Cherry	8. James Cooks	15.Jno LittleJohn
2. Jas Corneham	9. Wm Mixon	16. Charles Frazer
3. Thomas Huckobie	10. Carney Wright	17. Jesse Douglass
4. Isham Stroud	11. Wm Fields	18. Josiah Beasely
5. Jn McNatt	12. Jno Lee	19. Burrell Huggins
6. Thomas Godfrey	13. Jas Mason	20. James McCarly
7. Jacob Barringtine	14. Richard Green	

Ordered that the petit Jurors be drawn to serve next Sept. term from
No. 1 to No. 2.

1. John Stubbs	11. Alex Bodiford	21. David Steward
2. Duncan McRa	12. Burrell Whittington	22. Jesse Wilds
3. James Gillespie	13. Samuel Cox	23. George Smith
4. Jno Holecome	14. Edward Terrell	24. Jno Evans
5. Danl McIntire	15. Epraim Whittington	25. Wm Beasely
6. Thomas Conner	16. Thomas John	26. James Bolton
7. James Beasely	17. Jno Stroud	27. Wm Forniss

March term 1791

8. Jno Askew	18. James Stubbs	28. Benj David
9. Joshua Ammons	19. David Lee	29. Wm Leggett
10. Wm Cox	20. Welcome Hodges	30. Lockran Curry

Ordered that the court adjourn untill tomorrow Ten Oclock.

Tuesday March the eighth 1791. Court met according to adjournment.
Present Morgan Brown, Tristram Thomas and William Thomas, Esquires.

The State vs Wm Nichols. Hog Stealing. Ordered that the Grand Jurors
be called and sworn which was done accordingly. A True Bill. Barnebus
Hennagan, foreman. Ordered that the sheriff do take William Nichols
into custody....

certificate signed by Morgan Brown that he administered the oath of
justice of the peace to Thomas Evans and Drury Robertson.

Wm Thomas produced certificate that he administered the oath of justice
of the peace to Col. George Hicks, 8 March 1791.

Exors of Jno Mitchell vs Mathew Whitefield. Continued at plaintiff cost.

Benjamin Moore vs David Growter. Slander Jury sworn Thomas Cockran,
foreman; Samuel Sparks, Aaron Snoden, George Smith, John Feagan, Dampsey
Watson, Alexander Beverly, James Spears, Daniel Herring, Mackey McNatt,
Benjn David and Richard Edens. We find for the pltff Ь 5 damage with
cost of suit. Thomas Cockran, fm.

Samuel Brown Esquire one of the Justices came and took the oath prescribed
by the constitution.

The state vs Wm Nichols. Hog Stealing. The prisoner pleaded not guilty.

Mr. John Jones James returned an account of the expenditures of the
estate of Josiah Evans decd....

Mary Jones returned an account of the expenditure of the estate of Edward
Jones decd, but cannot make a final settlement with the court.

Court adjourned till tomorrow Ten Oclock.

Wednesday March 9th 1791. Court met according to adjournment. Present
Morgan Brown, Tristram Thomas and William Thomas.

Ordered that Jonathan John who was Empannelled on a Jury do Immediately
appear in court on the said Jury.

George Cherry vs Jno Lee & Jas Owens. Dismissed.

Isaac Perkins vs Thomas Oguin. Dismissed.

Eli John vs Jesse Wilds & Isham Hodges. Debt. Judgement by default
according to specialty with stay of execution three months.

Nathaniel Coggeshall vs Duncan McPherson & Adame Alexander. P. Summons.
Judgement confessed by Duncan McPherson for Ь 8 s 17d 4 sterling and
cost of suit.

Philemon Thomas vs Exors of Wm Hardick. Judgement by default for amt.
of bond being Ь 23 6/1 sterling with interested. As a judgement has
been obtained against Wm Coward for the same debt which last Judgement
when satisfied shall be a full discharge of this.

Isham Hodges vs Thomas Downer. Continued.

Nathaniel Coggeshall vs Eli John. Dismissed at Defts. costs.

March term 1791

Drury Robertson vs John Conner. Jury sworn. We find that the defts. real name is Hubbard tho he has been called John Stubbs, Long John....

Ordered that the sheriff do issue execution against all persons in arrears for the county tax for the year 1789.

Benjamin Moore vs David Growter. On motion of the defts. attorney for a new trial, not granted. appeal not granted.

Christian Due wife of James Due appeared and renounced her right of dower to 150 acres of land conveyed to Edward Crossland by deed 9 March 1791.

Ordered that the court do adjourn untill the first Monday in May next.

At an Intermediate Court held on the first Monday in May before the Honble Judges of said county.

Messers Moses Pearson & William Easterling appeared and was duly quali-fied as justices of the peace...

Then the court adjourned untill court in course.

Court held 1st day of Sept. 1791. Before Morgan Brown, Tristram Thomas, & William Thomas Esquires.

Ordered that the Jury be drawn to serve next term which was done. Ordered that the sheriff do make out a new Jury list.

John Daniel vs Wm Councell. This suit abates by the death of the deft.

St. David Society vs Wm Councell. This suit abates by the death of the deft.

Ordered that Nathaniel Coggeshall be permitted to retail Spiritous liquors within this county....

Ordered that David and Cornelious Manderville be permitted to retail Spiritous liquors within this county....

Then the court adjourned untill tomorrow 10 Oclock.

Tuesday Sept. the 2nd 1791. The court met according to adjournment present Morgan Brown, Tristram Thomas and William Thomas, Esquires.

Clothier Ratliff vs Wm Jordon. Continued at deft. cost. Ordered that the deft. in this case be ruled to special bale.

State vs Jonathan Gift. Assault & Battery. Grand Jury sworn. True bill. Carney Wright, foreman. Petit Jury sworn. Guilty. James Gil-lespie, foreman.

Lands Stanley vs John Windham. John Windham appeared and confessed Judgement according to specialty with cost of suit.

Exors of John Mitchell vs Mathew Whitfield. Continued at Deft. cost.

Isham Hodges vs Thomas Lowner. Continued at pltff. costs.

Isham Hodges vs Richard Stinson. Continued.

Isaiah Stuty vs Benjm Arnold. Agreed

Holden Wade vs Joseph Brown. Dismissed at plaintiff cost.

Ordered that Jonathan Gift be fined s 10 sterling in each of the bills of inditement agt. him.

Ordered that a process do issue vs Jonathan John empannelled as a Juror at the last court in a trial the state vs Wm Nichols who absented himself before returning the verdict without leave of the court.

Robert Hodges vs Alex Smith. The deft. confessed Judgement for ₺ 9 s 3 d 9 sterling with interest and cost of suit with stay of execution untill first of Jany next.

Ordered that the following children of John Hubbard decd be bound and placed in the following manner, VIZ. Agness and John to be bound to Peter Hubbard; William to be bound to John Little; and Peter to be placed with Anne Baker without binding untill further order from this court.

The State vs Wm Nichols. Hog Stealing. Ordered that a new trial be granted....

Ordered that Elinor Wise be allowed ₺ 5 for the support of her son Drury Wise.

Ordered that Joseph Perkins be allowed ₺ 3 sterling for the support of his wife...and that the receipts of the sd. Joshua & Elinor shall be recd in payment of all fines or county tax ..⸴

Then the Court adjourned untill court in course.

At a County court 1st March 1792. Present Tristram Thomas & William Thomas Esquires.

Ordered that the Jury be drawn to serve next Term, Grand Jurors from No 3 to No 4.   Names of Jurors

Jesse Douglas	1	Moses Murfee Jur.	11
Jesse John	2	Danl Herring	12
Richd Edens	3	James Gillespie	13
Jas Brown	4	Wm Lester	14
Jonh. Cottingham	5	Aaron Pearsor	15
Thos Burkett	6	Isham Davis	16
John McIntosh	7	Chas Frazer	17
Willis Williamson	8	Jesse Askew	18
Jos Costneham	9	Philip Clarke	19
Abram Baggett	10	Jacob Green	20

Petit Jurors from No 2 to No 1.

Moses Parker	1	George Cherry	11	Wm Leggett	21
Wm Edens	2	Henry Hill	12	Benj Bridges	22
Jesse Bethea	3	F Whittington	13	Joshua Ammons	23
Jesse Brown	4	John Brown	14	Robt Purnal	24
Lane Burkett	5	Andw Davis	15	John Bridges	25
David Mandeville	6	Jas Conner	16	Thos Conner	26
Wm Covington	7	Joshua Odam	17	James McGee	27
Saml Brown	8	Luke Pryor	18	James Walsh	28
Jesse Bethea Jur	9	John Pryor	19	James Water	29
James Rabon	10	John Manship	20	Moses Pearson	30

Holden Wade vs Thos Pearce Judgment confessed according to Specialty

Joseph Costneham vs Jno & Duncan McPherson. Agreed.

Ordered that John Murdock be permitted to keep a tavern within this County, William Fields & Wm Covington approved of as securities....

Ordered that Daniel Sparks be permitted to keep a tavern at Kolb ferry in the County... Court adjourned till 10 Oclock tomorrow.

Friday March 2nd 1792. Court met according to adjournment. Present the Hon. William Thomas.

March term 1792

Arter Evans vs Peter Ferrel & alie. debt. P. S. Richard Dunstan
appeared and confessed Judgment according to specialty with cost of
suit and stay of execution until 1 June next, decree by default agt
John Breeden, Peter Farell.

William Evans vs Aaron Pearson. Decree for the plaintiff ₺ 6 s 17 d 1¼
with cost of suit.

Michael Mason vs Herbert Smith & Wm Robertson Debt. Wm Robertson appeared and confessed judgment for the amt. of the note and interest
with cost of suit.

Isham Hodges vs Thomas Downer. Attachment Non suit.

Alexander Smith vs Aaron Snoden & Sam Terrell. Judgement by default,
according to specialty with cost of suit.

State vs Thomas Herringdine. Cow Stealing Grand Jurysworn. True bill.

On information of   Whittington it appears that Susannah Whittington
a bastard child of Elizabeth Whittington is like to become chargeable
to the county...therefore ordered that sd. child be bound to John
Stephens & wife untill she shall attain to the age of 18 years.

George Cherry was duly qualified as a Justice of the peace.

We the Grand Jurors for the County of Marlborough do present as a grievance the very bad repair in which the roads is kept at Phills Creek to
the emminent danger of women and children, and the great detention of
travelling.

We further present John Murdock for retailing spiritous liquors by the
half gallon contrary to law on Saturday 24th Dec last by the information
of Richard Stinson.

Ordered that a process do issue against John Murdock to show cause by
tomorrow ten oclock why an inditement should not be laid agt. him....

Clothier Ratliff vs William Jordon. Continued at deft. cost.

Then the court adjourned till tomorrow 10 Oclock.

Saturday March the 3rd 1792. Court met according to adjournment. Present
the Honble. Morgan Brown, Tristram Thomas and William, Esquires (sic)

State vs William Nichols. Hog Stealing Jury sworn. Not guilty.

Exors John Mitchell vs Mathew Whitfield. Continued at plaintiff cost
and ordered thatTristram Thomas Esqr. do take Jonathan John's examination
in this case on the deft. giving plaintiff legal notice.

Samuel Sparks vs Jonathan Gift. Decree for the pltff. ₺ 3 sterling with
cost suit.

Peter Smith vs Jesse Wilds. Continued at plaintiff cost.

Isham Hodges vs Richard Stinson. Decree for the deft. with cost of suit.

Evander McCallum vs Maloney Ayers. Trover Judgement by default and
order for writ of inquiry to be executed next court.

Isham Hodges vs John McCartey Attachment. Discontinued at pltff. cost.

Edmund Blackman vs Samuel Councell. Agreed.

State vs Thomas Herringdine. Corn stealing. Jury sworn. Not guilty.

March term 1792

John Bound vs Thomas Pearce. Discontinued.

James Moore vs John Smithhart. Contd. at deft. cost.

Ordered that the rule against John Murdock be extended untill Court.

William Pledger was elected sheriff.

Isham Hodges vs Thomas Downer. Welcome Hodges acknowledged himself
special bail for the deft.

Ordered that the court adjourn till court in Course.

Saturday, Sept. 1st 1792, at a County of Pleas and Sessions...before the
Hon. William Thomas, Tristram Thomas and Morgan Brown, Esquires.

Ordered that the Grand Jurors be drawn to serve next Term from No 3 to
No 4   Names of Grand Jurors.

John Moore	1	Duncan McCall	11
John Daniel	2	Isaiah Wodkins	12
David McCall	3	Christopher McRa	13
Alexander Bodiford	4	Robert Allison	14
Elisha Parker Jur.	5	Malchi Badgegood	15
David Curby	6	Adam Alexander	16
Burrel Whittington	7	Wm Brockington	17
Thos Vining	8	Richard Brockington	18
Wm Steward	9	Alexander Peterkin	19
Wm Mixom	10	Joseph Sister	20

Petit Jurors Names   drawn from No 1 to No 2

Thomas John	1	Dempsey Watson	16
John Stroud	2	Charles Cottingham	17
Joseph Owens	3	Jesse Stevens	18
Willeby Browton	4	Wm Morris	19
Eli King	5	James Parish	20
James Cook	6	John Askew	21
David Bethea	7	Edmund Brown	22
Isham Hagins	8	Daniel Sillivan	23
Joseph Cox	9	Morris Clark	24
Shadrach Easterling	10	John McIntire	25
Benj Evans	11	James Bolton	26
Henry Easterling	12	Azariah David	27
Reubin Cook	13	George Bland	28
David Harry	14	John McRa	29
Jesse James	15	Duncan McRa	30

In consequence of a state warrent being issued against John Washington
Stevens for passing to Jno McPherson a ten shilling bill supposed to be
counterfiet the said Stevens came voluntarily & delivered himself up a
prisoner to the court who ordered him into custody of the sheriff.

Ordered that a dedimus be directed to George Hicks & Drury Robertson
to examine Nancy Reid wife of James Reid touching her consent of dower
to a tract sold John Wilson Esquire by James Reid.

The Grand Jurors being called there not being sufficient number to do
business were dismissed and ordered to attend court on Monday next at
10 oclock.

Ordered that court do adjourn untill Monday next 10 Oclock.

Monday Sept. 3 1792. Court met according to adjournment. Present William
Thomas & Tristram Thomas, Esquires.

Clothier Ratcliff vs William Jordan. Case. Jury sworn. Ordered that
the verdict be recorded, we find for pltff. Ⱡ 9 s 6 d 8 with cost of
suit.

Sept. term 1792

Silas Pearse vs Jesse Wilds. P. Summs. Deft. came & confessed Judgment for amt of specialty with costs.

Eleazer Elizer vs Saml Blyth, Edw C. Debruhl & Edward Smith. P. S. Debt Judgment by default. Decree for pltff. for ℔ 9 sterling & 8/ with costs.

Sylvanus Crunk vs Daniel Curry. P. Summs. Judgment by default. Decree for pltff. ℔ 9 sterling & 8/ with cost.

Robert Allison vs Samuel Terrel. P. Sums. Deft. confessed Judgment for debt ℔- 7 s 6 d 6¼ sterlg. with costs.

Exrs. of John Mitchell vs Mathew Whitfield. P Sums. Nonsuit on amt of the specialty being debt Mislaid.

Richard Stinson vs John Murdock. Damage, agreed at deft. costs.

Richard Stinson vs John Murdock. Detinue, agreed at defts. costs.

Richard Stinson vs Samuel Brown. Assumpset. Nonsuit.

Samuel Brown vs Lucretia Studivent. on appeal, judgment reversed and judgment for plaintiff in the appeal.

William Smith vs Isom Hodges. Capias. Ordered that the verdict be recorded debt on specialty, we find for pltff. ℔ 12 s 8 d 2 sterling with cost of suit.

William Strother vs Jesse Wilds. Capias. Debt. The deft. appeared & confessed judgment for ℔ 12 sll d 4½ with interest from 24 Sept 1790 with cost & stay of execution from 1 March next.

Ordered that the court do adjourn untill tomorrow nine oclock.

Tuesday Sept. 4th 1792. Court met according to adjournment. Present William Thomas & Tristram Thomas, Esquires.

State vs William Goodwin. Corn stealing. a true Bill. James Gillespie, fm.

State vs Benjamin Arrandel. Assault. A True bill.

Edward c. Debruhl vs Levi Solomon. Case continued at Plaintiffs cost.

Aaron Daniel vs William Fields. Capias. Deft. confessed judgment for ℔ 8 s 18 d 5 sterling with cost of suit.

Peter Smith Sr. vs Jesse Wilds. P Sums settled at defts. cost.

Alexander Smith vs William Covington. Debt. Continued at defts. cost.

John Murdock vs Dunston Terrel. Attachment. Decree for the deft. & cost of suit.

Jesse James vs Robert Oliphant. Attachment. We find for pltff. ℔ 15 s 18 sterling with cost. Ordered that the sheriff do expose to public sale two feather Beds & furniture, one pewter dish, eight do plates, four ditto basons, a small parcell of earthen ware, one pine table, one cypress do, skillets & one copper tea kettel, the property of the deft.

State vs Benj Arrandel. Assault. Guilty. Moses Pearson, fm.
Ordered that the deft. be find ℔ 4 stg. & that he do give good security for his good behaviour for 12 month and one day....

State vs John White. Indictment for Counterfeiting. A true bill.

Sept. term 1792

Ordered that Wm Pledger sheriff do deliver John White to the Gaolar of the District Gaol at Greenville. [N. B. This is not Greenville County; this Greenville was the seat of Cheraws District--BHH.]

James Moore vs John Smithart. Trover. Process. Decree for pltff. Ŀ 3 with cost of suit.

Robert Allison vs John Murdock. Debt. Deft. confessed judgt. for Ŀ 15 s 14 with cost of suit.

State vs William Goodwin. Corn Stealing. Not guilty.

Exrs. of Robert Blair vs Aaron Pearson. Debt. Deft. confessed Judgment for Ŀ 53 s 16 d 6½ with cost of suit.

Lewis Malone Ayers vs Samuel & George Wilds. Debt. Judgment confessed by deft. for Ŀ 20 with lawfull interest from 1 January 1792 with one shilling damamge and cost of suit, with stay of execution till 1 March 1793.

State vs John Washington Stevens. Indictment for Counterfeiting. A true bill. Ordered that sd. John Washington Stevens be discharged with proclamation.

Ordered that Drury Robertson Esquire do bind over John McPherson & Robertson Carloss to appear at the next circuit court to be held at Greenville for the District of Cheraws on the 10th Nov next to give evidence on the part & behalf of tne state of S. C. vs John White for counterfeiting.

John Wilson vs Adams Alexander. Debt. deft. confessed judgment for the amt. of note interest & cost of suit.

Ordered that court do adjourn untill Court in Course.

At a County court held 1st March 1793. Before Tristram Thomas and William Thomaes, Esquires.

Ordered that the Grand Jury be drawn to serve next court from 3 to 4.
Names Grand Jurors

1	Samuel Cox	11	James Spears
2	Thomas Turner	12	John Hillson
3	Gulley Moore	13	Jas Pouncey
4	Mishack Ginn	14	Mathew Murfee
5	George Wilds	15	J. J. James
6	John Doughlass	16	Henry Dilling
7	Jno Smithhart	17	George Smith
8	Ephraim Whittington	18	Joseph Ellison
9	Aaron Snoden	19	Jesse Vining
10	John Holcomb	20	Samuel Thomas

Petit Jury from No 1 to No 2 Names of Petit Jurors

1	Azariah David	11	Moses Parker	21	John Huse
2	Edward Feagins	12	Zackery Ayers	22	Wm Morris
3	Joseph Dillport	13	Edward Crossland	23	Nath. Humphreys
4	Jonathan Cutler	14	James Reed	24	John Lee
5	Baron Poelnik	15	Joseph Jones	25	Wm Fields
6	Enoch Harry	16	George Stanton	26	Isham Hodges
7	Wm Forniss	17	Charles Barringtine	27	Lewis Holms
8	Wm Beasley	18	Jonh. Brown	28	John Willis
9	John Dyer	19	John Bohannan	29	Jarvis Stafford
10	Akillis Knight	20	Edwd C. Debruhl	30	Geo Trayweeks

Mordica M. Clarke vs John McGill. Assault & Battery. Ordered that judgment be entered by nonpross.

Robert Allison & wife vs Edward & Joseph Rowe. Process Judgment confessed by Joseph Rowe for debt amt of speciality and cost of suit.

March term 1793

William Thoms vs William Covington. Debt. Judgment confessed for amt. of specialty and cost of suit.

William Thomas vs Knight & Abbott. Debt. Decree for amt. of specialty with cost of suit when the above cases were tried only Tristram Thomas was present.

Moses Daniel vs Aaron Daniel. Judgmt. by default according to specialty.

Ordered that the court do adjourn till tomorrow 10 oclock.

Saturday March 2nd 1793. Court met according to adjournment. Present Tristram Thomas & William Thomas.

John M Coggeshall vs Alexander Peterkin. Judgement by default with a stay of execution till 10th Sept. next.

Isham Hodges vs Thomas Downer. Attachment. Judgement non suit.

James Conner vs Thomas Heringdine. Assault & Battery. Continued at defts. cost.

Orderd that Wm Edens be appointed constable for the ensuing year.

State vs Richard Armstead. Larceny for taking 6 yards Irish linen. Ordered that the prisoner be discharged on act. of the prosecutors non attendance.

Mackey McNatt vs Robert Campbell. Summons. Dismissed at plaintiffs cost.

John J. James vs Wilds & Seneath. Judgment by default.

John Evans vs Samuel Wilds. Judgment by default.

Brown & Coggeshall vs Mordica Johnson. Judgment by default.

Ordered that the County Treas. do pay Thomas Hodges 13/6 for his expences in apprehending Thomas Herringdine and searching for Stolen corn.

Ordered that the court do adjourn till Mon. 10 Oclock.

Monday March 4th. Court met according to adjournment. Ordered that court do adjourn until Court in course. Tristm. Thomas.

At a County Court held 2d Sept 1793 before William Thomas and Tristram Thomas Esquire.

Ordered that the Petit Jurors be drawn to serve Next Term from 2 to 1.

Turbill Cottingham	1	Jonathan Cottingham	16
Francis Bridges	2	John McNatt	17
David Watson	3	Daniel Cottingham	18
Philip Edens	4	Shadrack Fuller	19
David Steward	5	Thomas Cook	20
Aaron Knight	6	William Stubbs	21
Jacob Barrentine	7	Henry Beverly	22
Arthur Pearce	8	William Jordan	23
John Broidin	9	James Stubbs	24
Thomas Pearce	10	Simion Cherry	25
John Murdock	11	Benj Beverley	26
William Conner	12	James Smith	27
John Cook Jur.	13	Jesse Baggett	28
Hubbert Stephens	14	William Luke	29
Jacob Odom	15	Aaron Daniel Jr.	30

Thomas Evans vs Elias Hillson. P. S. Judgment confessed agreeable to specialty.

Moses Daniel vs Aaron Daniel Debts. Judgment confessed for amt. of
note and lawfull interest with cost of suit.

George McCall vs Aaron Daniel. Debt. Judgment confessed for amt. of
note and lawful interest with cost of suit.

Moses Murfee vs William Fields. Debt. Judgment confessed for amt. of
note and lawful interest with cost of suit.

Henry Coggshall vs William Evans. Debt. Judgment confessed for amt. of
note and lawful interest and cost of suit.

Ordered that court adjourn until tomorrow 10 Oclock.

Tuesday Sept. 3 1793. Present William Thomas, Tristram Thomas and Morgan
Brown, Esquires.

Alexander Smith vs William Covington. Debt. Jury sworn and retired.

William Thomas vs William Covington. Debt. Judgment confessed for amt.
of note and interest with cost of suit.

David Davis vs Nathl. Coggeshall. Debt. Continued untill next court
by consent.

Alexander Smith vs William Covington. Debt. We find for deft. ₤ 3 s 10
with cost of suit.

James Conner vs Thomas Herringdine. Slander. Settled by consent, cost
divided equally between them.

Robert Allison & wife vs Isham Hodges & Gully Moore. Debt. Continued
at defendants cost.

Henry Coggeshall & Co. vs William Hodges. Debt. Judgment confessed for
admt. of note with interest with cost of suit.

Henry Coggeshall vs John Dyer. Debt. Judgment confessed for amt. of
note and interest with cost of suit.

Richard Stinson vs Samuel Brown. Non suit.

Robert Allison & wife vs James Bolton. Debt Judgment confessed with
stay of execution untill March term.

Sylvanous Crunk vs Daniel Curry. Case   Continued.

Mackey McNatt vs Ezekel Brown. Attachment. We find for the Plaintiff
₤ 17 s 1 d 9½ with cost of suit. Ordered that the sheriff expose to
public sale one black horse, saddle, and bridle, the property of sd.
Ezekel Brown.

Henry Coggeshall & Co. vs Joel McNatt. Debt. Judgment by Default for
amt. of note and interest with cost of suit.

John Wilks vs Benjamin Hicks. Judgment by default.

Mary Jones vs Alexander Smith. Judgment by default for am.t of Note &
interest with cost of suit.

Ordered that court do adjourn untill tomorrow 10 Oclock.

Wednesday Sept 4 1793. Court met according to adjournment. Present
Tristram Thomas and William Thomas Esquires.

Richard Stinson vs David Bethea. Settled at the deft. cost.

Sept. term 1793

Edward C. Debruhl vs Levi Solomon. Case We find for the pltff. Ƚ 21 s 4 d 7 with cost of suit.

County Treasurer vs Stinson & Winfield. P. S.   Judgment for amt. of note and interest with cost of suit, the money to be paid to the Treasurer of said county.

Philip Philman vs Jesse James. Decree for the pltff. Ƚ 3 s 8 d 11 & cost of suit.

Isham Hodges vs Samuel Sparks. Fiere Facias. A writ of firi facias to issue by consent of deft. for amount of Judgment.

William German vs Saml Fields. Case. Continued.

James Collins vs Edwd Terral Dismissed.

Parish Self vs Stephen Ginn. Discontinued.

Isham Hodges vs Thos & Ann Stephen. Attachment. Edwd C. Debruhl appeared as garnishee in the above case.

State vs Wm Stubbs. Assault & Battery. Laid over until next court.

Ordered that Grand Jurors be drawn to serve March term 1794. drawn from No 3 to No 4   Names of Grand Jurors

Miles King	1	Aaron Daniel Senr	11
James Easterling	2	James Moore	12
Nathl Coggeshall	3	John Wilson	13
Silas Pearce	4	Stephen Parker	14
Peter Hubbert	5	Benj Williams	15
David Bethea	6	Enoch Evans	16
Richd Green	7	John Odam	17
Daniel Blue	8	Thomas Huckerby	18
Marnis Curgill	9	Barnabas Henigan	19
Joshua David	10	Robert Purnell	20

Edwd C Debruhl vs Levi Solomon. Ordered that the pltff. do shew cause to this court on first March why the Judgment in this case should not be arrested.

John J. James vs Adams Alexander. Attcht. Judgment by default.

Ordered that the Sheriff do forthwith proceed to sell the two Estrays Horses taken up by Isham Hodges and Saml Terrall agreeable to law.

Ordered that Court do adjourn untill court in course.

At a County Court held on Saturday 1st day in March 1794, before William Thomas and Tristram Thomas, Esquires.

Ordered that the Petit Jurors be drawn to serve next term. From No 2 to No 1   Petit Jurors

1	Joseph Delport	John Windham	16
2	Duncan McPherson	John Johnson	17
3	John Beesly	Simon Cherry	18
4	Joel McNatt	Jesse Perkins	19
5	John Daniel	William Robertson	20
6	Mathew Daniel	Thomas Cochran	21
7	Benjn David	Sion Hodges	22
8	James Falconer	John Mason	23
9	Alexander Beverly	Burrel Huggins	24
10	James Blanton (Stricken)	Abraham Rayborn	25
11	Alex John	Isham Stroud	26
12	John Smithart Junr	Thomas Godfrey	27

March term 1794

13 Daniel Evans		Sion Odom	28
14 Thomas Evans		Herbert Smith	29
15 Jacob Barringtine Junr		Lewis Stubbs	30

Ordered that the Grand Jurors be drawn to serve next term from No 3 to
No 4

Josiah Beesly	1	Richard Whittington	11
Saml Councill	2	Aaron Pearson	12
John LittleJohn	3	William Evans	13
Isaac Sumrall	4	Anthony Murfee	14
James Yoe	5	Robert Campbell	15
William Easterling	6	Thomas Ellison	16
John Evans	7	George Evans	17
William Beauchamp	8	James Pouncey	18
John Cox	9	Joseph Cosneham	19
Welcom Hodges	10	Charles Frazor	20

The Grand Jurors were called and sworn.   Names

John Wilson, F. M.	Thomas Huckerby
Nathl Coggeshall	Robert Burnell
David Bethea	James Easterling
Richard Green	Magniss Curgill
Joshua David	Benjamin Williams
Aaron Daniel	John Odom
James Moore	Silas Pearce

Ordered that the Grand Jurors be discharged untill Monday 10 Oclock.
Petit Jurors were called and discharged until Monday 10 Oclock.

Ordered that court adjourn untill Monday 10 Oclock.

Monday March 3rd 1794   Court met according to adjournment. Present
William Thomas and Tristram Thomas, Esquires.

State vs Joshua Wilds. Larceny. Ordered that Joshua Wise now in Gaol,
do give sufficient bail to the sheriff for his appearance to the next
court in course.

Sylvanus Crunk vs Daniel Curry. Case. Continued at Defts. cost.

Henry Coggeshall & Co. vs Isham Hodges. Debt. I confess Judgment for
amt. of within note contained and cost of suit.

Henry Coggeshall & Co. vs Jesse James. Debt. Judgment confessed....

Robt. Allison & wife vs Isham Hodges & Gully Moore. Debt. Continued at
the defts. costs.

Samuel Humphress vs William Stubbs. Discontinued.

William German vs Samuel Fields. Discontinued.

Darby Powers vs Joseph Thomas. Case Discontinued.

James Collins vs Edward Terrall. Battery   Discontinued.

John James Jones vs Adams Alexander. Attachment. Edward Terrall being
garnishee and failing to appear, ordered that judgment issue against
him....

Isham Hodges vs Thomas & Ann Stevens. Attachment. Continued.

Duncan McRa vs Isham Hodges. continued.

The Grand Jury being called there was no business before them, they
retired and returned with the following presentments.

We present as a grievance that such anormous sums are yearly imposed
upon the county for building the Gaol & Court House and that the Build-

ings are very indifferently done, for the sums paid and we further present the Sheriff for suffering the buildings to be made use of as Store Houses, instead of the use they were intended for very much to the damage of said buildings.   Jno Wilson, fm.

Thomas Sumrall vs Neal McNeal. Attach. Judgment be default. Ordered that the negro man Slave named London, attached in this case be sold....

Ordered that court do adjourn untill tomorrow 11 Oclock.

Tuesday March 4th 1794. Court met according to adjournment.

Ordered that the Sheriff do take into the custody & bring before the court Peter Boyer, Samuel Councel & Daniel Cottingham to be examined relative to the damage done to the court house in the course of last night.

Also that Benjamin Thomas, Thomas Pearce & George Cherry be bound to appear as witnesses in behalf of the state against the above....

Outlaw & Smith vs D & Saml Sparks. Sciri Facias. Continued Non Pross

Robert Hodges vs Alexander Smith. Ordered that the proceedings be revived.

Robert Wilson vs Samuel Terrall. Sciri Facias. Ordered that the proceedings be revived.

Ordered that Court do adjourn untill court in course.

At a County court held 1st September 1794, before Tristram Thomas and William Thomas Esquires.

Ordered thatthe Grand Jurors be drawn to serve next term.   Drawn from No 4 to No 3

1	Thomas Burkell	11	John Odom
2	James Spears	12	Enoch Evans
3	Willis Williamson	13	Benjamin Williams
4	Henry Willing	14	Stephen Parker
5	John Wilson	15	Barnabe Hennagin
6	Aaron Snowden	16	John Wilson
7	Ephraim Whittington	17	Drury Robertson
8	John Smithart	18	James Moore
9	Robert Purnell	19	Richard Green
10	Thomas Huckerby	20	Aaron Daniel Senr.

Ordered that the Petit Jurors be drawn to serve next term Drawn from No 2 to No 4

1	Leaven Weatherly	16	Joseph Thomas
2	John Twitty	17	Stephen McClendal
3	Wilson Conner	18	Thomas Sumrall Jur.
4	Jarvis Stafford	19	Thomas Sumrall Senr.
5	Hardy Flowers	20	Joseph Fuller
6	Joseph Taylor	21	Jonathan Meekins
7	Cornelius Mandeville	22	Samuel Evans
8	Thomas Stubbs	23	John Teague
9	Marmaduke Brantley	24	John Hubbard
10	Isaac Weatherly	25	George S Turner
11	David Haggins	26	Daniel Murfee
12	John Syllivan	27	Thos. Weatherley
13	Polson Haggins	28	Dill Cottingham
14	Hardy Clark	29	Josiah David
15	Nathaniel Knight	30	Samuel Terrall

Ordered that William Falconer be appointed county attorney....

Sept. term 1794

Ordered that the Grand Jurors be called which being done and the Business ready to lay before them, Ordered that they be discharged untill tomorrow 10 Oclock.

Ordered that the Petit Jurors be called...no business for them to do. Ordered that they be discharged untill tomorrow 10 Oclock.

David Kennedy is appointed constable for the County of Marlborough.

Simeon Bethea is appointed constable for the county of Marlborough.

Ordered that the court adjourn untill tomorrow 10 Oclock.

Court met according to adjournment. The Grand Jury appearing

Josiah Beesely	Thomas Ellison	Charles Fazor
William Easterling	George Evans	Aaron Snowden
John Evans	James Pouncey	Thos Evans
Robert Campbell	Joseph Cosneham	

There not being a sufficient number to compleat the Jury. Ordered that two tallies be drawn to compleat the Jury. Peter Hubbard Gully Moore. Thomas Evans appointed foreman.

The Petit Jury appearing

Duncan McPherson	Aley John	Burrell Huggins
John Beesley	Reece Luke	Abraham Raybon
Joel McNatt	Daniel Evans	Isham Stroud
John Daniel	Jesse Perkins	Thomas Godfrey
Mathew Daniel	Thomas Cochran	
Benjamin David	Sion Hodges	
Alexander Beverley	John Mason	
James Falconer	Sion Odom	

The Petit Jury drawn to serve this term.

Benjamin David	Mathew Daniel
James Falconer	Abram Raybon
Burrell Huggins	John Beasley
Joel McNatt	Sion Odom
Duncan McPherson	Rece Luke
Thomas Cochran	Sion Hodges

Benjamin David appointed foreman.

Robert Allison & wife vs Isham Hodges & Gulley Moore. We find for pltff Ь 14 s 4 stg. with interest & cost of suit.

The Grand Jury returned the following bills.

State vs Mary Bunt. Assault & Battery. No Bill
State vs John Bunt   Assault & Battery. No Bill

Admors of Niel Bethune vs Griffin Nunnery. P. S. Decree for deft.

John Askew is appointed constable for the county of Marlborough.

Admors of Niel Bethune vs Rachel Neveal. Process. Decree for pltff. Ь 1 s 2 stg. with cost of suit.

Nathl Coggeshall & Co vs Abraham Bloodgood. Continued.

Isham Hodges vs Thos & Ann Stephens. Attachment. Continued untill next term.

Edward Green vs Admors of Carny Wright. On motion of Mr. Falconer atty for Plff. ordered that a commission do issue in this case directed to examine Edward Gibson & Moses Crafford, witnesses in this case....

Sept. term 1794

Bailey Barrett vs William Barrintine. not to be found. Assault & Battery. Dismissed

James Falconer vs William Robertson. Debt. Settled at defendants costs.

Sarah James vs James Smart detinue. abated by the death of the plaintiff.

Mackey McNatt vs Robert Campbell. Continued.

Aaron Daniel Jr. vs James Jones. non suit.

Samuel Fields vs Edward Boothe. Non suit.

Robert Allison vs Samuel Terrall. Debt. Judgment confessed for amt. of debt, interest and cost of suit.

King & Allison ind'ee of Edwd Smith vs William Fields. discontinued.

King & Allison ind'ee of Edwd Smith vs William Fields. discontinued.

King & Allison vs David David. P S Decree for amt. of note and cost of suit.

Mathew Willis vs James Moore. P S Decree for pltff L 4 & cost of suit.

Robert Allison vs John Dyer. Debt. judgment confessed....

William Evans vs Samuel Sparks. Attach. abated by death of the pltff.

William Carter Ind'ee vs William Covington. Decree for pltff....

Thomas Cochran vs Jesse Doughlass. P S Settled at Defts. cost. Clerks fee 6/6 paid.

James Hudges vs Charles Barton. Judgment confessed, with stay of execution till January
Wit: Robert Lide   his
                                   Charles C Barton
                                             mark

Robert Allison vs Seneath & Mackey McNatt. Debt. Judgment confesed by McNatt and on Sineath by default.

Benjamin Hicks Esqr. was qualified as a Judge of the County Court of Marlborough.

State vs Thomas Herringdine. Felony. A true bill. Ordered that William Pledger sheriff do deliver sd. Thomas Herringdine to the Goal of the District at Greenville.

Evander McIver vs Samuel Chewning. Decree for pltff. L 5 with cost of suit.

Ordered court adjourn untill tomorrow 10 Oclock.

Wednesday Sept. 3rd 1794. Court met according to adjournment.

Solomon & Murdock vs Scizm & Thomas. Debt. Agreed at plaintiff cost.

Soloman & Murdock vs Dyer & Thomas. Debt. Agreed at plaintiff cost.

Henry William Herrington vs Carter Barnett & Others. Judgment confessed by Thomas Evans, John Dyer & Samuel Terrall and on Azariah David by default for amt. of note, interest & cost of suit.

James Brown vs Duncan McPherson P S Judgment for amt. of note, interest & cost of suit.

King & Allison vs Duncan McPherson. P S Judgement confessed for amt. of note, interest & cost of suit.

Henry Coggeshall vs Levy Gray. P S Judgment confessed....

Edmors of Niel Bethune vs John Punch P S Judgment be default for amt. of note....

Samuel Thomas vs Benjamin Williams. P S Decree for pltff. Ł 8 s 11 d 8 & cost of suit.

Mary Parish vs Willis Hodges. P S Judgement agreeable to specialty & cost of suit.

Abram Coker vs Thomas Godfrey P S Judgment be default for amt. of note....

Admors of Niel Bethune vs Moses Pearson Esquire. P Sums. Continued untill next term

Henry Coggeshall & co. vs William Covington. P S Judgment confessed....

Admors of Niel Bethune vs Moses Pearson Esqr. Plead Non assumsit.

Isham Hodges vs Thos & Ann Stephens. Attacht. Discontinued.

Edward C. Debruhl vs Levi Soloman. the pltff. shewing no cause why Judgment should not be arrested in this case, ordered that judgment be arrested.

State vs Joshua Wise. Larceny. A true Bill. Ordered that the sheriff take Joshua Wise into his custody.

State vs Margaret Stephens Corn stealing. No bill.

Mary Jones vs Thos Cochran Agreed at the defts. cost.

William Prue vs Jonathan Gift. Judgment confessed.   his
Wit: T. Godfrey.   Jonathan ⊥ Gift
                                                        mark

State vs Joshua Wise. Stealing slaughter hide. Guilty. Ordered that the sheriff take same Joshua Wise and inflict the punishment of 25 lashes on his bare back, well laid on.

Elizabeth Mason vs Drury Robertson. Debt. I do hereby consent that the Judgment heretofore given be revised the former being lost and that all payment heretofore made on the same be deducted. D. Robertson.

Nathaniel Coggeshall vs Edward Terrall. Attacht. Dismissed at pltff. cost.

John Dwiggins vs Saml Council. Attach. Continued.

Tristram Thomas & John Pledger exors of P. Pledger vs D & Saml Sparks. Attach. Continued.

Joseph Booth admor of John Edwards vs Saml Sparks. Debt. Judgment by default for amt. of bond, interest & cost of suit.

Admors of Niel Bethune vs Ebenezer Hayes. Judgment by default.

William Robertson ind'ee vs Isham Hodges. P S Dismissed.

Edward Jones vs Mims & wise. Dismissed.

Exors of Col. Hicks vs William Robertson. Settled at defts. cost.

Sept. term 1794

Benjamin Thomas vs John Murdock. Settled at plaintiffs cost.

Philip Pledger vs Aaron Daniel Jur. Judgement by default for amt.of note....

Ordered that court do adjourn untill court in course.

At a Court held on Monday 2d March 1795 before Tristram Thomas and Benjamin Hicks, Esquires.

Ordered that the Grand Jury be drawn to serve next Term from No 4 to No. 2.

1	Isaac Summerall	11	Magness Curgill
2	John LittleJohn	12	David Bethea
3	Jesse Vining	13	William Coward
4	Joseph Ellison	14	Silas Pearce
5	George Smith	15	Josiah Beesley
6	William Easterling	16	Mathew Murfee
7	James Youe	17	Joseph Lister
8	Daniel Blue	18	John Moore
9	Anthony Murfee	19	George Wilds
10	Joshua David	20	James Easterling

Ordered that the Petit Jury be drawn to serve next term from No 2 to No 1.

1	Baxter Smith	16	James Reed
2	William Ammons	17	David Harry
3	Mackey McNatt	18	Edmond Brown
4	Jonathan John	19	James Bolton
5	Jonathan Masine	20	Isham McIntire
6	Jesse Brown Junr	21	Edward Feagin
7	Younger Newton	22	George Bland
8	James Welch	23	William Mauris
9	John Stroud	24	Isham Haygin
10	Joseph Owens	25	Jacob Barrentine
11	George Stanton	26	Willerbee Broughton
12	George Traweeks	27	John Askue
13	Joseph Jones	28	Charles Cottingham
14	Edwd Crossland	29	Jesse Stephens
15	Dempsey Watson	30	Jesse James

Grand Jury called and discharged untill tomorrow 10 Oclock.
Petit Jury called and discharged untill tomorrow 10 Oclock.

Thomas Ammons vs Admors of Henry Councell decd. P Summs. Decree for pltff. for ℔ 3 s 11 d 0 3/4 & cost of suit.

Jonathan Brown vs Jesse James, Writ. settled.

Jonathan Brown vs Jesse James. Process settled.

Jno J. James vs Jonathan Brown. Process settled.

Admors Neil Bethune vs William Steward. Process decree for pltff. for ℔ 4 s 12 d 1 with cost.

Admors Neil Bethune vs Thomas Evans Esqr. Process. Judgment confessed for ℔ 9 s 2 with cost suit.

Robert Allison & wife vs Edwd & Joseph Roe. Sciri Facias. Ordered that the proceedings be renewed....

Ordered that court do adjourn untill tomorrow 10 Oclock.

Court met according to adjournment.

March term 1795

Ordered that the Grand Jury be called.

John Wilson   Robert Purnell
Thos Burkell   Thos Huckerby
James Spears   John Odom
Aaron Snowden   Drury Robertson
Aphraim Whittington   James Moore
John Smithart   Aaron Daniel Senr
                               Benjamin Williams

Ordered that the Petit Jury be called

Josiah Davis, foreman   Joseph Fuller
Wilson Conner   John Teague
Thos Stubbs   John Hubbard
Cohon Haygin   Samuel Terrall
Marmaduke Brantley   Jarvis Stafford
Isaac Weatherly
Leavin Weatherly

Edward Gin vs Admors of Carney Wright. We find for pltff with damages and cost of suit.

Tristram Thomas & John Pledger exors of P. Pledger vs Benjamin Hicks. discontinued.

Peter & Nathl Coggeshall vs William Bartlet. Attach. Discontinued at plff. costs.

Exors of Col. Hicks vs Philimon & Welcom Hodges. debt. Judgment confessed for balance due on the note in this case & cost of suit.

William Thomas Esqr. vs Cogges. & Evans. settled.

Isaac Frazor vs William German. Non Pross.

Ordered that the following persons be appointed constables for the ensuing year; Hugh McLerin Jr, Shadrack Howard, Joel Easterling and William Fields.

Ralph Dodsworth vs JohnMcIntosh. Debt. Judgment confessed with stay of execution until 2 Sept next.

Vernon & Mortimer vs John McIntosh. Debt. Judgment confessed with stay of execution until 1 Sept next.

Admors of Neil Bethune vs Ebenezer Hays. We find for pltff. Ⱡ 7 11/7 with cost of suit.

John Dwiggins vs Saml Council. Attacht. We find for pltff Ⱡ 3 15 0 with interest from 11 Feb 1794 with cost of suit.

same vs same We find for pltff Ⱡ 4 17 6 with interest from 5 Feb 1794 with cost of suit.

Admors Neil Bethune vs Aaron Snowden. Debt. We find for pltff Ⱡ 20 0 0 with interest from 1 Jan 1794 with cost of suit.

William Price vs Saml Thomas. Debt. We find for pltff Ⱡ 7 7 3 with interest from 1 Jan 1793 with cost of suit.

Thomas Ammons came into court and acknowledged a deed for 378 acres to Moses Parker.

William Price vs Mungo & Williams. Judgment confessed....

William Price vs William Fields. Judgment confessed.

William Price vs Joseph Thomas. Judgment confessed.

March term 1795

William Price vs Henry Hill. We find for pltff. upon the within note
Ḷ 22 6 6 with interest from March 22 1793 with cost of suit.

Henry Coggeshall & Co vs Bailey Mungo. Debt We find for pltff amt. of
within note....

Scott & Coggeshall vs David David. Process. Decree for pltff for Ḷ 4 s
1 d 10 with cost of suit.

Henry Coggeshall & Co vs Joseph Chewning. Debt. We find for pltff
Ḷ 11 10 with costs of suit.

Robert Hunter vs Admors William Elliott. Debt on Bond. Ordered that a
commission be directed to the Judges of Darlington County to examine
Morgan Brown esquire who is the witness to the bond above mentioned.

John Dyer vs Aaron Pearson the younger. continued.

Joseph Jones vs Aaron Pearson the younger. continued.

Edward Smith vs William Fields. Assumsit. We find for the pltff 50
Dollars with interest from 1 Dec 1792 with cost of suit.

Gift & Allison vs Dwiggins & Breeden Debt. Judgment confessed.
                                              his
                                    John   X   Breedin
                                            mark

Admors of Neil Bethune vs Moses Pears. Case assumsit. continued.

Edward Smith vs William Fields. Assumsit. We find for pltff 60 Dollars
with interest from 1 Dec 1792 and cost of suit.

James Spiller vs Dixon Pearce. Debt. We find for pltff Ḷ 10 with interest from 1 May 1792.

Admors of Wm Elliott vs Kennedy & Williams. Trover. Ordered that a commission do issue to two Justices in the State of North Carolina to
examine Thomas Williams a material witness....

Thomas Brown vs William Covington. Debt. We find for pltff. Ḷ 10 1 4
with interest from 3 Aug 1787 with cost of suit.

Ordered that the petit jury be discharged untill tomorrow 10 Oclock.

Wednesday March 4th 1795. Court met according to adjournment.

Henry Coggeshall & Co vs Abraham Bloodgood. assumpt. discontinued at
plaintiffs cost.

James Ware vs Richard Stinson continued.

Thomas & Ann Stephens vs Benjamin Beverley. Trover. continued.

Admors of Neil Bethune vs Abel Hodges. assumpt. continued.

Admors of Neil Bethune vs Moses Pearson. Debt. continued.

David Graham vs Edwd C. Debruhl. debt. continued.

Brit Goodwin vs John Dyer. Process agreed.

Benjamin Hicks Esquire produced his commission to this court which was
ordered to be recorded. (commission recorded in full, dated 21 Dec
1793)

Mackey McNatt vs Robert Campbell. Case.demerced in this case to the

74

March term 1795

to the plaintiffs declaration the court were of opinion that the declaration substantiates the cause of action...judgment entered for pltff ₺ 20 and cost of suit.

John Dwiggins vs Samuel Council. Attachment Judgement against Welcom Hodges garnishee in this case, for ₺ 4 s 17 d 6 with interest from 4 Dec 1794 with cost of suit.

James Crocker & others vs William Pledger. Trover we find for pltff. ₺ 15 0 0 with cost of suit.

Vernon Mortimer & Co vs William German. Judgment by default for amt. of note interest & cost of suit.

Vernon Mortimer vs Hodges & Cherry. Judgment confessed.

Ralph Dodsworth vs Samuel Thoams. Judgment confessed with stay of execution untill 1 Sept next.

Vernon & Mortimer vs James Yoes. Debt. Judgement by default for am.t of note, interest & cost of suit.

Ralph Dodsworth vs William Fields. Debt. Judgement confessed for amt. of note interest and cost of suit.

Ralph Dodsworth vs Joseph Thomas. Debt. Judgment confessed for amt. of note interest & cost of suit.

Nathl Coggeshall vs Aaron Daniel Jur. Debt. Judgement by default.

P & Nathl Coggeshall vs James Smart. Assumpsit. Judgement be default.

Robertson Carloss vs Michael Mason. Case settled.

John Bunt vs James Falconer. Assumsit. settled.

Nathl Coggeshall vs Aaron Daniel the younger. Assumpt Judgement by default.

Daniel Sparks vs William Fields. Process settled.

Ralph Dodsworth vs Benjamin Hicks Esqr. Judgment confessed for ₺ 5 s 4 with interest & cost of suit from 1 Jan 1793.

Ordered that a county Tax be levied on the inhabitants of this county equal to 1/5 part of the public tax for the year 1794 for the purpose of building a Gaol. To be paid by 1st Jan next.

Ordered that court adjourn untill court in course.

At a County Court held for Marlborough at the Court House on the 1st day of March 1796. Present Tristram Thomas Esquire. Thomas Evans Esq. produced his commission and was ordered to be recorded. (dated 20 Dec 1794)

The said Thomas Evans was legally qualified and took his seat accordingly.

The Hon. John Jones James produced his commission...dated 19 Dec 1795.

Grand Jurors from No 3 to No 4 for next term.

1	Jonathan Marine	8	Moses Parker	16	Wm Beesely
2	John Thomas	9	Wm Easterling	17	James Cook
3	Turbet Cottingham	10	Edmund Brown	18	David Steward
4	James Bolton	11	Jesse Douglas	19	Geo Wilds
5	Barnebas Hennigan	12	David Bethea	20	John David
6	Wm Conner	13	Wm Forniss		
7	Geo. Cherry	14	Nathan Thomas		
		15	James Gillespie		

75

March term 1796

Petit Jurors from No 1 to No 2 for next term

1	Daniel Murfee	4	Lewis Stubbs	7	Wm Davis Goodwin
2	Lochran Curry	5	Wm Williams	8	John Smithhart
3	Dill Cottingham	6	Shadrick Fuller	9	Daniel Cottingham

10	Dempsey Watson	21	James Feagin
11	Wm Adams	22	James Dunbar
12	Lockran McCall	23	Alex McRa
13	Charles Cottingham	24	Jonathan Meekin
14	John Douglass	25	Abraham Baggett
15	Wm Smith	26	Thos Weatherly
16	Thos Stubs	27	Reuben Cook
17	Edwd Cottingham	28	Stephen McClenon
18	Philip McRa	29	Thos Adam
19	Robert Purnel	30	Joshua Ammons
20	James Conner		

Andrew Paul made application for licence to retail spiritous liquor at Parkers ferry, which was granted....

John Murdock made application for licence to retail spiritous liquor at Marlborough Court House, which was granted.

Messrs King & Allison made application for permission to retail spiritous liquor at their store near Marlborough Court House, which was granted.

Ordered that court adjourn untill tomorrow 10 Oclock.

Wednesday March 2nd 1796. Court met according to adjournment. Present Tristram Thomas, Thomas Evans & John Jones James.

The Grand Jurors being called, and not appearing a sufficient number to proceed to business, they were discharged.

Ordered that all proceedings in criminal cases and all recognizances be continued over untill next court

Wm Price vs Benj Hicks Esqr. Judgment by default according to specialty.

Vernon Mortimor & Co vs Philip Pledger. Confessed Judgment....

Ralph Dodsworth vs James Welsh. Judgment confessed.

Nathaniel Coggeshall vs Philip Pledger. Settled at the Defts. cost.

Nathl Coggeshall vs William Fields. Judgment confessed.

Snowdon & Douglass vs Magness Curgill. Rule of reference. Ordered that Moses Pearson & Robertson Carloss be appointed as reference in this case, and in case of disagreement to choose an Umpire....

P. & Nathaniel Coggeshall vs John Darby & others. We find for pltff one Dollar and cost of suit. Jas.Bolton.

Guthridge Lyons Ind'ee vs Thomas Vining. Debt. We find for pltff. one Dollar and cost of suit.

Jesse Wilds vs Exors of Wm Evans. We find for pltff. one Dollar and cost of suit.

Solomon Lisenby vs William Fields. Judgment confessed.

Mehatabel Lide vs Azariah David. Judgment confessed.

Philip Pledger vs John Bridges. Ordered that this case be referred to Robertson Carloss & John LittleJohn & in case of disagreement to choose an Umpire.

Ralph Dodsworth vs Godfrey & Williams. Debt. We find for pltff. one Dollar damages & cost of suit.

Jesse Neavill assignee vs Philip Pledger. Debt. Judgment confessed.

Court proceeded to the election of Sheriff and Wm Thomas Junr is duly elected.

Ordered that Court do adjourn untill tomorrow 10 Oclock.

Thursday March 3rd 1796. Court met according to adjournment. Present Tristram Thomas, Thomas Evans.

William Little Thomas appeared and was qualified as deputy sheriff.

Exors Niel Bethune vs Abel Hodges. continued.

James Wear vs Richd Stinson. Judgment by default for Ŀ 6 with cost of suit.

P. & Nathl Coggeshall vs James Smart. We find for pltff $111.50 & cost of suit.

Messrs David & Cornelius Mandeville made application for permission to retail spiritous liquors at Cashuaway ferry, which was granted....

Vernon & Mortimer vs David & John Kennedy. Decree according to specialty against David Kennedy.

Izrael Snead made application for tavern licence which was granted....

Vernon & Mortimor & co. vs Saml & Joseph Thomas. Decree according to specialty with cost of suit.

Vernon Mortimor & Co. vs Joseph Thomas. P Sums. Judgement confessed according to specialty.

Henry Coggeshall & Co. vs Snowden & Evans. P Sums. Judgment confessed according to specialty.

Henry Coggeshall & Co. vs Dyer & Evans. Judgment confessed according to specialty.

William Ratliff vs Benj. Hicks. P Sums. Debt Decree according to specialty.

Thomas Quick vs Michael Mason. Decree for the plaintiff $14 and cost of suit. Ordered that the property attachd be sold.

Vernon & Mortimor vs Anthony & Saml Pouncey. Debt. Decree according to specialty.

King & Allison vs Azariah David. Settled at pffs. costs.

James Forniss vs Mackey McNatt. Dismissed at pff cost.

Robert Campbell vs Thomas John- Decree for the pltff. according to specialty.

Peter & N. Coggeshall vs Thomas John. Decree according to specialty for pltff.

Jesse Wilds vs Exors Wm Evans. The deft. attorney moved for a new trial which was overruled by the court on argument.

77

March term 1796

James Moore vs Thomas Stephens Defendants death. abated at pltff costs.

Deleisseline & Winfield vs Wm Covington. Attach. discontinued.

Robert Allison vs Wm Covington. Attach. Decree for pltff Ⱡ 7 s 7 d7 with cost of suit. Ordered that execution do issue agt. Jesse Councill garneshee in this case for Ⱡ 2 s 2.

Ordered that Mary Andrew do deliver to the sheriff one Mans saddle & seven head of sheep which was acknowledged to be in her possession as the property of Wm Covington.

Smith & Murray vs Benjamin Hicks Esqr. Judgment by default.

Exors Enoch Harry vs Mackey McNatt. Ordered that this case be referred to Col. Evans & Capt. James & in case of disagreement to choose an umpire....

Ordered that the court adjourn until tomorrow 10 Oclock.

Friday March 4th 1796. Court met according to adjournment. Present Tristram Thomas, Thomas Evans & J. J. James, Esqr.

Vernon Mortimor & Co vs Samuel Thomas. Debt Judgment confessed.

Exors Wm Evans vs Joseph Dilport. discontinued.

Dixon Pearce vs Thomas Dean. Referred to Tristram Thomas & Thomas Evans in case of disagreement to choose an umpire.

John M. Coggeshall vs Wm Covington. Judgment by default.

Richard Edens vs Harbert Smith. Case on note. Judgment by Default.

Magniss Cargill vs James Pouncey. Discontinued.

John M. Coggeshall survivor of Scott vs Jesse James. Judgment confessed for Ⱡ 3 s 15 d 7½

Brittain Goodwin vs James Moore. referred to Capt. John J. James & Capt. Allison & incase of disagreement to choose an umpire.

Wm Pledger vs Wm Barringtine. settled.

King & Allison vs John W. Stephens discontinued.

Samuel Terrall vs Exors Josiah Evans. Decree for pltff Ⱡ 8 16/2 with cost of suit.

Benjamin Williams vs Mary Andrews. Settled.

Henry Welsh vs James Welsh. Case Judgement by default.

Robert Allison vs Jeremiah Roper. Decree for pltff. Ⱡ 9 16/4 with cost of suit... Ordered that execution do issue agt. Thos Evans as garnishee.

Thomas Cochran vs Jeremiah Roper. Decree for pltff Ⱡ 3 15/2 with cost of suit. Ordered that execution issue agt. Thomas Evans as garnishee.

Robert Campbell vs Exor Wm Evans. P Sums. continued.

William Pledger vs Benjamin Hicks. Attachmt. Decree for pltff Ⱡ 9 s 12 d 6 with cost of suit. Ordered that Malichi N Bedgegood garneshee do deliver five cow hides, and Ⱡ 1 s 15

John Kimbrough vs Moses Murfee Debt. Order for special bail.

Ordered that the sheriff do retain in his hands the monies arising from the sales of property of Benjamin Hicks & Wm Covington, and apply the same to the payment of the eldest executions in his office against the sd. Benj Hicks & Wm Covington.

Ordered that the Court adjourn untill tomorrow 10 Oclock.

Saturday March 5th 1796. Court met according to adjournment. Present Tristram Thomas, John J. James & Thomas Evans Esquires.

Ordered that the sheriff do immediately collect the balance of the County tax laid in October 1793 and pay the same to Mr. Benj. Thomas or his attorney---and in case of default to issue executions . ordered that the county be assessed one third part of the public tax for the year 1795, and that the sheriff do begin to cllect the same by 1st January next....

Thomas James was duly qualified as deputy clerk of this county.

Robertson Carloss elected coroner.

Ordered that court do adjourn untill court in course.

At a court of Pleas and Sessions 1st September 1796 before Tristram Thomas, Thomas Evans and John Jones James, Esqr.

Grand Jurors drawn from No 3 to 4 for next term.

Josiah David	1	Welcome Hodges	11
Mackey McNatt	2	John Dewitt	12
John Lide	3	Wm Thomas	13
Silas Pearce	4	Drury Robertson	14
Ephraim Whittington	5	Isham Hodges	15
James McGee	6	Moses Pearson	16
Jesse Bethea Senr	7	Samuel Brown	17
Wm Leggett Junr	8	Magness Curgill	18
Thomas Dean	9	Aaron Daniel	19
Isaac Neavell	10	Aaron Pearson Senr	20

Petit Jurors from No 1 to 2 for next term

Joab Bensley	1	Philip Clarke	11	Elisha Parker	21
Joshua Dilling	2	Peter Way (stricken)	12	James Coward	22
Isaac Summerlin	3	Thomas Cook	12	Jos Cosneham	23
Elias Adams	4	Duncan McCall Junr	13	Joel Baggett	24
Cornelius Mandeville	5	James Blanton (stricken)		Wm Lester	25
David Mandeville	6	Danl McTyre	14	Bartee Smith	26
Ch McRa Junr	7	John Odam	15	Hardy Stewart	27
Jarvis Stafford	8	Edwd C. Debruhl	16	Wm Morrice	28
Francis Whittington	9	Benj Beverly	17	Wm Dabs	29
Francis Kennedy	10	Edwd Crossland	19	Stephen Lisonby	30
		James Stubbs	18		
		Ch Barringtine	20		

Ordered that the sheriff do return the writ of venire.

Defaulters of the Grand Jurors Jonathan Marine, James Gillespie, Geo. Cherry.

Ordered that Joseph Brevard Esqr. be appointed county attorney.

The state vs Richard Stinston. Indictment for stealing a cow & calf. A True Bill. Wm. Easterling, foreman.
Ordered that a writ of Habeas Corpus do issue to the Keeper of Cheraw District Jail to bring up the said Richd. Stinston by tomorrow 10 Oclock.

John Lide vs Moses Murfee. Judgment confessed.

Sept. term 1796

Solomon Cohen vs Moses Murfee. Judgment confessed.

John Kimbrough vs Moses Murfee. Judgment confessed.

David Graham vs Edwd C Debruhl. Judgement by default.

John M. Coggeshall vs Jesse James. Judgment confessed.

Vernon & Mortimer vs Wm Pledger. We find for pltff with one Dollar damage and cost of suit.

Robert Campbell vs Thomas John. Judgment confessed.

Smith & Murray vs Mackey McNatt. Judgment confessed.

Henry Welch vs James Welch. We find for the Plaintiff $64 with cost of suit. Chas Cottingham, fm.

Ordered that court adjourn till tomorrow 10 Oclock.

Fryday Sept. 2nd 1796. Court met according to adjournment. Present Tristram Thomas, John Jones James, Esqrs

Admors Niel Bethune vs Abel Hodges. Continued at pffs cost.

John Dyer vs Snowden & Evans. Judgment confessed by Arn. Snowden & Thos Evans.

Jesse Neavil vs Balir & Terrall. Judgement by default.

Duncan McRa vs Isham Hodges. continued.

Ordered that Jesse James be permitted to keep a Tavern at Level Green....

Ordered that Ephraim Whittington be permitted to retail spiritous liquors at his house in Cashuaway....

Admors Niel Bethune vs Moses Pearson. continued at plffs cost.

State vs Richard Stinston. Indictment for stealing of Cow. A True Bill.

Admors William Elliott vs Kennedy & Williams. (stricken)

State vs Wm Barringtine. Hog Stealing. A true bill.

State vs Wm Frazer. Hog Stealing. A true bill.

Abijah Porter was appointed constable and appeared and was qualified.

Robert Campbell vs Exors Wm Evans. Judgment confessed by Elizabeth Evans and Geo Evans.

same vs Same. Judgment confessed for Ⱡ 9 s 4 d 3 sterling & cost.

Admors Wm Elliott vs Kennedy & Williams. We find for pltff $142 with cost of suit.

State vs Wm Barrintine. Hog Stealing. Guilty of stealing a sow & five shoats. Sd. Wm Barringtine not being able to pay his fine, ordered that the sheriff give him 15 lashes on the bare back in the court yard immediately.

Admrs. Enoch Harry vs Mackey McNatt. Ordered that the award in this case be affirmed, and that Judgement be entered up agt. the deft.

Sept. term 1796

Joseph Dilport vs Exors Wm Evans. Agreed at pffs cost.

Ordered that court adjourn till tomorrow 10 Oclock.

saturday Sept. 3rd 1796. Court met according to adjournment. Present
Tristram Thomas, Thomas Evans & John Jones James, Esqrs.

State vs Thomas Waters. Indictment for Hog Stealing. A true bill.
On motion of the county attorney, ordered that as the offense is laid
to be committed in Darlington County, the deft. be removed these, or
bound over himself in L 10 in two securities each in the sum of L 5
for his personal appearance at next Darlington County Court....

State vs Wm Frazier. Hog Stealing. Guilty of stealing the sow & one
of the shoats metnioned in the indictment. Fine was L 10, prisoner
could not pay the same, therefore sentence him to receive ten lashes or
stripes on the bare back.

State vs Richard Stinston. Indictmen for stealing cow & calf. Deft.
plead not guilty. Petit Jury Sworn: Charleston Cottingham, fm; James
Dunbarr, Stephen McClendon, Abraham Baggett, Jonathan Meekins, Thomas
Weatherly, William Williams, Edwd Cottingham, Thomas Stubbs, Rhuben
Cook, James Cook & James Conner. We find deft. guilty...could not
pay the fine, ordered to receive immediately nine lashes or stripes on
his bare back, and to pay the cost of the prosecution.

Ordered that Court do adjourn till Monday 10 Oclock.

Monday Sept. 5th 1796. Court met according to adjournment.

Daniel McRea vs Dixon & Silas Pearce. We find for pltff with 1 Dollar
damage & cost of suit.

Smith & Murray vs Aaron Daniel. Judgment confessed.

Anne Elliot vs Admors of Neil Bethuen. continued at deft. cost.

Brittain Goodwin vs James Moore. Rule of reference last term. Ordered
that the award be affirmed, and judgment be entered up agt. pltff.

Nathaniel Coggeshall vs Exors Extrix Wm Evans. Judgment by default.

Ann Stephens vs Benj Beaverly. Petit Jury sworn. James Feagin, fm; Daniel Cottingham, Dempsey Watson, Dill Cottingham, Shadrick Fuller,
James Dunbarr, Abraham Baggett, Jonathan Meekins, Thomas Watherly,
William Williams, Edward Cottingham & Rueben cook. We find for pltff.
the negro man named Cato with one Dollar damage & cost of suit.

State vs Richard Stinson. Cow stealing. Jury sworn. We find deft. not
guilty.

Aaron Snowden vs Jesse Doughlass. Discontinued at plffs cost.

Philip Clarke vs William Hickman. Abated by death of the pltff.

Penelope Whittington vs Jarratt Whittington. discontinued.

Mary Lee vs Wm Field. Non suit.

Vernon & Mortimer vs Jonathan Gift. We find for plff with one Dollar
damage & cost of suit.

Ordered that court adjourn untill Tomorrow 9 Oclock.

Tuesday. Sept. 6th 1796. Court met according to adjournment. Present
Tristram Thomas, Thomas Evans, John Jones James,esqrs.

Sept. term 1796

Thomas Deen vs Wm Furniss. By consent on both sides continued.
Ordered that Col. Samuel Bentons deposition be taken upon interrogatory's.

Harry & Furness vs Mungo & Harry. Judgment confessed by Bailey Mungo
and David Harry. Wit: Thos A. James.

John Murdock vs Edwd Roe admor of Joseph Roe decd. Petit Jury sworn.
We find for pltff with one Dollar Damage & cost of suit.

Robert Campbell vs Aly Jesse John. We find for pltff. with one Dollar
damage and cost of suit.

John Dyer vs Aaron Pearson. Settled.

Moses Pearson vs James Pouncey. Judgment confessed.

Vernon & Mortimer & Co. vs Wm Pledger & Tristram Thomas. We find for
pltff with one Dollar damage & cost of suit.

Rebechah Hewson vs Aaron Snowden. Discontinued at plff cost.

Stephen Seizm vs Solomon Hughs. Non Pros.

Jamima Vickers vs Andrew Paul. Shff return non est Inventus. Ordered
that a Judicial attachment do issue in this case.

Aaron Daniel vs Peter & Nathl Coggeshall. Decree for deft.

Adam Marshell vs Thomas Dean. Judgement confessed with stay of execution
until 1 Feb next.

John Murdock vs admrs Joseph Roe. Debt on note. we find for deft. with
cost of suit. The plaintff. moved to suffer a non suit, when the
jury returned to the barr to deliver in thier verdict, which was overruled by the court, whereupon the pltff is granted an appeal to the
circuit court.

William Price vs Mary Andrews. Judgement confessed.

Wm Pledger vs Jonah Cutler. Discontinued at plff cost.

John Murdock vs Hodges & Harry. We find for pltff $43.03 with cost of
suit.

Robert Campbell vs Benj Hicks Esqr. We find for pltff $50 and cost
of suit. Ordered that execution do issue against Richard Dunson as
garnishee for the sum of $12.

Joseph Thomas vs Wm Covington. Dismissed at plff cost.

Henry Coggeshall & Co vs David Harry. We find for plff with one Dollar
damage & cost of suit.

Whereas it has been represented to the Court that the many delinquencies
and neglect have been committed by William Pledger the late sheriff of
this court, on motion of Mr. Falconer. Ordered that leave be given to
have his shff bond delivered up to be sued by each of those persons
who are entitled to a remedy thereon.

Similar complaint regarding James Moore, former sheriff....

Ordered that Court adjourn untill tomorrow 10 Oclock.

Wednesday Sept. 7th 1796. The court met according to adjournment.

Philip Pledger vs Benjamin Arrandall. Continued.

Sept. term 1796

Ordered that Jesse Doughlass admr. of Enoch Luke decd. be cited to
appear at the next intermediate court, in order to give an account of
his proceedings of the said estate.

Ordered that court adjourn untill court in course.

At a Court of Pleas and Sessions on 1st day March 1797. Present
Thomas Evans Esqr.

The Honble John Jones James produced in open court his commission as
one of the Judges of this county, and was duly qualified....

    Grand Jurors drawn from No 3 to 4 and from No 4 to 3.

1	Thomas Godfrey	11	John David
2	James Pouncey	12	Sam Brown
3	Dixon Pearce	13	Wm Easterling
4	Jas. Fuller	14	James Cook
5	Isaiah Walker	15	Wm Conner
6	Benj Rogers	16	Isaac Nevill
7	Peter Hubbard	17	Wm Leggett Junr
8	Jesse Vining	18	David Steward
9	Magniss Curgill	19	Moses Parker
10	James McGee	20	Josiah David

    Petit Jury from No 1 to No 2

1	Jesse Askew	7	Azariah David	13	Younger Newton
2	Jos Lister	8	Chrisr. McRa	14	Thos Huckabee
3	Lockran McClaren	9	Jos. Jackson	15	Jesse Brown
4	Lackran McClaren Jr	10	John Adam	16	David Watson
5	Wm Coward	11	John Haines	17	Saml Cox
6	Wm Stubbs	12	Thos Almonds	18	Zach'h Moreman

19	James Faulkner	25	Jacob Abbott
20	Philip Pledger	26	Alex Beverly
21	John Murdock	27	Luke Turnage
22	Thomas Rayfield	28	John McRa
23	George Smith	29	Rhodrick McRa
24	Robert Allison	30	Geo Evans

Ordered that the sheriff do make a new Jury list & return it next term.

Jonathan Gift vs Thomas Hodges. P Summons discontinued.

Deliesseline & Winfield vs Thomas Godfrey. Judgment confessed by T.
Godfrey.

Exors Philip Pledger vs Danl & Saml Sparks. (stricken)

John Wilson vs John Lide. Judgement confessed.

Ordered that Andrew Paul be permitted to keep a Tavern at Marlborough
Court House....

Ordered that court adjourn untill tomorrow 10 Oclock.

Thursday 2 March 1797. Court met according to adjournment.
Present Thomas Evans & John Jones James, Esqrs.

Exors Philip Pledger vs Danl & Saml Sparks. Non suit.

Admors Niel Bethune vs Moses Pearson. continued. Ordered that a dedimus issue to take the examination of Richard Howard & Bartho'w Whittington in this case.

William Thomas vs Philip Pledger. Judgement confessed....

March term 1797

Ordered that Messrs King & Allison be permitted to retail spiritous liquors at their store in this county.

William Covington vs Duncan McCall. Judgement confessed for Ł 8 3/4 & cost of suit.

Ann Elliott vs admors Neil Bethune. Jury sworn John Odom, foreman; Job Bensly, Benj Beverly, David Manderville, James Stubbs, Francis Kennedy, Stephen Lisonby, Hardy Stewart, Edwd Crossland, Wm Dabbs, Danl McIntire, Elias Adams. We find for pltff Ł 7 8/2 with cost of suit.

Silas Skipper vs John Polson. non suit.

Anthony Pouncey vs Exors Robert Blair. Non suit.

Duncan McRa vs Isam Hodges. Scire Facias. Ordered that execution do issue.

Duncan McRa vs John Pledger & others, Ordered that Joseph Brevard's Esqr. deposition be taken before the clerk to be read in evidence in this cause. Issue Joined.

Saml Councill vs James Cook non suit.

Winny Chalker vs Wm Pledger. Dismissed.

Robert Campbell vs M. N. Bedgegood plea nel debet Issue joined.

Joseph Dillport vs Abejah Porter. Issue Joined.

Robinson Carloss vs Thomas Godfrey. On motion of the pltff attorney, ordered that deft. file special bail in this case.

Deliesseline & Winfield vs James Pouncey. Judgement by default.

Deliesseline Robertson & Co. vs James Pouncey. Judgement by default.

Ordered that Orison Hinds be permitted to retail spiritous liquors by the small measure, at Cashuaway Ferry in this county....

Thomas Dean vs Wm Forniss. Dismissed at plaintiff cost.

Philip Pledger vs Benjn Arrandel. Continued.

Isam Hodges vs Admor & Admx. Jos Pledger. Non suit.

Duncan McPherson vs John Murdock non suit.

William Pledger vs Mal'a. N. Bedgegood. Decree for pltff Ł 7 8 4

John Murdock vs Israel Snead. Issue joined.

Abel Waddle vs Moses Murfee. Decree for plff according to specialty.

Isam Hodges vs John Murdock non suit.

Deliesseline & Winfield vs Solomon Quick. Decree for pltff.

Thomas Henry vs Wm Pledger. Issue Joined.

Lochran McCall vs Francis Holt. discontinued.

Mackey McNatt vs Thomas Evans. Dismissed.

Ordered that Mary Welsh be permitted to sue Edward Smith and Wm Pledger bond given for the maintenance of her bstard child.

<u>March term 1797</u>

Ordered that Israel Snead be permitted to keep a tavern at Marlborough Court House....

Mackey McNatt vs Wm Barringtine. Discontinued.

Ordered that the court do adjourn untill tomorrow 8 Oclock.

Friday 3d March 1797. Court met according to adjournment. Present John Jones James, Esq.

Azeriah David vs Col. Thos Evans. Non suit.

Orderd. that court adjourn for ten minutes.

Court met according to adjournment. Present Thomas Evans & John Jones James, Esqrs.

John Murdock vs Elijah Henson. Judgement by default. Whereas Thomas Hoges one of the constables of this county hath returned to this court, that he hath summond. Mary Andrews & George Hicks to answer as garnishees on the attachment in this case, who have failed to appear... sheriff to compel them to appear on first day of Sept next....

Ordered that the Clerk do furnish the Shff with executions against all persons indebted to the county, & that he proceed to collect them immediately.

Order'd that William Pledger late sheriff of this county be cited to appear at next June term in order to shew cause why an execution should not issue agt him for all monies which by law he ought to have collected belonging to the county.

Ordered that William L Thomas shff of this county do pay into the hands of the Hon. Thomas Evans Esqr. on or before the 2d Monday in April next all monies collected for county taxes for the year 1794 & 1795 and all other monies which he may collect belonging to the county....

Ordered that Benj Beverly and Thomas Cook be fined each one Dollar for Misbehaviour before the court.

Ordered that the court adjourn untill court in course.

Commission to John Jones James Esqr. to be a judge of the County Court of Marlborough, dated 20 Dec 1796.

At a Court of Pleas and Sessions firday Sept 1797. Present Tristram Thomas and Thomas Evans, Esquires.

Grand Jurors drawn from No 4 to No 3

1	Aaron Pearson	11	Silas Pearce
2	Wm Forness	12	Turbet Cottingham
3	Epriam Whittington	13	James Gillespie
4	Nathan Thomas	14	Jas Bolton
5	Thomas Dean	15	David Bethea
6	Isam Hodges	16	Welcom Hodges
7	Mackey McNatt	17	George Cherry
8	Jona'n Merine	18	John Thomas Senr
9	Barns. Henagan	19	Jesse Bethea Senr
10	John Lide	20	Moses Pearson

Petit Jurors drawn from No 1 to No 2

1	Joel McNatt	Jacob Odom	13	Duncan McCall Jr.	21
2	John McRae	Danel Sullivan		Sion Odom	22
3	John Moreman	Jno Killensworth	14	Jesse Baggett	23
4	Shadk Easterling	John McNatt	15	Wm Brown	24
5	John Dyer	Jas. Smith	16	David McColl	25

6	Burrel Whittington	Benj. Cox 17	Abner Miller	26
7	Alex Bodiford	James Spears 18	Jno Daniel	27
8	John Cox	Jesse Perkins 19	Jesse James	28
9	Laml. Burkett	Joseph Dilport 20	Wm Fields	29
10	David Kerby		Burwill Huggins	30
11	Wm Mixon			
12	Chs Barton			

Duncan McRae vs John Pledger & others. Judgment confessed for ℔ 37 6/5 with cost of suit, John Pledger, P. Pledger, William Fields.

Robert Campbell vs Malachi N. Bedgegood. Judgment confessed.

Ralph Dodsworth vs Wm Pledger. Judgment confessed.

R. Carloss vs T. Godfrey. Settled.

Stephen Parker vs Mary Andrews. Decree for pltff ℔ 7 2/2 & cost of suit.

Samuel Pouncey vs George Evans. Judgment confessed.

King & Allen vs George Evans. Judgment confessed for ℔ 5 15/11.

James Forniss & others vs Brittain Goodwin. Settled at plffs cost.
D. Mandeville.

John Shackelford vs John Evans. Discontinued.

John Shackelford vs Wm Whitfield. Discontinued.

Jeremiah Brown vs George Evans. Settled at plffs cost.

King & Allison vs George Evans. By consent, cause is referred to arbitration of Robert Campbell and Mackey McNatt....

Ordered that court do adjourn untill tomorrow 10 Oclock.

Saturday Sept. 2 1797. Court met according to adjournment.

Admors Niel Bethune vs Moses Pearson. Settled each paying their attorneys cost & dividing the court charges.

Admors Neil Bethune vs Abel Hodges. Settled at plffs cost.

Joseph Dilport vs Abijah Porter. Referred to arbitration of John Odom and James Gillespie.

John Murdock vs Israel Snead. Judgment confessed... Eras. Rothmahler, Defts. atty.

same vs same   Judgment confessed.

John Murdock indorsee of Richd Edens vs Israel Snead. We find for pltff $53.80 with cost of suit.

Ephraim Whittington vs Thomas Vining. By consent, referred to arbitration of Benjamin Rogers and Magnis Corgill....

Jamima Vickers Ind'ee vs Andrew Paul. We find for plaintiff within note & cost of suit.

Sept. term 1797

John Murdock vs Elijah Hinson. Judgment by default. Thomas Hodges a constable hath returned that he hath summoned Mary Andrews and George Evans to answer as garnishees, who have failed to appear...compell them to next court.

Elizth. & Geo: Evans vs Monger & Harry. Judgment confessed by David Harry & Baily Monger.

Harry Coggeshall vs John J. James. Judgment confessed.

John Murdock vs Edmund Sims. Decree for plff Ƚ 7 0/2 & cost of suit. Ordered that the sheriff do sell 200 bushels of corn attached in this case by John Bridges constable to satisfy the said debt and cost.

Wilds & Marshall vs Duncan McPherson. P Summs. It appearing to the court that the bail taken is not sufficient; ordered that deft. do file special bail.... Decree for pltff amt. of Note, interest & cost of suit.

Duncan McPherson vs John Murdock. Ordered that proceedings be stayed untill the cost of a former suit be paid.

Isam Hodges vs John Murdock. Ordered that proceedings be stayed untill the cost of a former suit be paid.

Mackev McNatt vs Edward Terrall. Judgment by default.

Joel Winfield & Co vs Wm Pledger. Declaration filed & issue joined.

John McClelland vs Jesse James. declaration filed.

John Murdock vs Simeon Bethea. Declaration filed & issued joined.

John Wilson vs D. Robertson. Declaration filed & issue joined.

Evander McIver admro. vs D. Robertson. Declaration filed & issue joined.

Arch Taylor vs Wm Whitfield. Declaration filed & issue joined.

Ephraim Whittington vs Thomas Vining. Umpire returned the following award...deft. Thomas Vining do pay unto the plaintiff Ephraim Whittington $118.36 with cost of suit. Wm Thomas.

Exor Josiah Evans. vs Aaron Snowden. We find for pltff.

James Bounds vs Richd Ballard. Decree for pltff Ƚ 8 stg. with interest & cost of suit. Thomas Dean   sworn as garnishee made oath that he has in his possession the following property of Richd Ballard: one cloth coat, one pair Breachers & 1 fine cocked hat and one short home made coat & waistcoat. Ordered that above property be sold by the sheriff.

James Forniss vs Philip Pledger. Continued.

Ordered that the sheriff pay to Genl. Tristram Thomas, Ƚ 40 sterling being the ballance due for building the gaol of this county.

Joseph Dilport vs Abijah Porter. Arbitrators returned: We James Gillespie and John Odom do award unto Joseph Dilport the plaintiff $11 and all cost....

Exors Geo Hicks vs Anthony Pouncey. Discontinued on the payment of cost.

Geo Beesely was qualified as constable.

Ordered that court adjourn untill court in course.

March term 1798

At a court of pleas and sessions held 1st March 1798. Present Tristram Thomas, Esqr.

Drury Robertson produced his commission as Judge of this court duly qualified.

Ordered that Lewis N. Cantelou be permitted to retail spiritous liquors by the small measure....

Elias Lister appeared and proved the last will and testament of Joseph Lister decd, proved by Edward Feagins. Dedimus be directed to Nathan Thomas Esq. to qualify Edward Feagins, James Feagins, Charles Cottingham, Daniel Murfee & Jesse Vining as appraisers.

Ordered that Samuel Wilds Junr Esqr. be appointed county attorney.

Archibald Taylor vs William Whitefield. Judgement confessed for debt & cost.

John Murdock vs Simeon Bethea. P Sums Settled. Ordered that the court adjourn untill tomorrow 10 Oclock.

Fryday March 2nd 1798. Court met according to adjournment. Present Tristram Thomas and Drury Robertson, Esq.

Thomas Evans, Francis Kennedy & George Hodges appeared and proved the last will and testament of George Cherry decd. The due execution of which was proved by the oath of Mrs. Elizabeth Evans. They being duly qualified as executors.
   Ordered that a dedimus be directed to William Whitefield Esqr. to qualify Benj Rogers, Samuel Brown, Isaiah Watkins, James McGee & C. Mandeville as appraisers to said estate.

State vs Sarah Barringtine. Inditement Hog Stealing No bill.

State vs Ann Elliott & James Stephens. Hog Stealing. A true bill against Ann Elliott.

State vs Thomas Brigman. Inditement for Hog Stealing. A true bill.

Ordered that sd. Thomas Brigman be committed to the district Gaol of Cheraw District....

John Shackelford vs Wm Whitefield. Judgment confessed for Ł 1 10/7 with cost of suit & stay of execution untill next Sept. Court.

Joseph Costneham appeared & was qualified as constable for this county.

King & Allison vs Edward Terrall. Decree for pltff Ł 6 s 8 d 8 with interest.

Joel Winfield vs Wm Pledger. Jury sworn. We find for plaintiff 50 cents with cost of suit. upon executing a writ of Inquiry in this case...we find damages for not performing the within condition the bond declared upon 2 March 1798 to be 105 dollars and the amt. of recp. of money paid to Mary Walsh for the maintinance of the child in the sd. condition by the county treasurer to be therefrom deducted.
                                                          John Dyer

Lewis Harper vs Jonathan Fart. Case referred to Moses Pearson, Wm Whitefield & Samuel Brown....

John McClelland vs Jesse James. We find for pltff with one dollar damage and cost of suit.

Wm Henry Pledger vs Jesse James. Decree for pltff Ł 6 and cost of suit. Ordered that the property returned by L. N. Cantelou as garneshee be sold.

March term 1798

Ordered court adjourn untill tomorrow 10 Oclock.

Saturday March 3rd 1798. Court met according to adjournment.

Survrs. Kershaw Brown vs Wm Strother. Judgement by default.

Ralph Dodsworth vs Robertson Carloss. Judgment confessed.

Wm Price vs RobertsonCarloss. Judgment confessed.

John Shackelford vs John Evans. Judgment confessed.

Minard Vanevery vs Jesse James. Decree for Ł 6 s 0 d 10 & costs.

Grand Jury from No 4 to 3.

1	Isaac Weatherly Senr	11	James McGee
2	Wm Beesely	12	John Lide
3	Edmond Brown	13	Silas Pearce
4	George Wilds	14	Jesse Vining
5	Wm Thomas	15	Sam Brown
6	John Williams	16	Moses Pearson
7	James Pouncey	17	Isaac Weatherly Jur.
8	David Stewart	18	John David
9	Jno Thomas	19	Barnebus Hennegan
10	Jonathan Marine	20	Peter Hubbard

Petit Jurors from No 1 to No 2

1	Aaron Snowden	11	Thos Cockran	21	Alex Peterkin
2	Thos Burkett	12	John McGill	22	John Beesely
3	Richd Adams	13	Willerby Broughton	23	Benj David
4	Philip McRa Senr	14	Mathew Murfee	24	Benj Williams
5	Wm Grier	15	Jesse John	25	Jas Easterling
6	John Williams	16	Jacob Odam	26	James Lister
7	John Wilson	17	Duncan McRa	27	John L. John
8	John Fridges	18	Wm Lucas	28	John Edens
9	Henry Dilling	19	Joshua David	29	Jno Breeden
10	Francis Bridges	20	Archd McIntire	30	Philip Pledger

Order'd that the sheriff do make out a new Jury list by the next court.

Joseph Jones returned a citation duly published praying for admn. on Edward Jones decd estate which was granted on his entering into bond with Philip Pledger & Jno Dyer security for Ł 150. Ordered that a dedimus be directed to John David Esqr. to qualify Samuel Terrall, Mackey McNatt, Azariah David, Edwd Terrall & John McNatt as appraisers.

John Murdock vs Elijah Hinson. George Hicks appeared & made oath that he did not owe the defendant.

Ordered that Abijah Porter be struck off the list of constables and the sheriff do serve him with this order.

Ordered that Andrew Paul be permitted to keep a Tavern at Marlborough Court House on his complying with the requisite of Law.

Ordered that Messrs. King & Allison be permitted to retail spiritous liquors by the small measure at their store.

Ordered that Donald McDerman be permitted to retail spiritous liquors at his store....

Philip Pledger vs Benj Arrandell. continued.

Ordered that Wm L Thomas be find Four Dollars for neglect of duty.

Ordered that the Court do adjourn untill court in course.

At a court of pleas and sessions held 1st day of September 1798.
Present Tristram Thomas, Thomas Evans and Drury Robertson, Esquires.

Grand Jurors drawn from No 4 to No 3.   Petit Jurors from No 2 to No 1

Grand Jurors

1 Samuel Brown (stricken)	11 James Bolton
2 Barnebus Hennegan (stricken)	12 Wm Beesely
3 Jesse Vining (stricken)	13 Wm Easterling
1 Magness Cargill	14 James Gillispie
2 Welcome Hodges	15 James Cook
3 George Wilds	16 William Leggett Junr
4 Isaiah Watkins	17 Mackey McNatt
5 Wm Furniss	18 Turbet Cottingham
6 Thos Dean	19 Isom Hodges
7 David Bethea	20 Aaron Pearson Senr
8 Moses Parker	
9 Benj Rogers	
10 Josiah David	
Isaac Neavill (stricken)	

Petit Jurors

1 Benj David	15 Jarvis Stafford
2 Jas Conner	16 John Murdock
3 Thos Cochran	17 Jos. Costneham
4 James Feagins	18 Rhuben Cook
5 Thos Adams	19 John McGill
6 Joshua David	20 David Mandeville
7 Philip McRa Junr	21 Thos Weatherly
8 John Wilson	22 Wm Lucas
9 Aaron Snowden	23 Francis Bridges
10 Jacob Abbott	24 Rhodrick McRa
11 Thos Stubbs	25 Burrell Whittington
12 Jacob Odam	26 Jesse Askew
13 Abraham Baggett	27 Wm Grice
14 Lackran McCall	28 Joshua Ammons
	29 Zachariah Moreman
	30 Lewis Stubbs

Defaults to be cited to appear at next court.

Ordered that Welcome Hodges be permitted to keep a tavern at his house.

Survrs. Kershaw Brown & Co vs Benjamin Rogers. Judgment confessed.

Survrs. Kershaw Brown & Co. vs Israel Snead. We find for pltff.

Zachariah Cantey vs Jacob Abbott. We find for pltff. one cent damage
and cost of suit.

Isaac Course Ind'ee vs William Pledger. Judgment confessed.

William Prue vs William Pledger. Judgment confessed.

Elizabeth Evans Ind'ee vs Jesse councell. We find for plaintiff with
one cent damage.

same vs same. Judgment confessed.

James McNatt vs Jesse James. Decree for plaintiff $16 and cost of suit.

Zachariah Cantey vs M. N. Bedgegood. Judgment confessed.

Ralph Dodsworth vs William Pledger. Judgment confessed for Ł 7 s 9 d 2
with interest from May 1795.

Elisha Woodward vs William Pledger. Judgment confessed for Ł 7 s 9 d 11.

Ordered that Messrs. Nettles, McCall & Company be permitted to retail
spiritous liquors at Cashuaway Ferry....

Orderd. that court adjourn untill Monday ten Oclock.

Monday Sept. 3rd 1798. Court met according to adjournment.

King & Allison vs Jesse James. Attachment N. L. Cantolou being
returned summoned as garnishee in this case and he being sick. Ordered
that this trial be continued.

Philip Pledger vs Benjamin Arrandell. Attacht. We find for pltff
$60 with cost of suit. Ordered that judgment be entered up agt. King
& Allison for Ŀ 6 s 7 d 6.

King & Allison vs Richard Edens. Decree for pltff $27.73 with costs
of suit.

The Grand Jury returned the following presentments.

We present as a grievance that so little attention of late, has been
paid to the public Roads of this County, and particularly that the
landing of Kolbs Ferry now is, and has been for some time past in such
a situation as to be almost impassable for carriages.

State vs Susannah Henry. Assault & Battery. A True Bill.

State vs Ann Elliott. Inditement for hog stealing. Ordered that a
bench warrant do issue against the said Ann Elliott.

Ordered that Aaron Snowden & Daniel Snead who were bound for her
appearance by summoned by scire facias, to shew why their recognizance
should not be forfeited.

Henry Coggeshall & Co vs McPherson & P. Pledger. Debt. Judgment confessed.

Jno Kershaw vs Drury Robertson. Decree confessed.

State vs Brummit Williams. Indictment for Reseous. A true bill.
Deft. pleaded guilty. Ordered that the prisoner be fined $10....

State vs Rabell Stafford & wife. On motion of Mr. Falconer, ordered that
the recognizances & papers in this case be quashed as having been impro-
perly issued and taken.

On motion of the county attorney, ordered that the recognizances which
are not particularly discharged be continued over untill the next court
of sessions.

William Thomas Ind'ee vs Thomas Evans. Judgement confessed.

Vernon & Mortimer & co vs William German. Capias ad satis. Sheriff returned that he had taken the body of the deft, and confirmed him in
gaol until he gave a bond with John Odam security....

William Dabbs vs Thomas Evans. Judgement confessed.

Thomas Henry vs William Pledger. Ordered that the deft's witnesses be
examined and their deposition taken by Drury Robertson Esq....

Lachlin McColl vs Francis Holt. Decree for the pltff, $20. Ordered that the property attached be sold.

King & Allison vs Peter Hall. Judgement by default.

Jonathan Gift vs McPherson & Hodges. Appeal continued.

Ordered that the overseer of the Kolb ferry be cited to appear at next court to shew cause why the said road is not kept in good order.

Ordered that court adjourn untill court in course.

At a court held 1st day of March 1799. Present Tristram Thomas, Thomas Evans, & Drury Robertson. Court met and adjourned until Sat. 10 Oclock.

Saturday 2nd March. Court met according to adjournment.

Andrew Paul vs Solomon Quick Decree for pltff. according to specialty.

Andrew Paul vs Landey Harwell. Judgment confessed.

Andrew Paul vs Thomas Evans. Judgment confessed.

King & Allison vs Elijah Burns. Judgment confessed.

Thomas Dean vs Peter Bowyer. decree for pltff.

Henry Oakman vs Benj. Williams. Judgement confessed.

Francis G. Delesseline vs Abijah Porter. Judgement confessed.

Henry Oakman vs Thomas Godfrey. Judgement confessed.

King & Allison vs Sion Hodges. Judgement confesed for the amt. of note

Andrew Smith vs Wm Covington. Ordered that the deft. in this case be ruled to special bail.

Andrew Paul vs William Bristow. Judgement confessed for ₺ 4 7/6 and cost of suit.

Elisha Woodward vs Abijah Porter. Judgment confessed.

King & Allison vs Abijah Porter. Judgment confessed ₺ 11 8 9½ with cost of suit.

Archibald Taylor vs John Odam. settled.

King & Allison vs Jesse James. Attachment discontinued.

Benj. Henry vs James McNatt. settled at defts. cost.

Francis Vanlandingham vs Thomas Sealy. settled.

Robert Allison vs Charles West. Judgement by default.

King & Allison vs Abraham Hall. Judgement confessed.

King & Allison vs Joseph Dillport. Juagement by default.

King & Allison vs Joel McNatt. Judgement confessed for ₺ 10 s 5 d 2 3/4 and cost of suit.

Andrew Paul vs George Evans. Judgement confessed.

Ordered that Messrs. Allison & Pledger be permitted to retail spiritous liquors at their store....

March term 1799

Ordered that William Param be permitted to keep a tavern at his House in this county....

Ordered court adjourn untill Monday Ten Oclock.

Monday March 4th 1799. Court met according to adjournment.

Grand Jurors drawn from No 3 to 4

1	Wm L.Thomas	11	Moses Parker
2	Moses Pearson	12	Thos A. James
3	Benj Williams	13	William Pledger
4	Thos Burkett	14	Duncan McColl
5	Joseph Jones	15	Donald McDermid
6	Saml Brown	16	Jesse John
7	Elias Adams	17	Andrew Paul
8	Malcom McRa	18	John Brittain
9	Grady(?) Steward	19	Abner Miller
10	Benj Beverly	20	Benj David

Petit Jurors from No 1 to 2

1	William Brown	16	David Kirby
2	Azariah David	17	Herbert Smith
3	Jesse Councell	18	William Grice
4	George Wilds	19	John Breedin
5	Jonathan Mickins	20	Saml Burkett
6	Henry Hill	21	Burrell Huggins
7	John S. Thomas	22	James Welsh
8	Thomas Huckabee	23	Thos Godfrey
9	Peter Easterling	24	Lackrin McClarrin Jr.
10	Peter Bowyer	25	Joseph Thomas
11	Wm Lister	26	Robert Lide
12	John Evans	27	Edwd Cottingham
13	William Fields	28	John Lide
14	Danl McClarrin	29	Stephen Lisonby
15	Charles Irby	30	Saml Pouncey

Ordered that John Dyer & William Stubbs Junr be appointed constables....

Ordered that Andrew Paul be permitted to retail spiritous liquors at his store....

Ordered that Donald McDermid be permitted to retail spiritous liquors at his store...

Ordered that the court do adjourn untill court in Course.

At a Court of Please and Sessions held for Marlborough on 2d Sept 1799. Present Tristram & Drury Robertson Esquires.

Ordered that the Grand Jury be called to serve this court.

William Pledger, fm.	Benj Beverly
Moses Pearson	Moses Parker
Joseph Jones	Thos A. James (excused)
Jesse John	Duncan McColl
John Brittain	Abner Miller
Elias Adam	Benj. David
Thos Burkett	Benjn. Williams
	Donald McDermid

Ordered that the petit Jury be drawn to serve this court.

1	David Kirby	7	Peter Bowyer
2	Burrell Huggins	8	Jonathan Meekins
3	Geo Wilds	9	Wm Grice
4	Danl McClarin	10	Joseph Thomas
5	John Breedin	11	Robert Lide

Sept. term 1799

6   John Lide   12 Thos Huckebee

Elisha Woodward vs   (torn)   Debt

Archibald Taylor vs John Evans. Judgment confessed.

Robert Campbell vs John Evans. Judgment confessed.

Nathan Thomas Ind'ee vs Robertson Carloss. Judgment confessed.

Survors. Kershaw Brown & Co. vs George Hicks. Judgment confessed.

Survors. Kershaw Brown & Co. vs George Hicks. Judgment confessed.

State vs Samuel Humphreys. Indictment Assault & Battery. True bill.

State vs William Barringtine Junr. Indictment. Stealing a Bell.
True bill.

State vs James Barringtine & Elizabeth Wallis. Hog Stealing. True
bill.

Daniel Makay vs William Neavil. Judgment confessed.

Archibald Kirby vs Exor Isaac Neavil. settled.

State vs William Barringtine. Larceny. True bill.

Ordered that court adjourn untill tomorrow 10 Oclock.

Tuesday 3rd Sept. 1799. Court met according to adjournment.
Ordered that the petit Jury be called. (same as on p. 92,
John Lide, fm.)

State vs James Barringtine & Elizabeth Wallis. Hog Stealing. Guilty.

State vs William Barringtine Junr. Indtictment for stealing a Bell.
Guilty.

STate vs William Barringtine Junr. Larceny. Guilty.

Andrew Smith vs William Covington. Judgment confessed.

State vs Samuel Humphrey. Nolle Preseque. entered. Ordered that the
deft. be discharged from his recognizance.

Thomas Henry vs William Pledger. discontinued at plaintiff cost.

King & Allison vs Brittain Goodwin. discontinued.

Ordered that William Barringtine Junr who having been found guilty of
stealing a Bell be taken into the Court Yard and receive ten lashes on
the bare back well laid on.

Ordered that William Barringtine Junr who having been found guilty of
stealing a hatchet be taken and there receive twenty lashes on the bare
back.

James Barringtine having been found guilty of Hog stealing be taken and
receive thirty lashes on the bare back well laid on.

Wm Zimmerman vs Joel Wingfield. Judgment confesed for $70 & cost of
suit.

James Furniss admr. of Enoch Harry vs Philip Pledger. Judgment confessed for debt and costs.

Sept. term 1799

Archibald Taylor vs Joel Winfield. Judgment confessed for amt. of note and cost of suit.

Ordered that Elizabeth Wallis who having been found guilty of stealing a Hog be fined in the sum of Five (sic) and she be discharged....

Ordered that court do adjourn untill tomorrow 10 Oclock.

Wednesday Sept. 4th 1799. Court met according to adjournment. Present Honble Tristram Thomas & Drury Robertson, Esquires.

Revel Stafford & wife vs Bedgegood & Fields. We find for pltff. $75 & cost of suit.

John McGill vs Ann Stevens. Appeal Judgment reversed.

Jonathan Gift vs Duncan McPherson & Isam Hodges. Appeal Judgment reversed.

John Odam vs Thomas Evans. Decree for Pltff $32.44

Wm L. Thomas vs German & Odam. We find for pltff. $72.10 & cost of suit.

Nathan Thomas vs Williams & Lide. Judgment confessed.

Indorsee of Taylor & McFarlan vs Malichi N. Bedgegood. Judgment confessed.

John Peburn vs Gadi Bullard. Decree for pltff $33 with cost of suit.

Robert Allison vs Charles West. We find for pltff $13 with cost of suit.

Thomas David vs Patrick Mahony. Judgement on Non Pros.

John Shackelford vs George Evans. Ordered that the dft. ruled to special bail.

Joseph Thomas Indee vs George Evans. Debt. Judgement by default.

Jesse Pouncey vs Jesse John. discontinued.

Jonathan Murphy vs Cottingham & Green. P Sums. Dismissed at Stafford Leadenham costs.

John McDaniel vs Benj Rogers. Judgement by default.

Archibald Taylor vs Benj Rogers. Judgement by default.

William Barringtine Junr & James Barringtine appeared in open court and made oath that they were not able to pay the cost in case of the state against them. Whereupon they were discharged.

King & Allison vs Samuel Snead. Decree for pltffs. $31.41, and ordered that the property attached be sold by the coroner.

Ordered that Court do adjourn untill Court in Course.

Wednesday March 9th 1791. A court was held for the County of Marlborough before the Hon. Morgan Brown, William Thomas, and Tristram Thomas, esqrs.

Mr. John Jones James returned an account of the expenditures of the Estate of Josiah Evans decd....

Mary Jones returned an account of the expenditures of the estate of Edward Jones dec'd but cannot make a final settlement with the court... Mary Jones do make a final settlement on next term.

Mary Andrews and Benjamin Hicks made application to the Court for joint Administration on the estate of John Andrews dec'd which was granted and entered into bond with Thomas Evans and William Pledger securities. Ordered that Drury Robertson, Thos Godfrey, William Covington, Benjamin Williams & Thomas Cochran, be appointed appraisers....dedimus to George Hicks to qualify appraisers.

Tristram Thomas Esq. returned an account of the estate of Philip Pledger dec'd....

Simon Cherry returned an account of the estate of Wm Cherry decd....

Samuel Brown Esq. returned an acct. of the estate of Jno. Brown decd....

John McNatt made application for admn. on Daniel Luke decd...dedimus to Thomas Evans to qualify appraisers.

Ordered that Samuel Brown admr. to the estate of Jno. Brown decd. be permitted to sell at public auction all the personal property of said estate except the slaves...as will raise Ł 16 sterling.

At a Court of Pleas and Sessions 1st Sept. 1791 before Morgan Brown, Tristram Thomas and William Thomas Esqrs.

Messrs. David & Cornelius Manderville made applicatn. for admn. of Wm. Murry decd. Ordered that the clerk take a bond with George Cherry and Nicholas Bogan security in the sum of Ł 1000 sterling.

Ordered that a dedimus be directed to Moses Pearson Eqr. to qualify George Cherry, Richd Brockington, Wm Brockington, N. Rogers and Isaac Perkins as appraisers to the sd. estate.

George Cogdell made application for admn. of David Dudley decd. Ordered that the clerk do take bond with Moses Fort and Thomas Cochran securities in the sum of Ł 100 sterling. Ordered that a dedimus be directed to Moses Pearson to qualify Robert Campbell, Eli John, Thomas John, Wm. Evans & John Evans as appraisers.

John McNatt returned an appraisement of the estate of Daniel Luke decd....

Ordered that the sd. John McNatt be permitted to sell at public out cry all the property belonging to the sd. estate on giving credit untill 1st Jany 1793.

Ordered that John Jones James be permitted to sell thirty five head of cattle belonging to the estate of Josiah Evans decd. on credit untill the 1st of Jan. next.

George Evans appeared and a non Cupitive will made by Elizabeth Evans decd the due exeution of which was proved by the oaths of Levy Gray, William Balldue & Ann Rayburn, the sd. George Evans was qualified as an

COURT OF ORDINARY

Sept. term 1791

admr. with the will annexed. Ordered that a dedimus be directed to Moses Pearson Esq. to qualify Robert Campbell, George Threeweeks, Magness Cargell, Jesse Vining and Thomas Vining as appraisers.

Jesse Councell appeared in open court and chose Wm Fields as his guardian. Ordered that letters of guardianship do issue on his assigning a bond with Wm Pledger and Philip Pledger securities.

the court adjourn untill court in course.

At an Intermediate Court on the first Monday in October 1790. Before Tristram Thomas and Wm Thomas Esqr.

David Mandeville returned the appraisement of Wm Murry decd estate....

Rachal Councell made application for admn. on Wm Councell decd which was granted...entered into bond for Ł 400 sterling with Thomas Cochran and Samuel Councell, securities. Ordered that a dedimus directed to Wm Easterling Esqr. to qualify Wm Robertson, James Bolten, Thomas Ammons, Wm Bennett and Robert Purnall as appraisers.

Ordered that George Cogdell admr. of David Dudley decd be permitted to sell such of the personal property of the decd...at Hunts Bluff.

Benjamin Hicks admor. of John Andrews decd returned the appraisement of the said estate.

Ordered that the Sheriff do take Elizabeth Driggers and give her ten stripes for being convicted of bastardy...and the sd. Mary Driggers made oath that she had not wherewith to pay her fees.

Ordered that a County Tax of one third of the public tax for the year 1789 is laid on the inhabitants of this county, to be paid to Bury'n Thomas whose receipt shall be good for the same in Indigo of first quality, 4/ Pork a 14/ P Corn a ¾ P Bushel.

Ordered that the Court do adjourn untill Court in Course.

At a County Court held on the 1st day of March 1792. Before Morgan Brown, Tristram Thomas & William Thomas, Esquires.

Christopher Vernon exhibited to the court a citation duly published on the estate of John Ponder decd. John Lisonbe entered a cavit on the sd. citation...the court decree the right of admn. was in John Lisonby, who entered into bond with Jacob Abbott and William Jordan in the sum of Ł 400 sterling... Ordered that a dedimus be directed to John Wilson Esqr. to qualify Jacob Abbott, Wm Jordan, Aaron Knight, Moses Knight & Nathn. Knight as appraisers.

Backter Smith made application for admn. on Millington Smith decd...entered into bond with David Steward and Barnebus Hennagan as securities. Ordered that a dedimus be directed to Wm Easterling Esq. to qualify David Steward, Barnabus Hennigan, Thomas Conner Sen, Turbet Cottingham & Edwd. Roll(?) Senr as appraisers.

Rachel Councell admx. of Wm Councell decd returned an Inventory and appraisement of the sd. estate.

On application ordered that sd. Rachal Councell be permitted to sell the personal estate of sd. decd.

At an intermediate court for Marlborough County 1st Monday in May before Tristram Thomas & William Thomas Esqr.

William Pledger Esqr. produced his commission as Sheriff of this county.

97

May term 1792

Robertson Careless was proposed to the court by the clerk as his deputy, whom they approved....

Edward Edwards returned an acct. of the estate of Thos. Harry decd....

David Mandeville returned an acct. of the estate of Wm. Murry decd....

George Evans returned an appraisement of the estate of Elizabeth Evans decd....

John Lisonby returned a dedimus and appraisement of the estate of John Ponder decd...John Lisonby be permitted to sell at public sales all the personal property of sd. estate.

Ordered that Samuel Brown admr. of John Brown decd. be permitted to sell at public sale all the personal property of sd. estate.

Baxter Smith returned an appraisement of the estate of Millington Smith....

Edward Smith returned an acct. of the estate of Frederick Smith decd....

Ordered that William Whittington a blind man, be allowed the sum of ₤ 5 sterling and that his receipt shall be taken in payment of all fines or county taxes to that amount.

John Jones James returned an acct. of the estate of Josiah Evans decd....

Ordered that Niel Bethune be permitted to retail spiritous liquors at George Cherry Esqr....

Ordered that letters of guardianship do issue to Phillip Pledger for John & Rebeccah Huson, who cose him, and the court appointed him guardian for William Huson, on his giving bond for ₤ 500 sterling.

Ordered that the sheriff do issue execution agt. all persons in arrears for county taxes.

Ordered that the Court do adjourn untill Court in Course.

At an intermediate Court held for the County of Marlborough on the first Monday in October 1792. Before Hon'ble Tristram Thomas, William Thomas, and Morgan Brown Esquires.

John Lisonby returned a schedule of the notes and accounts due the estate of John Ponder decd....

Mary Stubbs appeared in open Court and entered into bond with Jesse Doug= las security in the sum of ₤ 50 as admx. on Jno Stubbs estate...Saml Terrell, John Dyer, Wm Beesely & Aaron Daniel was qualified as appraisers.

Anne Briggs appeared in court and entered into bond with Samuel Terrell and John Odom as securities in the sum of ₤ 500 sterling for the admn. on Anthony Briggs decd. estate.
Wm Easterling, Jesse Bethea, Thomas Pearce and Thomas Dean appeared in court and was qualified as appraisers to said estate.

John Wilson, James Gillispie, and William Wright was duly qualified as admrs. to the estate of Carney Wright decd, and entered into bond with Benjamin Hicks & Thos Evans, securities in the sum of ₤ 900 sterling.

Miles King, Christopher Vernon, Lewis Malone & Benjamin Rogers appeared in court and was qualified as appraisers to the estate of Carney Wright decd.

Ordered that the County Treasurer do pay Drury Robertson Esqr. ₤ 4 ster- ling in consideration of money advanced by him for expenses in trying to apprehend Landtrip.

COURT OF ORDINARY

October term 1792

Mary Jones admx. of Edwd Jones decd. returned an acct. of said estate....

Ordered that court adjourn untill court in course.

March 1st 1793. At a court held before Honble Tristram Thomas & Wm Thomas, Esqrs.

William Pegues and Marcy Pegues appeared in open court and entered into bond in the sum of ₤ 12,000 sterling for the admn. of the estate of Claudius Pegues decd...dedimus directed to Benjamin Hicks Esqr. to qualify John Wilson, Thomas Godfrey, James Gillispie, Allen Chapman & Thomas Powe, as appraisers.

William Pegues, William Strother and Thomas Godfrey appeared and proved the last will and testament of George Hicks decd; the due execution of which was proved by the oath of William Covington.

Ordered that a dedimus be directed to Benjamin Hicks Esqr. to qualify James Gillispie, Miles King, Berry Williams, Wm Covington & Wm Fields as appraisers to the estate of George Hicks decd.

George Hicks, aged seventeen, appeared in court and chose William Pegues as his guardian.

Ordered that the court do adjourn till tomorrow 10 Oclock.

Monday March 4th 1793. Court met according to adjournment. Ordered that court do adjourn untill court in course.

At an Intermediate Court held for the County of Marlborough on the first Monday in May 1793 before Hon. Tristam Thomas and Wm Thomas, Esqrs.

John Willison Esqr. came into open court and was qualified as an exr. to the will of George Hicks decd.

William Pegues, Thomas Godfrey, William Strother & John Wilson exrs. to the estate of George Hicks, decd. returned an appraisement of the said decd....

Jesse Perkins appeared in court and entered into bond with James Gillispie and William Coward, securities for the due admn. on the estate of Athel Dempsey & Willis Perkins decd....

David & Cornelius Mandeville appeared in court and entered into bond with Thomas Evans security for the due admn. of the estate of William Elliott decd; a dedimus be directed to George Cherry Esqr. to qualify Benj. Rogers, Richd. Brockington, Wm. Brockington, Hezekiah Ellison & Isaiah Watkins as appraisers....

Edey McDonald appeared in court and entered into bond with Thomas Hodges & Barnebus Powers securities for the admn. of the estate of Andrew Mc-Donald decd....

Thomas Hodges appeared in court and entered into bond with Wm Fields security for the admn. of the estate of John Petterkin decd and sd. Thomas Hodges was duly qualified as admr.

Thomas Cochran appeared in court & entered into bond with John Wilson & Benjamin Thomas securities for the admn. of the estate of Rachal Councell decd....

Ordered that court do adjourn till tomorrow 10 Oclock.

Tuesday May 7th. Court met according to adjournment. Present Hon. Tristram Thomas Esqr.

May term 1793

Mary Harper appeared & entered into bond with Mackey McNatt security
for the admn. of the estate of John Harper decd....

Admn. granted to Shadrach Fuller on the estate of John White decd.
Shadrach Fuller appeared and entered into bond with Joshua Ammons,
security for admn. of the estate of John White decd.

James Faulkner appeared and entered into bond with William Fields, security for the admn. of the estate of Edward Faulkner decd.

Isham Hodges appeared in open court and entered into bond with William
Fields, security, for the due performance of the admn. of the estate of
Turtle McCloud, Joab Hodges, Mark Hodges, Edmond Hodges, and Charles
Steward decd....

Ann Elliott appeared in open court and entered into bond with John
Pledger security, for the admn. of the estate of Francis Stephens decd....

Solomon Hues appeared and entered into bond with Aley John and Aaron
Snowden securities for the admn. of the estate of William Thornell decd....

Aley John appeared and entered into bond with Alexander Peterkin security
for the admn. of the estate of Elisha Watson decd....

Ordered that William Perason be permitted to retail spiritous liquors
at the fork of the Walsh Neck and Cheraw road and that the clerk do furnish him with License.

Ordered that William Robertson be permitted to retail spiritous liquors
at Drury Robertson lower saw-mills, by the quart.

John Dyer appeared in court and entered into bond with James Hodges security for the admn. of the estate of Edward Williams decd....

William Luke appeared in open court and entered into bond with John Dyer
and Benjamin Thomas securities for the admn. of the estate of William
Obryan(?) decd....
Ordered that a Dedimus be directed to Thomas Evans Esquire to qualify
John James, Mackey McNatt, Azariah David, Aaron Snowden and Samuel Terrall
as appraisers to appraise the estate of William Obryant decd.

Philip Pledger appeared in open court and was qualified as deputy sheriff
for the county of Marlborough.

Ordered that court adjourn until court in course.

At a County Court held on the 2d day of September 1793 before Honble.
William Thomas and Tristram Thomas, esqrs.

Thomas Cochran returned the inventory and appraisement of the estate of
Rachal Councell decd which was ordered to be recorded.

Ordered that Thomas Cochran amdr. of Rachel Councell decd. be permitted
to sell the estate of said decd....

Solomon Dosson appeared & proved the execution of the last will & testament of Moses Cranor in due form....

Thomas Cochran appeared in open court and was qulaified as admr. of the
goods and chattels which are not administered which were of Henry Council
at the time of death with the will of sd. Henry Councell decd. annexed.

Ordered that a dedimus be directed to Thomas Evans Esquire to qualify
Robert Allison, John Murdoch, Benjamin Thomas, Edward Crosland and Isham
Hodges as appraisers to the estate of Henry Councell decd.

Ordered that court do adjourn untill tomorrow 10 Oclock.

COURT OF ORDINARY

October term 1793

At an Inetrmediate Court for the County of Marlborough held on the first Monday in October 1793, before Tristram Thomas and William Thomas, esqrs.

Christopher & Edward Mortimer appeared and entered into bond with James Gilliespie and David Manderville securities for the admn. of the estate of Neil Bethune decd....

Ordered that a dedimus be directed to George Cherry Esqr. to qualify David Mandeville, Cornelius Mandeville, William Brockinton & Benjamin Rogers as appraisers to appraise said estate.

Ordered that all the personal property of the estate of George Hicks not mentioned in his will be sold on the 1st of January next.

Thomas Cochran admr. of Rachal Councell decd. returned the amt. of sale....

Thomas Cochran admr. of Henry Councell returned the appraisement of sd. estate.

Ordered that one Negro fellow the property of Henry Councell decd be sold by the admr. on a credit untill 1st of Jan. next.

David & Cornelius Manderville admrs. of the estate of William Elliott returned an appraisement of said estate.

Thomas Cranor appeared and qualified as exr. to the will of Moses Cranor decd.

Ordered that a dedimus be directed to William Easterling Esqr. to qualify John Hues, Shadrach Fuller, Daniel Murfee, Joseph Lister & Edward Feagin as appraisers to the estate of Moses Cranor decd.

Ordered that Thomas Evans Esquire do bind James Fearson to Saml Terrall untill he arrives to the age of 21 years, and do give him 18 months schooling.

Ordered that Thomas Evans Esquire do bind Bently Fearson to David Bethea untill he arrives to the age of 21 years, and do give him 18 months schooling.

Ordered that Thomas Evans Esquire do bind John Fearson to William Pledger untill he is 21 years, old, and do give him 18 months schooling.

Philip Pledger guardian for William Fearson returned an inventory of said estate....

Sarah Luke, aged 17 years, appeared and chose Aaron Snowden as her guardian. Ordered that letters of guardianship issue, and security in the sum of ₤ 100 sterling.

Ordered that the county be assessed to the admt. one third part of the public tax for the year 1792, and that the same be paid unto the sheriff of the county on or before the first day of February next....

Ordered that the court adjourn until court in course.

At a court holden on Saturday the first of March 1794, before Hon. William Thomas and Tristram Thomas, Esquires.

March term 1794

Ordered that the receipt of William Whittington a blind man be recorded by the sheriff in lieu of cash for the county tax next hereafter to be laid to the amount of ₤ 10.

Ordered that the Court do adjourn untill Monday 10 Oclock.

Monday March 3rd 1794. Court met according to adjournment.

Ordered that a dedimus be directed to Thomas Evans Esquire to qualify Thomas Godfrey, William Robertson, William Covington & Isham Hodges as appraisers to appraise the estate of William Terrall decd.

Ordered that court do adjourn untill tomorrow 11 Oclock.

Court met according to adjournment.

Robert Lide was proposed to the court by the sheriff as his deputy whom they approved of....

Ordered that court do adjourn untill court in course.

An an Intermediate Court held for the County of Marlborough on Monday the 5th of May   1794. Present Hon. Tristram Thomas and William Thomas.

Nancy, wife of James Reed, came into court, declared that she did freely renounce her right of dower in a certain tract of land conveyed by her husband & self to John Wilson for 150 acres on 22d August 1792.

James Reed came into court and acknowledged a deed of conveyance to Abner Miller for 150 acres.

Rachael Perkins returned a citation published praying for the admn. of the estate of Isaac Perkins decd....
Ordered that a dedimus be directed to Samuel Brown Esq. to qualify George Cherry, David Mandeville, Cornelius Mandeville, Benjamin Rogers, and William Neville as appraisers of the estate of Isaac Perkins decd.

Christopher Vernon & Edward Mortimer returned the appraisement of the estate of Neal Bethune decd. Also returned the amt. of sales of property of said Neal Bethune.

William Fields admr. of the estate of William Terrall decd returned a dedimus, warrant of appraisement and appraisement of the estate of William Terrall decd....

Ordered that Isaac Neville be appointed guardian for Thomas Perkins son of Isaac Perkins decd, bond for ₤ 100 sterling with David Mandeville security.

Sarah Harry and James Forniss came and was qualified as admx. & admr. to the estate of Enoch Harry decd....

Ordered that a dedimus be directed to Thomas Evans Esquire to qualify Azariah David, Philip Pledger, John David, Benjamin Thomas and David Bethea, as appraisers to appraise the estate of Enoch Harry decd.

Elizabeth Evans and George Evans appeared in open court and proved the will of William Evans decd, the due execution of which was proved by the oath of Aaron Pearson, one of the wit....

Ordered that a dedimus be directed to Moses Pearson Esquire to qualify Aaron Daniel Senr, Aaron Pearson Senr, Aaron Pearson Junr, Robert Campbell and Mackey McNatt as appraisers to appraise the estate of William Evans decd.

Jesse Askue came into court and proved the will of John Askue dec'd the due execution of which was proved by Aaron Pearson Senr....

May term 1794

Ordered that a dedimus be directed to Moses Pearson Esquire to qualify Aaron Pearson Senr, Magness Curgill, Jesse Vining, William Whitfield and James Pouncy as appraisers to appraise the estate of John Askue decd.

Robert Allison came into court and was qualified as admr. to the estate of Benjamin Evans decd....

Ordered that a dedimus be directed to Thomas Evans Esquire to qualify Benjamin Thomas, Thomas Cochran, Benjamin David, Isham Hodges, and David Bethea as appraisers to appraise the estate of Benjamin Evans decd.

Ordered that James Forniss be appointed guardian for John Reed, the said James Forniss to give bond for Ł 100 sterling, with Philip Pledger security.

Ordered that James Moore be appointed guardian for Abraham Paul he giving bond for Ł 50 sterling with Philip Pledger security...

Ordered that court adjourn untill tomorrow 10 Oclock.

Tuesday May 6th. Court met according to adjournment. Present the Hon. William Thomas and Tristram Thomas Esquires.

Thomas Cranor admr. of the estate of Moses Cranor decd. returned a dedimus, warrant of appraisement and appraisement of the estate of sd. decd.

Solomon McColl came into court and entered into bond with security for the admn. on the estate of John McColl decd.

Ordered that a dedimus be directed to Thomas Evans Esquire, to qualify Benjamin Thomas, Zachias Ayers, David Bethea, Thomas Cochran & Robert Allison as appraisers to appraise the estate of John McColl decd.

Elizabeth Mason and John Mason came into court and entered into bond with security for the admn. of the estate of Joseph Mason decd.
Ordered that a dedimus be directed to Thomas Evans Esquire to qualify Robert Campbell, James Pouncey, Magness Curgill, Aaron Pearson Senr and Aaron Pearson Junr as appraisers.

Ordered that Thomas Evans Esquire do bind John Fearson to David Bethea untill he arrives to the age of 21 years, and that the sd. Bethea do give him 18 months schooling.

Ordered that Thomas Evans Esquire do bind Bentley Fearson to Jesse Bethea untill he arrives to the age of 21 years and that the said Jesse Bethea do give him 18 months schooling.

Ordered that court adjourn untill court in course.

At a county court began for the county on 1st day of September 1794.

Elizabeth and John Mason returned a dedimus, warrant of appraisement and appraisement of the estate of Joseph Mason decd....

Elizabeth and George Evans extx & exr. of the will of William Evans decd returned a dedimus, warrant of appraisement & appraisement of the estate of William Evans decd which was ordered to be recorded.

Jesse Askue returned a dedimus, warrant of appraisement and appraisement of the estate of John Askue decd....

Mary James and Thomas Godfrey appeared in court and produced a citation legally published praying for admn. on the estate of William James decd... entered into bond with Drury Robertson and John Lide securities....
Ordered that a dedimus be directed to Thomas Evans Esquire, to qualify John David, Philip Pledger, Mackey McNatt, William Forniss and Samuel Terrall as appraisers to appraise the estate of William James decd....

Sept. term 1794

Ordered that court do adjourn untill tomorrow 10 oclock.

Sept. 3rd 1794. Court met according to adjournment.

Rachel Perkins admx. to the estate of Isaac Perkins decd. returned a
dedimus, warrant of appraisement, and appraisement of the estate of sd.
decd which was orderd. to be recorded.

James Forniss & Susannah Harry admx. & admr. of the estate of Enoch Harry
decd returned a dedimus, warrant of appraisement and appraisement....

Robert Allison admr. of the estate of Benjamin Evans decd, returned a
dedimus, warrant of appraisement and appraisement of the estate of sd.
decd....
Ordered that Robert Allison do sell all the estate of Benjamin Evans
decd on a credit untill first day of April 1795.

Ordered that the executors of the estate of William Evans decd have permission to sell the following Negroes,belonging to said estate viz Will
and wife Flora and child, Moses and Nero, Bill and wife, Nanny and
her child, on a credit untill 25 Sept 1795...also such perishable property
as they shall think necessary....

Ordered that Rachel Perkins admx. of the estate of Isaac Perkins decd do
sell all the personal estate of said decd, on a credit untill 1st Jan
1796.

Ordered that court adjourn until court in course.

At an Intermediate court held for the county of Marlborough on the 1st
day of Dec. 1794 before William Thomas Esq.

Ordered that Isaac Neavel be appointed guardian for Thomas Perkins, he
being appointed last May term with an ordered...David Mandeville security;
the sd. Mandeville not complying therewith...William Neavill security....

Ordered that the whole of the remaining personal property the estate of
William Evans decd be sold by the exors....

Nancy Conner returned a citation legally published praying for the admn.
on the estate of Lewis Conner. Nancy Conner enterd into bond in the
sum of Ł 300 with Charles Cottingham and James Spears securities....

Ordered that a dedimus and warrant of appraisement be directed to William
Easterling to qualify Turbel Cottingham, Edward Feagin, Isaiah Weatherly,
James Bolton and Nathan Thomas as appraisers to appraise the estate of
Lewis Conner decd.

Rachel Perkins returned an acct. of the sale of the personal property
of the estate of Isaac Perkins decd.

Martha Hodges aged 11 years came into court and voluntarily chose Tristram Thomas and William Pledger as her guardians. (stricken)

Ordered that Tristram Thomas and William Pledger be appointed guardians
for Martha Hodges, they giving bond in the sum of Ł 500....

David Harry and Isham Hodges returned a citation legally published for
the admn. on the estate of Ann Thompson decd...entered into bond with
Benjamin Thomas and James Moore securities....

Ordered that a dedimus be directed to Thomas Evans Esquire to qualify
William Fields, John Dyer, David Bethea, Josiah David and Robert Allison
as appraisers to appraise the estate of Ann Thompson decd.

William Fields returned a citation legally published praying for the
admn. on the estate of Sylvanus Crunk, which was granted, and entered

Dec. term 1794

into bond with William Pledger and James Moore securities....

Ordered that a dedimus be directed to Drury Robertson Esq. to qualify
John Odom, George Greyer, Joseph Dilport, Thomas Stubbs and James Welch
as appraisers to appraise the estate of Sylvanus Crunk decd.

Robert Allison returned an acct. of the sale of the estate of Benjamin
Evans decd. which was ordered to be filed.

Ordered that Court adjourn until tomorrow 10 oclock.

Court met according to adjournment. Present William Thomas, Esquire.

John Huson, Rebekah Huson, and William Huson came into court and made
choice of Jesse Douglas as their guardian in the room of Philip Pledger
heretofore chosen...Jesse Douglas do give bond for Ƚ 500 sterling with
William Fields, James Moore and James Forniss securities....

Christopher Vernon & Edward Mortimer admrs. of the estate of Neil Bethune
decd. returned the receipts and expenditures....

Mary James & Thomas Godfrey admx. & admr. of the estate of William James
decd. returned a dedimus, warrant of appraisement, and appraisement of
said estate.

Ordered that court adjourn untill court in course.

At a court held for the County of Marlborough on Monday 2nd March 1795.
before Tristram Thomas & Benjamin Hicks, Esquire and Wm Thomas.

Arthur Harris aged 16 years and Mary Harris aged 15 years came into
court and chose James Hart as their guardian....

Ordered that James Hart be appointed guardian for William Harris, and said
Hart do give bond for Ƚ 300 sterling.

William Fields returned a dedimus, warrant of appraisement and appraisement
on the estate of Sylvanus Crunk decd...ordered that personal property
be sold except one Horn by the admr....

Thomas Twitty & William Twitty returned the citation legally published
praying for the admn. of the estate of John Twitty decd...security in
the sum of Ƚ 800 sterling. Ordered that a dedimus be directed to Drury
Robertson Esquire to qualify James Gillispie, John Wilson, Thomas Godfrey, Thomas Lide & William Thomas Senr as appraisers....

Ordered that court adjourn untill tomorrow 10 Oclock.

Court met according to adjournment.

David Harry returned a dedimus, warrant of appraisement, and appraisement
of the estate of Ann Thompson decd....

Elizabeth & George Evans extx & Exr. of the estate of William Evans returned a schedule of the amt. of sales of the personal property of said
decd....

Ordered that William Fields admr. of the estate of William Terrall decd
do sell all the personal property except the Negroes....

Ordered that the court adjourn untill court in course.

At an Intermediate court held on the 1st day of June 1795 before Tristram
Thomas and Benjamin Hicks, esquire.

William Fields returned a schedule of the sales of the estates of William
Terrall and Sylvanus Crunk decd as administrator to sd. estates....

COURT OF ORDINARY

June term 1795

Thomas Twitty acting admr. of the estate of John Twitty decd returned a
dedimus, warrant of appraisement, and appraisement of the estate of the
said decd....

Edward Roe Senr returned a citation legally published praying for the
admn. on the estate of Joseph Roe decd which was granted and at the same
time entered into bond for Ł 200....

Ordered that a dedimus be directed to Nathan Thomas Esqr. to qualify
Edward Feagin, Turbell Cottingham, Charles Cottingham, Isaac Weatherly
and Thomas Weatherly as appraisers to appraise the estate of Joseph Roe
decd.

David Stewart came into court and acknowledged a deed to John Buchannon
for 200 acres in Marlborough County on Reedy Creek.

Ordered that court do adjourn untill court in course.

At a court of pleas and sessions held on the 1st day of March 1796.
Present Tristram Thomas, Thomas Evans & John Jones James, Esquires.

Edward Roe admr. of Joseph Roe decd returned an appraisement of the
estate...ordered that sd. Edward Roe be permitted to sell all the property,
except one negro Girl.

Samuel Pouncey and Anthony Pouncey returned a citation duly published
praying for the admn. of Roger Pouncey decd estate, which was granted
on their entering into bond in the sum of Ł 1400 with Magness Curgill,
James Pouncey & Thomas John, security.
Ordered that a dedimus be directed to Moses Pearson Esqr. to qualify
Benjamin Rogers, Jesse Vining, Aaron Pearson, Samuel Brown & Wm Whitfield
as appraisers to said estate.

Ordered that court do adjourn untill tomorrow 10 Oclock.

Wednesday March 2nd 1796. Court met according to adjournment.

Thomas Evans & William Pledger securities for Benj Hicks & Mary Andrews
for the due admn. of John Andrews estate, petitioned the court to be
release from sd. admn. bond.

Ordered that sd. Benj Hicks & Mary Andrews do appear tomorrow 10 oclock
to answer the sd. petition.

Robertson Carloss & Elisha Woodward returned a citation duly published
praying for admn. on the estate of Henry Leavenworth decd, which was
granted on their entering into bond with Wm Pledger & Malichi N. Bedgegood security in the sum of Ł 150....

Ordered that a dedimus be directed to John Wilson Esquire to qualify
James Gillispie, C. Vernon, Thos Lide, Isaac Course and Thomas Twitty
as appraisers to sd. estate.

Saturday 5th March 1796. Present Tristram Thomas,Thos Evans and John
Jones James,Esqr.

Ordered that Nathan Thomas Esqr. do bind to James Feagins, Silas Hillson
an orphan boy about 12 years old, the said boy to have one year schooling
and to be free at the age of 21 years old.

Ordered that Wm Easterling Esqr. do bind out to Moses Parker the following
children Mary Slay, eleven years old; Isha Slay, six years old; each
to have one year schooling & to be free at sixteen. Thomas Slay, three
years & six months old; Wm Slay, one year and six months old; to have
one & half years schooling and to be free at the age of 21 years old.

March term 1796

Ordered that Robert Allison Esqr. do bind out to the Hon. John Jones
James, Peter Hubbard an orphan boy eight years old, to have one year
schooling, and to be free at the age of 20 years old.

Ordered that Thomas Evans & Wm Pledger securities for Benjamin Hicks &
Mary Andrews on the estate of John Andrews decd be allowed to take into
their possession all the property belonging to said estate, and retain
the same in their hands, untill sd. Benjamin Hicks & Mary Andrews shall
give other sufficient securities to be approved of by the court.

Ordered that court do adjourn untill court in course.

At an Intermediate court held 1st June 1796 before Thomas Evans & John
Jones James.

Elisha Woodward & Robertson Carloss returned an appraisement of the estate
of Henry Leavenworth decd. Ordered that the admors. be permitted to sell
all the property belonging to said estate.

William Little Thomas produced his commission as sheriff of this county,
and entered into bond with Benj Williams and Joel Campbell securities
in the sum of Ł 1500.

Joel Winfield, clerk of this court, entered into bond with Benjamin
Rogers, Benj Williams & Wm Little Thomas securities for Ł 1000 for the
due performance of this office....

Ordered that Samuel Brown Esqr. do bind out to Benjamin Rogers, James
Murray an orphan boy untill he arrives to the age of 17 years, the same
boyto have six months schooling.

Ordered that Samuel Brown Esqr. do bind out to Cornelius Mandeville,
Elijah Murry, an orphan boy, untill he arrives to the age of 20 years.

Ordered that Drury Robertson do bind to the Honble John J. James, Peter
Hubbard an orphan boy eight years old, to have one year schooling and be
free at the age of 20 years.

Ordered that the court adjourn untill court in course.

At a court of pleas and sessions began and held on the 4th day of Sept.
1796.
Present Tristram Thomas, Thomas Evans and John James Esqr.

Ordered that the exrs. of Josiah Evans dec'd be permitted to sell at
public auction on the 1st day of Feb. next....

Ordered that Mary Andrews admx. of John Andrews decd be permitted to sell
at public auction for cash as much of the personal property of sd. decd.
as will be sufficient to raise Ł 132 to be appropriated to the payment
of the debt due from said estate.

Ordered that court adjourn untill court in course.

Thursday December 1st 1796. Court met according to adjournment. Present
Tristram Thomas, Esqr.

Ordered that court adjourn untill court in course.

Thursday March 2nd 1797. The court met according to adjournment. Present
Honble Thomas Evans & John Jones James Esqr.

Robert Thomas & Nathan Thomas appeared in open court and proved the will
of John Covington decd. the due execution of which was proved by the oath
of Robert Thomas Junr.
Ordered that a dedimus be directed to John Wilson Esqr. to qualify James
Gillispie, William Easterling, Wm Covington, John Lide & Hubbard Smith as

appraisers to said estate.

Ordered that court do adjourn untill court in course.

At an Intermediate court held on first day of June 1797 before Tristram
Thomas, Thomas Evans & John Jones James, Esquires.

The Sheriff proposed to the court Thomas Godfrey as deputy Shff, which
was approved of....

Ordered that William Whitefield & Fereby Clark be permitted to admr.
on the estate of Philip Clark.

John Easterling appeared and was qualified as constable.

Ordered that the admn. of Philip Clarke estate be granted to Wm Whitefield
& Fereba Clark, who entered into bond with George Evans & John Townson
securities.... Ordered that a dedimus be directed to Samuel Brown Esqr.
to qualify John Brittain, Simon Cherry, John Askew, Francis Kenendy &
Francis Brittain as appraisers to sd. estate.

Sarah Manship appeared and proved the will of Aaron Manship decd, the due
execution of which was proved by the oath of Edward Feagin, subscribing
witness....

Ordered that a dedimus be directed to Wm Easterling Esqr. to qualify
Edward Feagins, Edmond Brown, Matthew Boykin, Jervis Stafford & Thomas
Cook, as appraisers to said estate.

James Due appeared and proved the will of Mary Jordan decd, the due
execution of which was proved by the oath of James Gillispie a subscribing witness....

Ordered that a dedimus be directed to John Wilson Esqr. to qualify James
Gillispie, Wm Wright, Joseph Wright, Thomas Lide & Robert Lide as appraisers to said estate.

Lewis Stubbs appeared in open court and was qualified as constable.

Ordered that court adjourn untill tomorrow 10 oclock.

The court met according to adjournment.

Nathan Thomas one of the exrs. of the will of John Covington decd returned the acct. of sales and expenditures of said estate....

Ordered that court do adjourn untill court in course.

At a court of pleas and sessions held on 1st day of Sept 1797, before
Honble Tristram Thomas & Thomas Evans, Esquires.

Charles K.Benninfield returned a citation duly published praying for
admn. with the will annexed on Charles Benninfield decd estate, which was
granted on his entering into bond for Ł 200 with John Lide & Thomas Lide
securities....

Ordered that court adjourn till tomorrow 10 oclock.

Saturday Sept. 2nd 1797. Court met according to adjournment.

Sarah Manship extx. of Aaron Manship decd returned and inventory & appraisement of the estate....

William Whitefield and Ferebee Clark admor & admx. of Philip Clark decd
returned an inventory & appraisement of the estate of Philip Clark....

Sept. term 1797

Ordered that William Pledger be appointed guardian to Hartwell Ayers, Charlotte Ayers, James Ayers & Thomas Ayers on his giving bond & security for Ł 500 sterling.

Ordered that William Fields be appointed guardian to Ginny Ayers on his giving bond, security in the sum of Ł 150....

Ordered that court adjourn untill court in course.

At an intermediate court held 1st day of June 1798. Present Honble Tristram Thomas & Drury Robertson.

Susannah Cherry appeared and was duly qualified as extx to the last will of George Cherry decd.

Lucy Fuller appeared and proved the will of Shadrick Fuller decd, the due execution of which was proved by oaths of James Feagin...Ordered that a dedimus be directed to Wm Easterling to qualify Turbell Cottingham, Joshua Ammons, Robert Purnall, James Feagin, Robert Thomas as appraisers to said estate.

Elias Lister returned an appraisement of the estate of Joseph Lister decd.

Nathan Thomas returned an acct. of the receipts & expenditures of the estate of John Covington decd which was approved of except James Bulgin & Co & Elizth Bishop which stands over untill proper vouchers are produced agreeable to Law.

Ordered that the extx & extors of George Cherry decd be permitted to sell at public sale all the property belonging to the said estate....

James Due returned an appraisement of the estate of Mary Gordon decd....

Ordered that William Whitefield be appointed guardian for Isaac Clarke son of Philip Clark decd, and that he enter into bond in the sum of Ł 100 with Francis Kennedy & David Kennedy, securities....

The court approves of Andrew Paul as deputy clerk....

Ordered that court adjourn until court in course.

Monday September 3rd 1798. The court met according to adjournment. Present Honble Tristram Thomas & Drury Robertson Esquires.

Sarah Pearce returned a citation duly published praying for admn. on the estate of Thomas Pearce decd...Ordered that Sarah Pearce & James Stubbs secty do entered into bond for Ł 50...Ordered be directed to John David Esquire to qualify James Cook, Lewis Stubbs, Charles Cottingham, Silas Pearce and John Thomas as appraisers to said estate.

Ordered that court do adjourn untill court in course.

At an Intermediate court held 1st day of Decm. 1798.

On application of William Pledger, guardian for Hartwell, Charlotte, James & Thomas Ayers, ordered that he be permitted to sell at public auction a negro wench Rachel the property of said orphans....

William Little Thomas Esqr. sheriff appeared and resined his commission as sheriff. Then proceeded to the election, it appears that Robert Allison is duly elected.

Robert Allison appeared in open court and was qualified as deputy sheriff of this county.

Ordered that James Walsh be appointed constable for this county and that John Wilson be required to qualify him.

Dec. term 1798

Ordered that court adjourn untill Mondy 12 oclock.

Monday Dec. 3rd 1798. Court met according to adjournment.

Mary Hodges and Edmond Hodges returned a citation duly published praying for adm.n on the estate of Isom Hodges decd which was granted, ordered that they enter bond with David Mandeville & Aaron Pearson securities for Ƚ 1500....

Ordered that a Dedimus be directed to John David Esqr. to qualify Josiah David, Joseph Cosneham, John Dyer, Welcome Hodges, and Mackey McNatt as appraisers to sd. estate.

Jonathan Fuller an orphan boy appeared in open court and voluntarily chose Joshua Ammons his guardian, Ordered that Joshua Ammons do enter into bond with Isaac Weatherly, security for Ƚ 100....

Ordered that Drury Robertson Esqr. be permitted to retail spiritous liquors by the small measure at his distillery in this county....

Orderéd that Robert Allison Esqr. be permitted to retail spiritous liquors by the small measure at his house in this county....

Ordered that Joshua Ammons be permitted to retail liquors by the small measure at his house in this county....

William Neavil appeared in open court and proved the will of Isaac Neavill decd, the due execution of which was proved by George Shanks. Ordered that a dedimus be directed to Benjamin Rogers Esqr. to qualify Cornelius Mandeville, Frances Whittington, Francis Burton, David Kirby and John Windham as appraisers.

Ordered that the court do adjourn untill court in course.

Monday March 11th 1799. Court met according to adjournment. Present Tristram Thomas, Thomas Evans & Drury Robertson Esquires.

Mary Hodges & Edmond Hodges returned an appraisement of the estate of Isom Hodges. Ordered that the sd. admx. & admor be permitted to sell one waggon and one cow and calf.

Sarah Pearce admx. returned an appraisement of the estate of Thos Pearce Ordered that she be permitted to sell a certain negro wench Rachal....

Robert Allison produced his commission as sheriff...enterd. into bond with Joel Winfield & Thomas Alexander James, securities, in the sum of Ƚ 1500.

The sheriff proposed William Henry Pledger as Deputy Sheriff who was approved of....

Ordered that court ao adjourn untill court in course.

At a court held on 2nd Sept. 1799. Present Tristram Thomas & Drury Robertson, Esquires.

Jennett Watkins returned a citation duly published praying for admn. on the estate of Isaiah Watkins decd which was granted on her entering into bond with Samuel Brown and Alexander Gregg, securities. Ordered that a dedimus be directed to Moses Pearson to qualify James McGee, George Hodges, Joseph Ellison, Samuel Brown & John Windham as appraisers.

Ordered that court adjourn untill tomorrow 10 Oclock.

At an intermediate court held on the 1st day of June 1799.

Sarah Pearce admx. of Thomas Pearce returned an acct of the sales....

COURT OF ORDINARY

June term 1799

Ordered that Francis Brittain be appointed constable and Moses Pearson
Esqr. be requested to qualify him.

Ordered that George Webber be permitted to retail spiritous liquors by
the small measure near Muddy Creek in this county....

The Court proceeded to the election of a Coroner and it apears that
Robertson Carloss is duly elected.

Ordered that Thomas Townsend be appointed constable and William Whitefield Esqr. be requested to qualify him.

Ordered that the court do adjourn untill court in course.

The court met according to adjournment. Present Tristram Thomas & Drury
Robertson

Mary Odam returned a citation duly published praying for admn. on the
estate of Joshua Odam decd....entering into bond with James Thornnwell &
Saml Pouncey securities in the sum of ₺ 200 sterling.
Ordered that a dedimus be directed to Moses Pearson Esq. to qualify
Jesse Vining, James Pouncey, Jesse Hendly, John Askew & Anthony Pouncey
as appraisers....

Ordered that the admx. & admor. of Isom Hodges be permitted to sell 12
head of cattle and 2 head of horses....

Phillip Pledger returned a citation duly published praying for admn.
with the will annexed on the estate of Josiah Evans..into bond with
David Mandeville, security for ₺ 300 sterling.

Ordered that court do adjourn untill court in course.

At an Intermediate court held 1st day of Dec. 1799. Present Tristram
Thomas, esquire.

John McClarin returned a citation duly published praying for admn. of
Lachlan McClarin estate...sd. John McClarin & Hugh McClarin entered into
bond for ₺ 100 sterling....
Ordered that a dedimus be directed to David Stewart Esqr. to qualify
Daniel McClarin, Daniel McIntyre, Archibald McIntyre, Lachlan McClarin,
& Duncan McColl as appraisers.

Nancy Conner returned a citation duly published praying for admn. of the
estate of Wm Conner decd...entered into bond with Lewis Stubbs & James
Bolton security for ₺ 250...
Ordered that a dedimus be directed to James Frazier Esqr. to qualify Isaac
Weatherly, Turbel Cottingham, Thomas Weatherly, Edward Feagins & Robert
Thomas Senr as appraisers....

Ordered that the Court do adjourn untill court in coruse.

Proceedings & Minutes by Joel Winfield, Ordinary for the district of
Marlborough and state of South Carolina. March 18th 1800.

John McClarin admr. of Lachlan McLarin returned an appraisement of the
estate, and prayed for permission to sell the personal property....

On application of Mary Odom admx. of Joshua Odom decd, a dedimus directed
to Wm Whitefield Esqr. to qualify Anthony Pouncy, James Pouncey, Jesse
Hendley, Jesse Ryals & William Jones as appraisers.

June 2nd 1800 Nathan Thomas executor of John Covington decd produced his
accts of the receipts and expenditures of the estate of John Covington...

John Carraway Hubbard an orphan boy son of John Hubbard decd upwards of
14 years chose Peter Hubbard his guardian. sd. Peter Hubbard entered into

June 2nd 1800

bondwith Lewis Malone, security for $200.

June 12th 1800. Elizabeth Evans extx of William Evans decd. produced
an account of the receipts and expenditures of sd. estate....

June 20th 1800. Phebe Vining, widow of Jesse Vining, returned a citation
duly published for the admn. of sd. decd; entered into bond with William
Pledger & Aaron Pearson Jr., security in the sum of L 1000; dedimus
issued to Nathan Thomas Esqr. to qualify General Tristram Thomas, Edward
Feagin, Aaron Pearson, Burrel Huggins & James Pouncey as appraisers.

June 27th 1800. Phebe Vining returned an appraisement of the estate of
Jesse Vining decd...ordered that she be permitted to sell some property
(enumerated).

Sarah James produced the last will of Thomas Alexander James decd, which
was proved by the oath of John Dewitt Junr. Sarah James entered into
bond with John Dewitt Junr & Samuel Wilds Junr securities for $10,000.
dedimus issued to Genl Tristram Thomas to qualify Thomas Evans, David
Mandeville, James Furness, Benjamin David & George Wilds as appraisers....

Charles Ham, Bronus Poelnitz & Thomas Evans applied for admn. on the
estate of Col. Thomas Evans which was granted; entered into bond with
David Mandeville, Harris Dewitt & Tristram Thomas, for $15,000; dedimus
directed to John David Esq. to qualify James Furness, Josiah David,
Benjamin David, Joseph Burch & John Murdoch as appraisers...dedimus to
Hugh Lide Esqr. of Darlington district to qualify James Lide, Hugh Lide,
James Pugh, James Holloway & Jacob Buckles as appraisers, to appraise
such property as ly in Darlington.

John Evans applied for admn. on the estate of Ann Evans deceasd. his
mother which was granted, and sd. John Evans & John Dyer entered into
bond....

John Evans returned an appraisement of the sd. estate....

February 1801. Charles Poelnitz & Thomas Evans admrs. of Col. Thomas
Evans decd made application to sell a quantity of corn belonging to the
estate which was granted.

April 22nd 1801. Charles Poelnitz & Thomas Evans admrs. make application
to sell cattle....

April 29th 1801. Phebe Vining admx. of Jesse Vining made application
to sell 11 head of cattle.

May 5th 1801. On application of Phebe Vining admx. of Jesse Vining,
ordered she have permission to sell all stock of cattle.

Wm Henry Pearson produced the last will of Moses Pearson Esqr. decd.
which was proved by the oath of Light Townsend, a witness. Wm Henry
Pearson entered into bond with Wm Whitefield, David Mandevill & Francis
Britton, for $8,000; dedimus issued to Col. Benj. Rogers to qualify
Samuel Brown, James Pouncey, Robert Campbell, Harris Dewitt & John
Windham as appraisers.
Ordered that the admrs. of Col. Thomas evans be permitted to sell 490
bushels of corn....

July 24th 1801. Mary Hodges admx. of Isom Hodges decd. made application
for sale of 2 head of cattle and one feather bed.

August 18th 1801. William Henry Pearson admr. of Moses Pearson decd made
application for an order of sales for property (enumerated)....

Nov. 7th 1801. Pearce Stevens appeared and chose Ann Stevens as his
guardian; the sd. Ann Stevens entered into bond with Dixon Pearce, security in the sum of $500.

Nov. 17th 1801. On application of the admrs. of the estate of Thomas
Evans decd orderd. that they be permitted to sell nine head of horses,
etc.

January 16th 1802. Nathan Thomas & John S. Thomas proved the last will
of Thomas Bingham decd, the due execution of which was proved by the
oath of Genl. Tristram Thomas.

January 22nd 1802. Susannah Bingham appeared and was qualified as
extx of will of Thos Bingham decd.

11th Feb. 1802. On application of Samuel Wilds Junr. admr. of Doct.
John M. Wilds, ordered that he be permitted to sell all the personal
belongings....

15th Feby 1802. On application of admors. of Col. Thos Evans decd ordered that they be permitted to sell 500 bushells of corn at Cashuaway,
also 350 bushells corn at the plantation.

29th May 1802. An application of James Thornwell admr. of Moses Thornwell decd, ordered that he be permitted to sell all the property....

April 29th 1803. James McDaniel appeared & produced the last will &
testament of Joseph McDaniel decd, which was proved by the oath of James
Feagin Esqr, a subscribing witness. A dedimus issued to James Feagin
Esqr. to qualify ....

April 30th 1803. Jinny Odom widow of John Odom deceased, returned a citation duly published praying for admn. of said decd; entered into bond
with Josiah David & Jacob Odom, securities in the sum of $2,000; dedimus
issued to John Rogers Esqr. to qualify Edward Feagin, Aaron Pearson
Senr, John Killingsworth, William Beasley & David Mandeville as appraisers.

May 2nd 1803. Sarah David & James Pouncey returned a citation duly published for the admn. of the estate of Benjamin David decd; Sarah David &
James Pouncey entered into bond with John Rogers & Harris Dewitt, sec.
in the sum of $10,000; didimus to Thomas Evans Esqr. to qualify....

May 6th 1803. Jinny Odom admx. of John Odom returned an appraisement of
sd. estate.

June 15th 1803. Sarah David & James Pouncey made pplication to sell a
parcell of corn.

Proceedings and Minutes by William Easterling ordinary for the District
of Marlborough and State of South Carolina.

December 31st 1803. Mary Marler Winfield and Majr. Drury Robertson
produced the will of Joel Winfield Esqr. decd; proved by Elizabeth Moor
a witness....

27th of January 1804. Malachi Nicholas Badgegood entered a citation duly
published for the admn. of the estate of Christopher Vernon decd...
entered into bond with Drury Robertson & Robert Carloss, securities for
$20,000; dedimus issued to Wm Pledger to qualify Thomas Godfrey, Benjamin
Williams, Charles Irby, George Hicks & William Fields as appraisers in
Marlborough District and to Miles King Esq. to qualify William L. Thomas,
Nicholas Rogers, Erasmus Powe, Lewis Mitchell, and William Ellibe appraisers in Chesterfield District.

February 24th 1804. Sarah Pledger chose Wm H. Pledger for her guardian;
entered into bond with Charles Strother and Robertson Carloss securities,
for $2,000.

16th February 1804. John David returned a citation duly published for
admn. on the estate of Jesse David decd; entered into bond with James
Pouncey and Anthony Pouncey, sec. for $1500. Dedimus issued to John
Rogers to qualify Thomas Evans, Lewis Stubbs, Josiah David, Mackey McNatt,

16th Feb. 1804

& Aaron Pearson as appraisers.

March 20th 1804. Joseph U.Dyer returned a citation duly published praying
for admn. on the estate of John Dyer decd; entered into bond with Robertson Carloss and Samuel Terrel, sec. for $1000. Dedimus issued to Thomas
Evans Esqr. to qualify James Keel, James Forness, Samuel Ervin, Josiah
David & Mackey McNatt appraisers.

19th of May 1804. Joseph U. Dyer petitioned for an order of sale....

May 17th 1804. Cornelius Mandeville returned a citation duly published
praying admn. on the estate of Rachel Tyler decd which was granted; entered into bond with David Mandeville and William Nevil, sec. for $2000;
dedimus issued to George Hodges Esqr. to qualify Hezekiah Ellison,
Thomas Knight, David Kirby, Francis Whittington & Jesse Cooper as apprs.

Cornelius Mandeville petitioned the court for order to sell the personal
property of sd. estate....

May 19th 1804. William Fields returned a citation legally published for
the admn. on the estate of Peter Bowyer which was granted; entered into
bond with John Terrell and William Bristow, securities for $3000; dedi-
mus issued to William Pledger to qualify George Mathews, Joel Matthews,
James Webster, John Terrel and Charles Irby to appraise sd. estate.

Sept. 8th 1804. Josiah Parrish returned a citation duly published for
admn. of estate of John McDonald decd; enterd. into bond with Joshua
Ammons, John Roe, Nathan Stucky for $1000; dedimus issued To William
Bristow to qualify Joshua Ammons, Turbett Cottingham, Edward Roe, James
Bolton, Nathan Stucky as appraisers.

December 22d 1804. Josiah Parrish petitioned for liberty to sell the
personal property of Jno McDonald decd.

October 8th 1804. Rachel Windham produced the will of John Windham decd
which was proved by William Neavil, one of the wit; widow Rachel Windham
& John Windham extx. & exor; dedimus issued to William Neavel to qualify
John Cooper, Thomas Knight, Hezekiah Ellison, Francis Whittington, and
George Hodges as appraisers.

Nov. 2nd 1804. Will of William Forniss proved by Robertson Carloss,
qualified James Forniss executor.

October 27th 1804. James Picket returned a citation duly published for
admn. on the estate of Richard Adams decd; entered into bond with John
Adams & William Adams, sec. for $500; dedimus issued to William Bristow
Esqr. to qualify Joshua Ammons, Thomas Cottingham, James Feagin, Welcome
Hodges & Turbitt Cottingham as appraisers.

Nov. 2nd 1804. Proved will of William Forness late of Dist. of Marlborough planter, by Robertson Carloss; dedimus issued to Thomas Evans to
qualify Tristram Thomas, Josiah David, Thomas Cochran, Samuel Ervin,
James Keel appraisers.

Jan. 26 1805. Charles Irby Esqr. returned a citation legally published
for admn. on the estate of Mahetable Lide late of Marlborough District
widow decd; entered into bond with David Mandeville and Robertson Carloss,
sec. for $3000; dedimus issued to William Pledger Esqt. to qualify Thomas
Godfrey, Malachi N. Badgegood, William Fields, John Terrell and George
Hicks as appraisers.

March 18th 1805. Elizabeth Frizel Kerby returned a citation duly published
for admn. on the estate of David Kirby late of Marlborough District decd;
entered into bond with Francis Whittington and David Mandeville, sec. for
$5000; dedimus to George Hodges Esq. to qualify Wm Neavil, Francis Whit-
tington, John Cooper, William Brown and James Megee as appraisers.

May 28th 1805. Will of Tho. A. James late of Marlborough District decd proved by oath of James Keel, wit; qualified John Dewitt, Saml Wilds & Edwd Edwards exrs; the will then was in possession of Mr. Saml Wilds who says he cannot give it up to me by reason for his having promised to return it again to Mr. John Winfield.

June 22d, 1805. William Dewitt & Samuel Ervin returned a citation legally published praying for admn. on the estate of John Jones James decd; entered into bond with Samuel Wilds and John Dewitt Junr, for $50,000; dedimus issued to Charles Irby to qualify Tristram Thomas, William Thomas, Drury Robertson, James Forniss and Josiah David as appraisers.

August 5th 1805. Charles Strother and Lucy Strother returned a citation duly published praying for admn. on the estate of William Strother late of Marlborough District decd; entered into bond with Thomas Godfrey, Thomas Evans and Robertson Carloss, sec. for $10,000.

11th March 1807. Charles Strother and Lucy Strother admrs. of estate of William Strother decd petition for permission to sell personal property.

August 30th 1805. Duncan McLaurin, Hugh McLaurin, blackmisth, & John McLaurin returned a citation published praying for admn. on the estate of Lauchlin McLaurin late of Marlborough District decd; entered into bond with Lauchlin McLaurin, John McLaurin, sec. for $500; dedimus issued to David Steward Esq. to qualify David McColl, John McLaurin, Hugh McLaurin, John McLaurin & Neal McLaurin as appraisers.

Nov 5th 1805. William John returned a citation for adm.n on the estate of Jesse John decd with his will annexed; entered into bond for $500 with Danl McDearmed and Francis Britton sec; dedimus issued to James Pouncey Esqr. to qualify John Killingsworth, Aaron Pearson Senr, Aaron Pearson Junr, Francis Bridges, and Elijah Thomas as appraisers.

Oct. 9th 1805. Sarah Conner returned a citation for admn. on the estate of James Conner late of Marlborough district, planter, decd; entered into bond with John Conner & Benjamin Townsend for $500; dedimus issued to Nathan Thomas to qualify Jonathan Meekins, John Conner, Benjn Townsend, James Spears, and Jonathan Cottingham as appraisers.

Nov. 29th 1805. Proved will of Abner Miller late of Marlborough Dist. deceased by oath of Robt. Lide one of the subscribing wit. to the same, and qualified Sarah Miller, extx.

4th Feb 1806. Angus Colquhoun appeared and produced the will of Margaret Colquhoun which was proved by Nathan Thomas Esq.; qualified Angus Colquhoun exr; dedimus issued to Nathan Thomas to qualify Charles McRae, Jonathan Meekins, John McLucas, Charles McIntire and William Covington as appraisers.

5th Nov 1805. Wm Pledger returned a citation for admn. on the estate of Isaac Davis late of sd. district decd; entered into bond for $300 with Lewis Melone and Leon Hodges; dedimus issued to Jesse Bethea to qualify Jesse Bethea, Tristram Bethea, John Pinner, John Hammer and Robt Thomas Senr.

29th March 1806. James Fields chose William Fields as his guardian; William Fields entered into a bond with Malachi N. Badgegood and Dickson Pearce, for $1000.

28th Nov 1805. Proved will of Abner Miller by oath of Robert Lide, a wit; dedimus issued to John Wilson Esqr. to qualify John Lide, Charles Strother, Robert Lide, Robert Potter and James Welch as appraisers.

March 3rd 1806. Francis Whittington produced the will of Elizabeth Whittington late of Marlborough District decd; proved by Elizabeth Frizzell Kerby, a wit; qualified Francis Whittington exr; dedimus issued to William Neavel Esq. to qualify George Hodges, John Cooper, Ezekiah Ellison, Baker Wiggins, and Thomas Purkens as appraisers.

March 31st 1806. Elizabeth McTyer returned a citation for admn. on the estate of William McTyer decd; entered into bond with Francis Whittington and Nathan Whittington for $5000; dedimus issued to William Neavil Esq. to qualify George Hodges, John Cooper, Ezekiah Ellison, Baker Wiggins and Thomas Purkins as appraisers.

23rd May 1806. On application Elizabeth McTyer admx. that she be permitted to sell whole of the present property of sd. estate.

May 11th 1806. Juliana Cottingham returned a citation for admn. on the estate of Dill Cottingham decd; entered into bond with John McRae and Daniel Cottingahm, for $200; dedimus issued to David Stewart to qualify Tristram Bethea, Joshua Ammons, Daniel McKay, Daniel Cottingham and John McRae appraisers.

May 17th 1806. On application of Juliana Cottingham admx. ordered that she be permitted to sell the whole of the personal estate....

May 23rd 1806. Granted to Robt Cochran a citation for admn. on the estate of William Jones decd.

June 7th 1806. Robert Cochran returned a citation duly published for admn. on the estate of William Jones decd; entered into bond with Thos Cochran, Robertson Carloss, for $3000; dedimus issued to James Pouncey to qualify Anthony Pouncey, Wm Gallaway, John Britton, Francis Britton, and Burrell Huggins as appraisers.

March 31st 1806. Proved will of Elizabeth Whittington late of Marlborough Dist. widow decd; by Elizabeth Frizel Kerby a wit; qualified Francis Whittington, exr.

July 23rd 1806. Provd will of Duncan McColl late of Marlborough District by oath of Daniel Mcrae, a wit; qualified Duncan McColl and James McQueen exrs; dedimus issued to David Stewart to qualify Lachlin McLaurin, Lachlin McColl, Duncan McColl, John Douglas and Danl McIntyre appraisers.

July 29th 1806. Proved will of Mary Edwards decd by oath of Louisa Lewis a wit who says that she saw Mary Welch the other witness thereto sign her mark to the same; Joshua Lewis one of the exrs. named refused to take upon him the burthen of acting as exr. On 2d Aug 1806 William Fields the other exr. refused. Issued a citation to Nathan Morris and Penelopy his wife.

July 29th 1806. James McQueen and Duncan McColl exrs. of Duncan McColl decd returned an appraisement and made applicaton for an order to sell....

On 8th day of August 1806 Robert Cochran returned an appraisement of the estate of William Jones decd.

August 8th 1806. Nathan Morris returned a citation for admn. on the estate of Mary Edwards late of Dist. of Marlborough decd (with her will annexed); entered into bond with William Morris and Peter Stubbs, for $500; dedimus issued to William Pledger to qualify William Morris, Peter Stubbs, Joshua Lewis, Thomas Stubbs and William Stubbs Sen. as appraisers.

August 22n d 1806. Josiah David returned a citation for admn. on the estate of Benjamin David decd; entered into bond with Thomas Evans and Charles Irby for $20,000; ordered that Josiah David be permitted to sell all perishable property except the negroes....

December 24 1806. James Wright appeared and chose Alexander McDaniel as his guardian; on 12 Jan 1807, entered into bond with John McDaniel and John Way securities for $1000.

January 27th 1807. Tristram Bethea and Anna Bethea returned citation for admn. on estate of Jesse Bethea Junr decd; entered into bond for $10,000 with Philip Bethea and David Bethea sec; dedimus issued to Wm Bristow

<u>Jan. 27 1807</u>

to qualify James Leggitt, John McKay, Wm Morris, Moses Parker and Joshua
Ammons as appraisers.

Feby 9th 1807. Tristram Bethea adm and Anna Bethea admx. petitioned
to sell all property except the negroes on the estate of Jesse Bethea....

14th April 1807. John Thomas and Stephen Thomas returned a citation
for admn. on the estate of Betty Mendenhall decd; entered into bond
with Thomas Wilcuts and John Thomas Junr sec, for $500; dedimus issued
to Wm Bristow to qualify Thomas Wilcuts, Daniel Dawson, John Mendenhall,
William Adams and Thos. Morris as appraisers.

14th April 1807. John & Stephen Thomas Admrs. of Betty Mehdenhall petitioned for an order to sell all personal property of sd. estate...

Benjamin Beverly and James Jones returned a citation for admn. on the
estate of Benjamin Beverly decd; entered into bond with Robert Cochran
and James McDaniel for $500; dedimus issued to William Bristow to qualify
William Way, James McDaniel, John Breeden, Luke Robertson and Robert
Cochran as appraisers.

7th May 1807. James Feagin returned a citation for admn. on the estate
of JosephMaxwell decd with his will annexed; entered into bond with
Robert Cochran and William G. Feagin for $200; dedimus issued to Nathan
Thomas to qualify Charles Cottingham Senr, Jonathan Cottingham, Isaac
Weatherly, Thos Weatherly & Benjamin Bridgers to appraiser the estate.

7th May 1807. will of Joseph Maxwell was proved by oath of William G.
Feagin.

May 18th 1807. James Feagin, admr. of Joseph Maxwell with his will annexed, petitioned for permission to sell personal property.

August 7th 1807. Aqualla Quick & Thos Quick exrs of Levi Quick petitioned
for   liberty to sell a part of the stock....

Sept. 1st 1807. James Jones and Benj Beverly admrs. of Benjamin Beverly
decd petitioned for order to sell....

October 10th 1807. Elizabeth Quick returned a citation for admn. on the
estate of Solomon Quick decd; entered into bond with Burrell Quick and
John Scipper, for $10,000; dedimus issued to Thomas Godfrey to qualify
Drury Robertson, William Fields, Charles Bright, John Stubbs and Shadrach
Easterling as appraisers.

October 21st 1807. Proved will of Giles Newton, late of Dist. afsd.,
planter, by oath of Charles Bright, a wit; qualified Younger Newton &
Benjamin Handon exrs; dedimus issued to Wm Bristow to qualify Charles
Bright, Wm Adams,Shocklet Adams, Tho Huckabee & John Stubbs appraisers
in Marlborough District; also a dedimus issued to Wellcome Chapman Esqr.
to qualify George Bullard, Gilbert Purvis, John Craig, George Watkins &
Jno McNeal as appraisers in the Dist. of Chesterfield.

27th Oct 1807. Edward Merchison returned a citation for admn. on the
estate of John Murchoson; entered into bond with Daniel McLennan and
John McRae sec, for $200; dedimus issued to Nathan Thomas to qualify
Daniel McLannan, Charles McRae, Alexander Gilbert McRae, and Morgan
Brown as appraisers.

December 8th 1807. Mary Williams returned a citation for admn. on the
estate of William Williams decd; entered into bond with Robert T. Thomas,
and Nathan Stackey sec, for $500; dedimus issued to Nathan Thomas to
qualify Thomas Weatherly, Nathan Stuckey, George Bolton, Edwd Roe and
James Gray as appraisers; 31st Dec 1807. petitioned for order to sell.

Nov. 11th 1807. Major Drury Robertson returned a citation for admn. on
the estate of William Sturges decd; entered into bond with Robertson

Nov. 11th 1807

Carloss and Solomon McColl sec. for $500; dedimus issued to Wm Fields
to qualify Shadrach Easterling, James Webster, William Smith, John Stubbs,
and Benjamin Moore as appraisers. petitioned for permission to sell....

16th Jan 1808. Proved will of James Marler late of District of Marlborough by oath of George Cherry; qualified Levi Gray, exr; dedimus issued
to George Hodges to qualify Joseph Gourley, Hezekiah Ellison, John E.
Murry, George Cherry and Oliver Ellison as appraisers.

18th Jan 1808. Joseph Gourley returned a citation for admn. on the
estate of Thomas Gaddy decd; entered into bond with Francis Whittington
and John C. Gourley for $1000; dedimus issued to _____

Feb. 12th 1808. Sarah Grooms returned a citation for admn. on the
estate of Rachel Grooms late of Marlborough District decd; entered into
bond with Morgan Brown, Colson Grooms, for $500; dedimus issued to William
Whitefield to qualify Morgan Brown, Thos Brown Junr, Gilbert McRae, Daniel McLennon & Roderick McRae as appraisers. 28th May 1811. Petitioned
for permission to sell personal property....

March 10th 1808. Right Bruce returned a citation for admn. on the estate
of William Bruce, late of Marlborough dist. decd; entered into bond with
William Brown and Hezekiah Alison for $600; dedimus issued to George
Hodges to qualify Francis Whittington, Wm Neavel, Joseph Gourley, James
Megee and William Brown as appraisers.

March 24th 1808. A marriage license granted to Matthew Morris to
celebrate the ties of Matrimony with Julina Cottingham the same day
they were married by the Rev. Mr. Robert Thomas.

April 16th 1808. Elizabeth Pouncey returned a citation duly published
for admn. on the estate of Anthony Pouncey decd; entered into bond with
Francis Britton and William Henry Pearson, sec. for $3000; dedimus issued
to George Hodges Esq. to qualify Wm. H. Pearson, F. Britton, James Pouncey, Moses Hasque and Zacchariah Hasque, as appraisers.

May 21st 1808. Elizabeth Pouncey admx. of Anthony Pouncey petitioned
for permission to sell personal property except Negroes, and items mentioned.

April 25th 1808. Bethsheba Cooper, widow of Jno Cooper returned a citation
for admn. of the estate of John Cooper decd; entered into bond with
Francis Whittington and Hazekiah Allison sec for $800; dedimus issued
to George Hodges Esqr. to qualify Francis Whittington, Joseph Gourley,
John Brown, James Megee, Hezekiah Alison, as appraisers.

August 2nd 1808. Mandeville Polson returned a citation for admn. on the
estate of Barnabas Clark late of said district decd; entered into bond
with Thomas Hodges and John Polson, for $200....

4th Oct 1808. Will of Hugh Thompson was proved by the oath of Angus
Colquhoun a wit; qualified Danl Thompson and Neil Thompson, exrs; dedi-
mus to Nathan Thomas to qualify Angus Colquhoun, Jonathan Meekins, Chas.
McRae, and Alexander Henderson, to appraisers.

October 13th 1808. Hamlet Fuller returned a citation for admn. on the
estate of Joseph Fuller decd; entered into bond with James Parham and
Joshua Ammons for $1000;dedimus issued to Wm Bristow Esq. to qualify
Joshua Ammons, John Hamer, James Feagin, Robert Purnal, and Robert
Cochran as appraisers.

October 28th 1808. William Grice returned a citation for admn. on the
estate of William Grice Senr. decd; entered into bond with George Shanks
and William Neavel for $400; dedimus issued to Wm Neavel to qualify Fran-
cis Whittington, Nathaniel Whittington, Arthur Tomkins, Daniel Baker and
George Hodges Esqr. as appraisers.

13th of October 1808. Will of Magness Corgell was proven by the oath of Edward Feagins, wit; James Pouncey exr. refused to qualify; Tho. A. Corgell to admr. with the will annexed.

Dec. 27th 1808. James Feagin returned a citation duly published for admn. on the estate of Turbit Cottingham decd; entered into bond with Joshua Ammons & William G. Feagin, for $3000; dedimus issued to Wm Burton Esqr. to qualify Thomas Weatherly, Joshua Ammons, James Cook, James Parham & Joseph McDaniel as appraisers.

January 1st 1809. Thomas A. Corgill returned citation for admn. with the will annexed of Magnas Corgill decd; entered into bond with James Pouncey and Barnabas Henagan for $5000; dedimus issued to James Miles Esqr. to qualify Tho. Evans, Barnabas Henegan, Jesse Rials, James Pouncey and Francis Britton appraisers.

Jan. 4th 1809. Abel Jones returned a citation for admn. on the estate of Joseph Jones decd; entered into bond with James and Burrel Huggins for $3000; dedimus issued to Thomas Evans Esq. to qualify John Rogers, James Foris, Aaron Pearson, Burrel Huggins and Francis Bridgers as appraisers.

Jan. 19th 1809. Abel Jones admr. of Joseph Jones petitioned for an order for sales of the whole of the personal property....

July 1st 1809. Elizabeth Knight & Aaron Knight returned a citation for the admn. of the estate of Achilles Knight decd; entered into bond with William Pegues and Solomon Rye, for $2000; dedimus issued to Malachi Pegues to qualify William Thomas, James Pegues, E. Parker Junr, James Gillispie & John Lide as appraisers; petitioned court for permission to sell a part of the perishable property.

11th Aug 1809. will of John W. Covington decd was proved by oaths of Elias Jones and Robert Covington, subscribing wit; qualified James Gilispie, Malachi Pegues Esq. and Francis Gilispie, exrs; also, a codicil to last will annexed, appointed John Lide an exr. was proved by oath of George Strother Junr, a subscribing wit; dedimus issued to John Lide to qualify William Thomas, Benjamin Williams, Thomas Lide, Robert Lide and Alexander Lamb as appraisers.

Aug. 15th 1809. William Parham returned a citation for admn. of the estate of William Parham Senr, late of the district of Marlborough decd; entered into bond with James Feagin & Richardson Feagin for $500; dedimus issued to William Britton Esq. to qualify Charles Cottingham, Thomas Weatherly, Joseph McDaniel, Silas Pearce, and William Feagin appraisers.

Sept. 9th 1809. William Parham admr. petitioned for liberty to sell the whole of the personal property.

7th Oct 1809. Proved will of David McColl late of Marlborough District decd by oaths of Archibald Thompson and Hugh McLaurin; qualified Hugh McColl, exr; dedimus issued to William Bristow to qualify Hugh McLaurin, Daniel McIntyre, John McLaurin, David Stewart, and Lachlin McLaurin Junr appraisers.

Oct. 13th 1809. Hugh McColl exr. of David McColl petitioned for liberty to sell part of the perishable property....

Nov. 18th 1809. Proved will of Joseph Macy by the affirmation of Henry Macy and Henry David two of the wit; qualified William Way, exr; dedimus directed to William Bristow to qualify John Thomas, John Thomas Junr, William Adams, Shockley Adams & Obediah Harris appraisers.

16th Dec. 1809. Lamuel Boykin returned a citation for admn. on the estate of Matthew Boykin late of Marlborough Dist., decd; entered into bond with William Fields and William Seals for $1000; dedimus to Majr. William Fields to qualify William Bennet, John Adams, William Adams,

16th Dec. 1809

James Newton & Jonathan Merine Junr to appraise the sd. estate.

28th Dec 1809. Lamuel Boykin admr. of the estate of Matthew Boykin petitn. for order of sale.

Jan. 12th 1810. John Pinner returned a citation for admn. on the estate of Joseph Williams late of Marlborough District decd; entered into bond with David Montgomery and James McDaniel for $200; dedimus issued to William Fields to qualify Drury Robertson, Malachi N. Badgegood, Thomas Hodges, George Ferguson & James B. Ferguson as appraisers.

Feb. 5th 1810. John McRae and Alexander McRae returned a citation for admn. on the estate of Capt. Malcom McRae late of Marlborough Dst. decd; entered into bond with Charles McRae and Roderick McRae for $2000; dedimus issued to Nathan Thomas to qualify Chas. McRae Esqr., Thomas Weatherly, Roderick McRae, Hugh McLaurin and Nathan Stuckey as appraisers. petitioned court for order of sale

March 16th 1810. Edward Crosland returned a citation for admn. on the estate of Israel Crosland decd; entered into bond with Robertson Carloss and M. G. Brown for $1000; dedimus issued to Wm Pledger to qualify John David, Joshua David, Wm. A. Pledger, Thos Cochran & Mathew Hustes as appraisers.

April 11th 1810. Wm. H. Pearson & Sarah Pearson returned a citation for admn. of the estate of Griffin Steed decd; entered into bond with Saml Pearson & Wm. H. Pledger for $10,000; dedimus to Francis Miles to qualify Barnabus Henegan, Francis Britton, William Brown, John Brown & William Whitefield as appraisers.

April 25th 1810. Catherine McColl & John McColl returned a citation for admn. on the estate of Lachlin McColl late of sd. district; entered into bond with Hugh McLaurin Esq. and Lachlin McLaurin Senr, for $10,000; dedimus issued to Hugh McLaurin to qualify John McLaurin, Lachlin McLaurin, Danl McIntyre, Duncan McColl & John Douglas appraisers.

August 20th 1810. Joseph Purkins returned a citation for admn. on the estate of George Smith, late of Marlborough District, decd; entered into bond with John Johnston and Noah Whittington, for $500; dedimus issued to Malachi Pegues Esq. to qualify Capt. Benjamin Williams, Peter Nicholson, James Gilispie, James Coward and James Welch as appraisers.

Dec. 15th 1810. Elizabeth Covington relict & widow of John Wall Covington petitioned the court for a division of the personal estate agreeable to the will of her husband, that the exrs. should choose five freeholders of good character; the exrs. Viz. James Gillispie, Malachi Pegues and Francis Gillespie; they chose the following: William Thomas, Thomas Lide, Alexander Lamb, Robert Lide and William Pegues.

Feb. 23rd 1811. Aaron Knight & Elizabeth Rye (formerly widow of Achilles Knight) admx. and admr. of the estate of sd. Achilles Knight petitioned for liberty to sell remaining part of the estate.

March 5th 1811. John & Alexander McRae admrs. of Malcom McRae petitioned for liberty to sell the whole of the remaining unsold part of the personal property....
April 3rd 1811.
Edward Edwards returned a citation for admn. on the estate of James McDonald late of Chesterfield District decd; entered into bond with Tristram Thomas & Evander McIver for $20,000; dedimus to Charles Irby to qualify Thos Evans, John Rogers, David Mandeville, James Forniss & Nicholas Nicholson to appraise the part of the personal estate which is in Marlborough District. Also a dedimus issued to Maj. John Dewitt to qualify Threshly Chapman, Robert Bevill, John Edwards, William Michael & Isaac Webb to appraise that part of the personal estate which is in Chesterfield District.

March 31st 1812.   Edward Edwards petitioned for liberty to sell part of the personal property of James McDonald decd....

April 8th 1811.   Will of David Stewart, late of Marlborough District decd. was proved by oath of William Bristow Esqr., John Sands Thomas and James cook, witnesses to the same; qualified Nathan Thomas Esqr. & Hugh McLaurin Esq. executors; dedimus issued to William Whitefield Esq. to qualify William Bristow, John McKay, John S. Thomas, Robert Covington & Joshua Ammons as appraisers.

Oct. 3d 1811.   Will of Isaac Brigman, late of Marlborough District was proved by oath of Majr. Bethea, one of the wit; qualified Fereby Brigman extx & John Brigman, exr.

Oct. 8th 1811.   Ann Stephens, Wm. Fields, and Peter Pelham returned a citation on the admn. of the estate of Thomas Stephens decd; entered into bond with James Jones and Robert Johnston for $1000;

Jan. 6th 1812.   Elizabeth Henagan returned citation for admn. on the estate of John Hennagan decd; entered into bond with Barnabas Henegan and Francis Miles for $2000; dedimus issued to Francis Miles to qualify William Whitefield, John Brown, William Brown, John Miles & Jesse Miles as appraisers.

10th Jan 1812.   Elizabeth Henagan petitioned for liberty to sell the whole of the personal property....

Jany 12th 1812.   Nathan Thomas Esqr. exr. & Nathan B. Thomas & John Thomas heirs of the estate of Thomas Bingham decd petitioned court for permission to sell a negro man named Prince, for the purpose of effecting a division agreeable to the tenor of the will....

Feb. 11th 1812.   Paul May returned a citation for admn. on the estate of Matthew May decd; entered into bond with Wm May and John May for $10,000; dedimus to Wm Fields to qualify Silas Pearce, Wm. Bristow, John Herndon, John Breeden Jun and Joseph McDaniel as appraisers.

May 6th 1812.   Elizabeth Beverly returned a citation for admn. on the estate of Anthony Beverly decd; entered into a bond with Lewis Stubbs and James Stubbs Junr for $500.

6th June 1812.   Charles McRae returned a citation for admn. on the estate of Daniel McRae; entered into bond with Duncan McRae for $500.

Nov. 3d 1812.   Louisa Lewis & James Griner returned a citation for admn. on the estate of Revd. Joshua Lewis decd; entered into bond with Tristram Thomas, Wm. Pledger & John Lide.

1812 Jany 22.   James Pouncey returned a citation for admn. on the estate of Benjamin Daniel decd; entered into bond with Thos A. Corgill for $3000.

1813 Feby 25th.   Drury Robertson returned a citation for admn. on the estate of Bolton Steagel; entered into bond with William Pledger for $1000.

1812. April 25th.   Will of Jesse Bethea Senior was proved by the oath of Tristram Bethea, John Pinner and Joel Eastering; qualified Elizabeth Bethea, exorx and David Bethea, exr.

1812. December 22d.   Will of Luke Robertson decd was proved by William Bennett, Thomas Lide and Henry Beverly, all wit; qualified William Adams and Shockley Adams, exrs.

1813. Jany 2d.   Josiah J. evans Esq. returned a citation duly published for admn. on the estate of Philip Pledger decd; entered into bond with John Terrell and Tristram Thomas for $1000.

1813 April 22nd. Will of Aquilla Quick was proved by Noah Whittington and Joseph England; qualifyed Thomas Quick Jr., exr.

1813. Apl 12th. James Fields returned a citation for admn. on the estate of Goodwin Mitchel; entered into bond with John Terrell and John David Jr. for $1000.

June 1st 1813. Will of John Lide Esquire decd was proved by the oath of Doctor Oliver Haws, one of the wit; qualified Mrs. Elizabeth Lide, extx.

Nov. 8th 1813. Hannah Thomas returned citation for admn. on the estate of Benjamin Thomas; entered into bond with John Parnel for $2000.

1814. Feb. 11th. Elizabeth Pearce returned citation for admn. on the estate of Silas Pearce decd; entered into bond with William Pearce and John McDaniel for $10,000.

1814. June 28th. John Herndon returned a citation for admn. on the estate of Benjamin Herndon decd; entered into bond with John Breeden Junr, William Herndon & James M. Smith for $5000.

July 23d 1814. Will of Malachi N. Bedgegood was proved by the oath of Major Drury Robertson; qualified Malachi Pegues, William Vernon, Enoch Handford and Thomas Robertson, exrs.

Sept. 20th 1814. Will of Mary B. David was proven in Williamsburgh District before William Hedleston Esquire, by the oath of Benjamin Britton, one of the wit; on 6th day of October 1814, John G. Britton and Francis Britton of Marlborough District, qualified exrs. in Marlborough District.

August 6th 1814. James N. Pouncey returned a citation for admn. on the estate of Anthony Pouncey decd with his will annexed; entered into bond with Samuel Pearson and Burch Huggins for $2000.

October 13th 1814. Will of William Bennett was proved by David Montgomery; Thomas Stubbs and Moses Parker executors.

October 24th 1814. Samuel Sparks and Alexander McDaniel returned a citation praying for admn. on the estate of John McDaniel; entered into bond with William Pearce and William Bristow for $4000.

Nov. 10th 1814. Joseph Gourley returned a citation for admn. on the estate of John C. Gourley; entered into bond with Right Bruce and Oliver Alison for $2000.

1815 January 28th. Will of Anthony Pouncey was proved before John Rice Esqr. one of the Justices of the peace for Coleton County by oath of James A. Harper.

February 7th 1815. William Jones returned a citation for admn. on the estate of Abel Jones; entered into bond with John Rogers and Thomas A. Corgill for $5000.

February 27th 1815. James N. Pouncey returned a citation for admn. of the estate of Anthony Pouncey with his will annexed; entered into bond with Burwell Huggins and John Haskew for $5000.

7th March 1815. Selah Megee returned a citation for the admn. of the estate of John Megee; entered into a bond with Burwel Quick and William Grant for $500.

1815 April 3rd. John Luke appeared and chose John Rogers for his guardian; sd. Rogers entered into bond with James Forniss & Aaron Pearson for $1000.

1815 April 4th. Edw. W. Jones chose John Rogers his guardian; sd. Rogers entered into bond with Robertson Carloss and William Jones for $10,000

1815 May 1st. Elizabeth Megee and Hartwell Megee returned a citation for admn. on the estate of James Magee entered into bond with Francis Britton & George B. Wickfield for $5000.

May 3rd 1815. Gilbert Sweat returned a citation for admn. on the estate of Naomi Driggers; entered into bond with Benjamin Sewat and Solomon Sweat for $250.

1815 May 25th. Mary Clark returned a citation for admn. on the estate of Joseph Clark; entered into bond with Duncan McLaurin for $500.

July 31st 1815. Will of William Smith was proven by Giles Newton; qualified Thomas Stubbs, exr.

October 2d 1815. Mary Griner chose James Griner as her guardian; sd. James entered into bond with William Pledger and James Fields for $2000.

October 30th 1815. John Dunham returned a citation for admn. on the estate of John Peter Dunnam; entered into bond with Jesse Bethea & Robertson Carloss for $20,000.

Nov. 11th 1815. John Brigman returned a citation for admn. on the estate of Thomas Purkins; entered into bond with Merida Mixon and John Miles for $1000.

John Brigman returned a citation for admn. on the estate of Jehu Purkins decd; entered into bond with John Miles & Merida Mixon for $1000.

Jan. 9th 1816. Elizabeth Odom returned citation for admn. on the estate of James Odom decd; entered into bond with William Odom, Isham Turner and James Odom for $3000.

Jan. 27th 1816. Alexander Smith chose John Smith for his guardian; sd. John entered into bond with Giles Newton & Henry Easterling for $2000.

March 2d 1816. John Hasskew returned citation for admn. on the estate of Jesse Haskew; entered into bond with James Pouncey & William Bristow for $500.

March 15th 1816. Celia Megee chose Burwell Quick for her guardian; entered into bond with John Chavis for $100; same day Burwell Quick entered into bond with James Odom security to Celia Megee admx. of estate of John Megee in the sum of $53.25 for the securing of payment of $26.62½ to Dicy Megee it having been deposited in the hands of sd. Quick for sd. Dicey as her part of the estate of John Megee decd &c.

August 26th 1816. Will of Francis Whittington was proved by William Neavil; at same time qualified Hezekiah Allison exr.

October 16th 1816. Jesse Bethea chose David Bethea as his guardian; sd. David entered into bond with Moses Parker and Tristram Bethea.

December 26th 1816. Will of Sion Hodges decd was proved by Shadrach Easterling; qualified George Bristow and John H. David, exrs.

December 31st 1816. Nathan Thomas Esqr. returned a citation for admn. of the estate of Benjamin Thomas decd; entered into bond with Robert H. Thomas and John S. Thomas for $500.

January 20th 1817. Elizabeth Pearce returned a citation for the admn. of the estate of Dickson Pearce decd; entered into bond with Tristram Bethea and William Pearce for $1000.

March 17th 1817. Malachi Hagan returned a citation for admn. of the estate of Colson Hagan decd; entered into bond with Samuel Townsend and William Stapleton for $5000.

March 31st 1817. Will of Sarah Wright was proved by oaths of James Gil-

March 31st 1817

lespie, James Irby and John R. Due, witnesses thereto; qualified William
Wright and Joseph Wright exrs.

April 21st 1817. Charles Manship returned a citation for the admn. of
estate of Aaron Manship decd with his will annexed; entered into bond with
Isaac Pipkin & Eli Willis for $3000.

August 22d 1817. David Montgomery returned a citation for admn. of the
estate of Samuel Montgomery decd; entered into bond with Isaac Pipkin and
John McColl for $2000.

September 29th 1817. Will of Robert Covington decd was proved by Eli
Thomas; qualified Nathan B. Thomas exr, and on the   day of 181   came
Thomas Covington and qualified as executor.

October 13th 1817. David Mandeville and Bartholomew Cosnahan returned a
citation for admn. on the estate of Doctor Alfred Yeomans; entered into
bond with John Burch and James Forniss for $10,000.

Ann Lide and Charles Irby Lide returned a citation for admn. on the estate of Thomas Lide; entered into bond with William Pledger and John
Terrell for $1000.

July 18th 1817. Elizabeth John and Daniel John returned a citation for
admn. on the estate of Thomas John; entered into bond with John Haskew
and Malcom McBride for $5000.

Nov. 4th 1817. Josiah J. evans Esq. returned a citation for admn. on
the estate of John A. Evans; entered into bond with Robertson Carloss and
Charles Irby Esqres. for $20,000.

Nov. 6th 1817. Robertson Carloss and Margaret Britton returned a citation for admn. on the estate of Francis Britton; entered into bond with
William H. Pearson and Lamuel Pearson for $40,000.

Nov. 7th 1817. Will of Charleston Cottingham was proved by Patrick Mon-
roe; qualified Jonathan Cottingham & William Bridges, exrs.

Nov. 10th 1817. Josiah David returned citatn. for admn. on the estate
of Josiah David; entered into bond with Joshua David Jr. & Alexander
Lamb for $10,000.

Nov. 13th 1817. Thomas Bristow returned a citation for admn. on the
estate of Nancy Woodley; entered into bond with William Pearce and James
Parham for $200.

Nov. 15th 1817. Joseph Thomas and James C. Thomas returned a citation
for admn. on the estate of Tristram Thomas; entered into bond with Robert
T. Thomas for $40,000.

Nov. 20th 1817. David Stubbs and Silas Stubbs returned a citation for
admn. on the estate of John Stubbs decd; entered into bond with George
Bristow and Alexander McDaniel for $15,000.

December 1st 1817. Will of Thomas Ammons decd was proved by Jesse Ammons;
qualified Joshua Ammons, exr.

December 5th 1817. John Breeden at the return of a citation obtain by
Lindsey Breeden, came into court and demanded the admn. of the estate of
John Breeden Jr. deceased as having the prior right, which was granted;
entered into bond with William Lester & David Montgomery for $10,000.

December 8th 1817. Arthur T. Whitehead came and chose Captn. Duncan
McLaurin for his guardian; entered into bond with Shockley Adams & William Lister for $1000.

1818 January 5th. John David returned a citation for the admn. of the

COURT OF ORDINARY

1818 January 5th

estate of John David Jr. deceased; entered into bond with James Forniss and John Rogers for $20,000.

January 28th 1818. Elizabeth Pearce returned a citation for the admn. on the estate of Silas Pearce; entered into bond with William Pearce and James H. Pearce for $5000.

March 21st 1818. Margaret McRae & John McRae returned a citation for the admn. on the estate of Christopher McRae decd; entered into bond with Charles McRae & Roderick McRae for $10,000.

April 3rd 1818. Ephraim Sweat returned a citation for the admn. of the estate of Caleb Peavy; entered into bond with   for $500.

March 30th 1818 Will of Henry Hodges decd was proved by Francis McBride and William Townsend; qualify'd George B. Whitfield exr.

April 3rd 1818. Mary Graham & Duncan McColl returned a citation for admn. on the estate of William Graham decd; entered into bond with Daniel Dunbar & James Easterling for $3000.

April 7th 1818. Mary Pearson, Wm. H. Pearson and Samuel Townsend returned a citation for admn. on the estate of Samuel Pearson; entered into bond with Robertson Carloss & Geo B. Whitefield for due performance....

April 13th 1818. Will of William Dunnam was proved by William Carloss; qualifyed Robertson Carloss exr.

May 1st 1818. Will of Thomas Cochran was proved by oath of Thomas D. Mason; on 17th Oct 1818 qualifyed Phillip Bethea and John Hamer, exrs.

June 20th 1818. Hezekiah Thompson returned a citation for admn. on the estate of William Mitchel; entered into bond with Saml Townsend and John Alexd. Evans for $500.

July 2nd 1818. James Peavey chose James Easterling for his guardian; sd. Easterling entered into bond for $500.

1818 July 6th. Will of David Harry was proved by Morgan G. Brown; one of the exrs. dead and Tristram Thomas and the others refused to qualify; john Thomas renounced his executorship.

July 6th 1818. Mary Harry & David H. Harry returned citation for admn. on the estate of David Harry with his will annexed; entered into bond with Joseph Thomas and Tristram Thomas for $12,000.

July 5th 1818. Mary Watson returned a citation for admn. on the estate of Demcy Watson decd; entered into bond with William Fields and James Watson for $5000.

August 13th 1818. Will of Elizabeth David was proved by oath of Margaret Megee; qualifyed Elizabeth Hodges extx.

August 20th 1818. John McKay returned a citation for admn. on the estate of John Smith; entered into bond with Jepthah Robertson & Charles Manship for $5000.

September 7th 1818. Will of John Evans was proved by Abner Tarlton; qualifyed Thomas A. Evans and Morgan G. Brown exrs.

December 11th 1818. Duncan Rankins returned a citation for admn. on the estate of Daniel Comron decd; entered into bond with John McLaurin and Hamlet Fuller for $10,000.

January 18th 1819. Daniel L. Britton and Sarah Britton returned a citation for admn. on the estate of William H. Pearson; entered into bond with William Pouncey and Chs. F. Stewart for $20,000.

February 12th 1819. Jane Thomas and Philip P. Thomas returned a citation on the estate of Robert T. Thomas decd; entered into bond with Joseph Thomas and Philip Thomas for $10,000.

August 23rd 1819. Will of Absolom Burn proved by Majr. Drury Robertson; qualifyed Nancy Burn extx & Joseph Wright, exr.

April 5th 1819. Mary Evans returned a citation for admn. on the estate of William Evans decd; entered into bond with Aaron Pearson & William Pouncey for $5000.

April 13th 1819. John Townsend returned citation for admn. on the estate of Amey Hayse; entered into bond with JohnTownsend Junr & Jabish Townsend for $1000.

May 28th 1819. Will of Duncan McColl was proved by William Bristow; qualified John McColl exr.

July 8th 1819. Alexander Quick chose Benjamin Quick as his guardian; sd. Benjamin entered into bond with Levi Quick and Levi Quick Jr. for $5000.

September 19th 1819. John Rogers Esqr. returned a citation for admn. on the estate of Elizabeth Cochran decd; entered into bond with William Bristow and Joshua David for $10,000.

December 1st 1819. William Bristow Esquire returned citation for admn. on the estate of Peter Pelham; entered into bond with Arthur Bright and John Stubbs, for $2000.

December 15th 1819. Nancy Willis returned citation for admn. on the estate of Eli Willis; entered into bond with Legitt Robertson and Charles Manship for $6000.

December 15th 1819. Silas Stubbs returned a citation for admn. on the estate of Alexander McDaniel; entered into bond with James Stubbs and Charles M. Smith for $5000.

1820. January 4th. Francis Hinds returned a citation for admn. on the estate of Zaccheriah Ayer; entered into bond with Josiah David and Benjamin Stubbs for $5000.

February 4 1820. Alexander McRae returned a citation for admn. on the estate of James McRae; entered into bond with Charles McRae and Roderick McRae for $20,000.

February 16th 1820. Peter Pelham chose Shockely Adams for his gdn; sd. Shockely entered into bond with John McCollum and Joshua Fletcher for $1000.

March 17th 1820. Samuel Townsend returned a citation for admn. on the estate of Margaret Britton; entered into bond with James R. Ervin and George B. Whitefield for $10,000.

April 18th 1820. Jepthah Robertson returned citation for admn. on the estate of Ann Boyer decd; entered into bond with Shockley Adams and John McCollum for $1000.

1820 June 15th. James Stubbs returned citation for admn. on the estate of Sarah Miller decd; entered into bond with George Bristow and Alexander Stubbs for $5000.

July 12th 1820. Daniel L. Britton having married to Sarah Pearson widow and admx. of William H. Pearson decd; now the sd. Sarah and Samuel Townsend the co administrator with her desiring the admn. should be in the hands of sd. Sarah and sd. Danl Britton; entered into bond with James R. Ervin and George B. Whitefield for $5000.

July 29th 1820. Will of Capt. Robert Campbell proved by Mr. Donald

July 29th 1820

McDearmid; qualified Robert Campbell and James Campbell, exrs.

August 3rd 1820. Will of Mrs. Rhoda Neavel proved by William Barton; qualified Nathaniel Whittington and John Whittington and Rachel Windham, exrs.

September 19th 1820. Mary Thompson returned citation for admn. on the estate of James Thompson decd; entered into bond with Joseph McDaniel and James McDaniel for $500.

October 6th 1820. Daniel McRay returned citation for admn. of the estate of Doctr. John McRae; enterd into bond with John Donaldson and Shockley Adams for $5000.

October 30th 1820. Will of William Thoms deceased was proved by Genl. Erasmus Powe and William Pegues; qualifyed Benjamin Chears and Pleasant H. May Esquires, exrs.

1820 November 9th. Will of Doctr. James B. Hill was proven by William J. Forniss; qualified Mary E. Hill extx.

November 13th 1820. Rebecca Cosnehan and Daniel Crosland returned a citation for admn. on the estate of Bartholomew Cosnehan; entered into bond with John Rogers and Donald McDearmed for $50,000.

Nov. 22nd 1820. Major Pledger and Jane Hinds returned citation for admn. on the estate of Dawson Hinds; entered into bond with Joseph David and Edward Wright for $1000.

1821 January 9th. Mary David returned citation for admn. on the estate of John David; entered into bond with Charles S. Strother and William Jones for $10,000.

January 9th 1821. Richard Carlisle returned citation for admn. of the estate of Lewis Terrell; entered into bond with Mr. James and Wm. Bristo for $1000.

February 6th 1821. Martha Terrel returned citation for admn. on the estate of James Thornwell; entered into bond with John Terrel and Jacob Strickland for $5000.

February 15th 1821. John Murdoch Junr returned citation for admn. on the estate of James Murdoch Esquire decd; entered into bond with Wm Bristow & John Murdoch Senr for $10,000.

February 15th 1821. Will of Samuel Winds (sic) proved by Majr. Pledger and William Pledger Senr, not subscribing witnesses but swore to the handwriting; Thos Winds admr. with will annexed.

March 5th 1821. Thomas Winds returned citation for admn. on estate of Samuel Winds with his will annexed; entered into bond with Jas. Gillispie & Jno. J. McColloch for $5000.

1821. April 2nd 1821. Catherine McColl and John McLaurin returned a citation for admn. on the estate of John McColl; entered into bond with Charles McIntyre and John S. McColl for $1000.

May 7th 1821. Will of MasonLee decd proved by Captn William Pouncey; qualified Robertson Carloss Esquire executor.

May 31st 1821. Daniel McLaurin returned citation for admn. on the estate of Alexander McDaniel; entered into bond with John S. McLaurin and Captn. John McColl for $5000.

June 4th 1821. Elijah Spencer returned citation for admn. on the estate of Isham Wood; entered into bond with Joshua David Junr & H. Whickear (sic) for $1000.

June 19th 1821. Burwell Quick returned a citation for admn. on the
estate of Dorcas Quick; entered into bond with Elizabeth Quick and John
Dunn for $200.

June 19th 1821. A dedimus issued to Arthur Bright to qualify Joseph
Lockeler, Moses Turner, Wm Odom, Jas. Hewett and Benjn Williams to
appriase the estate of Burwell Quick;;sale to be 2nd July at the house
of Elizabeth Quick.

July 25th 1821. Will of Edmund Brown proved by William Bundy; qualified
John Graham Esqr. and Edmund Brown, exrs; dedimus to John Donaldson Esq.
to qualify John McKay, Moses Parker, Joshua Fletcher, Leggett Robertson
& Shockley Adams as appraisers.

At a court of ordinary holden the 28th day of November 1831.
James McDaniel, George Dudley vs John Jefferson Williams. Summons to
appear to shew cause why sd. Thomas McDaniel & Geo Dudley should not be
released from his securitiship in the bond given by sd. William for
admn. on the estate of Ann Williams with her will annext.

John Williams having been cited to appear this 28th of Nov 1831 and
shewing no cause ; admn. is revoked.

"TRANSCRIBED INTO BOOK C this Dec 24th 1839"

February 12th 1835. Will of Daniel Douglas was proved by John L. McLaurin

Feb. 18th 1835. qualified Duncan Douglas & Duncan McLaurin, exrs.
                                        L. E. Stubbs, O. M. D.

May 4th 1835. Will of Rebecca McFarlin was proven by John Campbell.

July 20th 1835. E. L. Henegan Shff. returned citation served on Dr.
William McQueen to appear in the court of Ordinary at Bennettsville on
the first Monday in August next to shew cause why the will of Rebecca Mc-
Farlan as proved & recorded should not stand as a matter of record.

July 20th 1835. E. L. Henegan Shff returned citation duly served on
Mary McQueenby the acceptance of Dr. Wm. McQueen for the same purpose....

July 20th 1835. E. L. Henegan Shff returned a citation duly served on
Robt McTier to appear to shew cause why Simon Emanuel should not be
released from securityship to the admn. bond of Catherine Irby & Robt
McTier, on the estate of John Irby decd.

July 20th 1835. E. L. Henegan Shff returned a citation served on Catherine Irby to shew cause why Simon Emanuel shold not be released....

July 20th 1835. Catherine Irby & Robt McTier not having appeared, sd.
Simon Emanuel is therefore released.

September 4th 1835. Vernon Dubose et ux et ali vs Ch. McRae et all.
Application to prove will in the solemn form.
Simon Dubose & Lucretia his wife and Elhanan Henagan some of the heirs
at law of Barnabas Henagan Senr decd having made application to cite
the exrs. of the will of sd. Barnabas Henagan in the solemn form.
On motino of Dargan atty for the applicants, ordered that exrs. of will
of Barnabas Hennegan to appeared before me on 14th Sept instant at
Marlboro C house to prove the sd. will and that notice be given to all
the legatees & heirs at law....   Lewis E. Stubbs, Ordy of M. D.

1835. Sept. 10th. Qualified before me William Cooper as exr. of the
will of Rebecca McFarlane late of Marlborough District decd.

Sept. 14th. The case of Simon Dubose et ux et ali vs Charles McRae et
ali is continued to a day to be hereafter appointed for want of witnesses

August 3rd 1835. Dr. Wm. McQueen & Mary McQueen for her daughter
Rebecca McQueen failing to appear as legally required to shew cause
why the will of Rebecca McFarlane, late of Marlboro: decd. should not
stand, it is therefore decreed that it does stand....

"Transcribed January 1st 1840 By L. E. S. O. M. D."

Index prepared by Mrs. A. W. King, Chapel Hill, N. C.

Abbott, _____ 64
  Jacob 11(2),15,21,24,40,47,
    50-51,52-54,56,83,90(2)
Abernethie, Thomas 32
Adam, John 83
Adams, Elias 79,84,93(2)
  John 114,119
  Richd. 89,114
  Shocklet 117
  Shockley 119,121,124,126,127,
    128
  Thos. 76-90
  William 76,114,117,119(2),121
Allen, _____ 86
  Mark 19
Alexander, Adame 57,61,66,67
Alison, Hezekiah 118(2),123
  Oliver 122
Allison, _____ 71,74,76-78,84,
    88,89,91,92,94
  Elizabeth 20,47
  Hezekiah 118
  Joseph 8
  Robert 20-21,26-28,47,61-63(2),
    65(2),67,69-70,72,78(2),
    83,92,95,100,103(2)-105,
    107-110(2)
  Sarah 47
  Thomas 39
Almonds, Thos. 3,13,15,83
Alvan, Elizabeth 23
Ammons, _____ 7
  Jesse 124
  Joshua 48,57,59,76,90-109,
    110(2),114(2),116,117,118,
    119,121,124
  Thomas 1,18,20,48,124
  William 72
Andrew, John 72
Andrews, John 2,23,25,35,38(2),
    96,97,106,107(2)
  Jno. 22
  Mary 18,78(2),82,85,86,87,96,
    106,107(2)
Arler, John 54
Armstead, Richard 64
Arnold, Benjamin 33,35,58
Arrandall, Benj. 43,45,82,84,
    89,91
Arrandel, Benj. 62(2)
Arrandell, Benj. 47,50,52,54(2),
    55
Asken, Hugh 52
Askew, Jesse 24,59,83,90
  Jno. 57
  John 3,8,61,108,111
Askue, Jesse 102-103
  John 72,102,103
Audabesh, Josiah 47
Auston, Wm. 5
Ayer, Thos. 47
  Zaccheriah 126
Ayers, Charlotte, 109(2)
  Ginny 109(2)
  Hartwell 109(2)
  James 109(2)
  Lewis Malone 63

Ayers Continued
  Maloney 60
  Thomas 109(2)
  Zachias 103
  Zackery 63

Badgegood, Malchi 61
  Malachi N. 114,115,120
  Malachi Nicholas 113
Bagan, Patrick 50
Baggett, Abraham 81(2), 90
  Abram 59,76
  Jesse 8,38,39,48,64,85
  Joel 79
Bainbridge, Peter (Rev.) 43-45,46
Baker, Anne 59
  Daniel 118
Balir, _____ 80
Ballard, Rich. 87
Balldue, William 96
Barnett, Carter 70
Barrentine, Jacob 72
Barrett, Bailey 70
Barringtine, Charles 24,63,79
  Jacob 22,56,64,67
  James 94(2)-95
  Sarah 5,88
  William 5,34,70,78,80,85,94
  Wm. Jr. 94,95
Bartlet, William 73
Barton, Charles (C.) 70,86
Bathea, Jesse 22-42-48
Bay, Elihu H. 35
Beasely, John 3,8,14,20,37-69
  Sinah 32
Beasley, James 32-56
  Josiah 56
  Wm. 56,63,113
Beauchamp, William 67
Beaverly, Alexander 29
  Benj. 81
Bedgegood, _____ 95
  Malichi N. 78,84,86,90,95,106,
    122
Beesely, Geo. 87
  Wm. 53,75,89,90,98
Beesley, John 18,66,69,89
  Josiah 22,29,53,67,69,72
Bennet, James 15
Bennet(t), Wm. 4,97,119,121,122
Benninfield, Charles H. 108
Bensley, Joab 79
Bensly, Job 84
Benton, Col. 2
  Samuel 82
Bethea, Anna 116,117
  David 61,65,66,67,72,75,85,90,
    101,102,103(2),104,116,121,123
  Elizabeth 121
  Jesse 3,4,25,59,79,85,98,103,115,
    117,121,123(2)
  Jesse Jr. 21,22,55,59,116
  Maj. 121
  Philip 116,125
  Simeon 69,87,88
  Tristam 117,121
  Tristram 115,116,123

130

Bethune, Neil 69,71(2),72,73,
  74(2),77,80(2),81,83,84,86,
  98,101,102,105
Bevel, William 43
Beverley, Benj. 8,15,54,64,74,
  79,84,85,93(2)
Beverly, Alexr. 5,57,66,96,83
  Anthony 121
  Benj. 9,17,117(2)
  Elizabeth 121
  Henry 64,121
Bevill, Robert 120
Biggard, Robert 52
Bingham, Susannah 121
  Thomas 4,14,16,31,34,113,121
Bishop, Elizth. 109
Blackford, Rachel 30
Blackman, Edmund 60
Blair, James 9
  Lucy 9
  Robert 3,29,63,84
Blalock, _____ 17,33,36
  Lewis 3,8,12,34,38
Bland, George 61,72
Blanton, James 15,19,47,66,79
Bloodgood, Abraham 69,74
Blue, Daniel 66,72
Blythe, Saml. 62
Bodiford, Alex 56,61,86
Bodyford, Alex 9,15
  Wm. 6,7
Bogan, Nicholas 96
Bohannan, John 63
Boid, Thomas 8
Bolton, George 117
  James 8,24,56,61,65,72,75,76,
  85,90,97,104,111,114
Booth, Charles 31
  Edward 70
  Joseph 43,45,71
  Mathew 9
Botsford, Edmund 16
Boulton, James 33
Bound, John 61
Bounds, James 87
Bowyer, Peter 92,93,114
Boyer, Ann 126
  Peter 68
Boykin, Lamuel 119,120
  Matthew 108,119,120
Braner, Elias 38
Branham, _____ 13
  William 9,29,34,43
Brantley, Marmaduke 68
Brassier, Elias 48,56
Breeden, John 117,121,124
  John Jr. 122,124
  Lindsey 124
Breedin, John 93(2)
Breedon, Jns. 89
  John 60,74
Brevard, Joseph 79,84
Brewer, Sterling 40,41,42,43
Bridges, Benj. 59
  Francis 37,64,89,90,115
  John 28,33,59,76,89
  William 124
Bridgers, Benjamin 117
  Francis 119
Briggs, Anne 98

Briggs Continued
  Anthony 98
Bright, Arthur 126-128
  Charles 117(2)
Brigman, Fereby 121
  Isaac 121
  John 121,123
  Thomas 88
Bristow, George 123-124
  James 127
  William 92,114(3),116,117(2),118,
  119,121,122,123,124,126(2),127
  (3)
Brittain, John 93(2),108
Brittian, Francis 108,111,112
Britton, Benjamin 122
  Daniel L. 125,126
  Francis 115-116,118,119,120,122,
  123,124
  John 116
  John G. 122
  Margaret 124-126
  Sarah 125
  William 119
Broach, _____ 13
  Abner 8,9,14,15(2)
Brockington, Richd. 15,18(2),22,27,
  35,61,96,99
  William 53,61,96,99
Brockinton, William 101
Broidin, John 64,87
Broughton, Job 12
  Mary 12
  Willerbee 72
  Willerby 89
Brown, Daniel 46
  Edmund 35,48,51,61,72,75,89,108,
  128
  Edwd. 9
  Eliza'th. 10,30
  Ezekel 65
  Francis 47
  Jas. 14,59,70
  Jeremiah 86
  Jesse 23,40,56,59,72,83
  Jno. 9,11,21,63,96
  John 2,14,47,59,98,118,120
  Jonathan 72
  Joseph 9,18,40,42,43,47,50,58
  Josiah 53
  Kershaw 89,90,94
  M.G. 120
  Morgan 1,2(2),3,4,6,10,11,12,13,
  14
  Morgan 1-4,6,10-22,24,25,28,30-34,
  37,39,41,45-49,51,52,56-58,60,
  61,65,96-98,117,118
  Morgan G. 125
  Moses 25
  Samuel 6,9,21,23,27,28,31,33,35-
  39,41-44,46-49,51,52,54,59,65,
  79,83,88,89,90,93,96(2),98,102,
  106,107,108,110,112
  Thomas 74,118
  William 85,93,114,118,120,121
Browton, Willeby 61
Bruce, Right 118,122
  William 118
Buchannon, John 106
Buckholds, Jacob 8

Buckles, Jacob 112
Bulgin, James 107
Bullard, Gadi 95
  George 117
  Joel 16
Bundy, William 128
Bunt, John 69,75
  Mary 69
Burch, John 124
  Joseph 112
Burke, Adamus 36
Burkell, Thomas 68-73
Burkett, Laml. 86
  Lane 59
  Samuel 53,93
  Thomas 59,89,93(2)
Burn, Absolom 126
  Nancy 126
Burrell, Robert 67
Burns, Elijah 92
Burrel, _____ 38
Burrill, _____ 19
Burton, Francis 110
  Wm. 119
Butler, Peter 6,26

Calvin, Arnold 31
Campbell, Alexander 20,21,41(2),
    42,43,45(2)
  James 127
  Joel 107
  John 128
  Robert 29,64,67,69,70,74,77,
    78,80(2),82(2),84,86,94,96,
    97,102,103,112,126,127
Cannon, _____ 26
  David 27,30
Cantelou (see Cantolou)
  Lewis N. 88
Cantey, Zachariah 90
Cantolou, N.L. 91
Careless (see also Carloss)
  Robertson 98,123
Cargill, Magness 47,53,90,97
  Magnis(s) 29,78
  Sarah 26
Carlisle, Richard 127
Carloss, R. 86
  Robert 113
  Robertson 63,75,76,79,89,94,
    106,107,111,113,114(2),115,
    116,118,120,122,124,125,127
  Robinson 84
  William 125
Carter, William 70
Chalker, Samuel 3
  Winny 84
Chamless, Pnepsilla 7
Chanery, Isaac 11
Chapman, Allen 99
  Threshly 120
  Wellcome 117
Chavis, John 123
Chears, Benjamin 127
Cherry, _____ 75
  George 3,7,9,17,21,27,32,33,
    35,36,39,40,41,44,49,53,54,
    57,59,60,68,75,79,85,88,96,
    98,99,101,102,109(2),118
  Simion 64

Cherry Continued
  Simon 15,22,40,53,56,66,95,108
  Susannah 109
  Wm. 1,3,36,40,56,95
Chestnut, John 26
Chewning, Samuel 70
Chewing, Joseph 74
Christie, Finlay 26,41,45,49,50
Clark, Barnabas 118
  Cooper 37
  Fereba 108
  Ferebee 108
  Fereby 108
  Hardy 68
  Jerimiah 4
  John 9
  Joseph 123
  Mary 123
  Morris 61
  Philip 108(2),109
Clarke, Isaac 109
  John 24
  Mordica M. 63
  Philip 59,79,81,108
Clary, Etheldred 11,19
  Robert 48,49,50
Clayter, Lawson 24
Clerk, Nathan 31
Clinton, Thomas 39
Cochran, Elizabeth 126
  Robert 116,117,118
  Thomas 8,10,11,13,18,20,23,26,27,
    32,34,35,41,42,53,66,69,70,71,
    90,96,99,100,101,103,114,116,
    120,125
Cockran, Thomas 29,57,78,89
Cogdell, Capt. 1
  George 42,96,97
  John 27,42,43(2),44,45
Coggs, _____ 73
Coggeshall, _____ 39,57,58,64,74
  Harry 87
  Henry 65(3),67,71(2),74(2),77,82,
    91
  John M. 64,78,80
  Nathl. 45,46,65,66,67,69,71,75(2),
    77,81,82
Coggshell, _____ 19,54
Cogshell, Nathaniel 27
Cohen, Solomon 80
Coker, Abram 71
Cole, David 35
Collins, _____ 42
  James 66,67
  Robt. 23,24,26,27
Colquhoun, Angus 115-118
  Margaret 115
Comron, Daniel 125
Coner, Thomas 16
Conn, Thomas 2,8,10,18
Conner, James 15,33,48,50,51,53,
    59,64,65,76,81,90,115
  James Jr. 29
  John 58-115
  Lewis 18,32,104
  Nancy 104,111
  Sarah 115
  Thomas 15,17,19,56,59,97
  William 22,29,35,64,75,83,111
  Wilson 68

Cook, Abram 7
  James 5,7,8,11,22,56,61,75,
    81,83,84,90,119,121
  John 19
  John Jr. 64
  Lewis 11
  Reubin 61,76,81
  Rhuben 81,90
  Thomas 64,79,85,108
Cooper, Bethsheba 118
  Jesse 114
  Jno. 118
  John 114(2),115,116,118
  William 12,128
Corgell, Magness 16,119
  Thos. A. 119
Corgill, Magnis 86
  Margness 3
  Thomas A. 121,122
Corneham, Jas. 56
Cornish, _____ 32
Cosnaham, Bartholomew 124,127
Cosneham, Joseph 35,59,67,69,79,
  110
Cosnehan, Rebecca 127
Costneham, Joseph 49,59,88
Cotingam, Daniel 1
Cotingham, Margaret 3
Cottingham, Charles 8,24,48,61,
    72,76,80,88,104,106,109,
    117,119
  Charleston 81,124
  Daniel 24,44,52,64,68,76,81,
    116
  Dill 24,35,44,45,68,76,81,116
  Edwd. 76,81(2),93
  Jonathan 29,59,64,115,117,124
  Juliana 116,118
  Thomas 114
  Turbel(l) 104,106,109,111
  Turbet(t) 85,90,97,114
  Turbill 64,75
  Turbit(t) 64,75
Couglass, Jesse 8
Coulson, _____ 13
  John 3,45,54,55
Councel, _____ 68
  Wm. 3
Councell, Henry 72,100-101
  Jesse 12
  Rachal 97(2),99,100,101
  Samuel 60,68,97
  William 9,18,32,58,97
Council, Saml. 71,73,75,84
  William 22,24,26,32,35
Councill, Jesse 78,90
  Saml. 67
  Wm. 2,31
Course, Isaac 90,106
Covington, Elizabeth 120
  John 108,109,111
  John W. 119
  John Wall 120
  Robert 119,121,124
  Thomas 124
  William 12,15,16,18,22,29,34,
    35,37,40,48,53,56,59,62,64,
    65,70,71,74,78(2),79,82,84,
    92,94,96,99,102,107,115
Coward, James 79,120

Coward Continued
  Will 17
  William 21,27,28,29(2),44,53,56,
    57,72,83,99
Cox, Ben 49
  Benj. 52,86
  Emanuel 3
  John 67,86
  Joseph 61
  Samuel 48,56,63,83
  Wm. 48,57
Crawfford, Moses 69
Craig, John 117
Cranor, Moses 100-101-103
  Thomas 103
Crocker, James 75
Crosland, Daniel 127
  Edward 6,15,63,72,84,100,120
  Israel 120
Crossland, Edward 8,18,22,24,37,53,
    58,79
Crunk, Sylvanus 62,65,67,104,105(2)
Curby, David 61
Curgill, Magness 72,76,79,103,106
  Marnis(s) 66,67,83
Currie, Lauchlan 29
Curry, Daniel 62,65,67
  Lochran 53,57,76
Cutler, Jonah 82
  Jonathan 63

Dabbs, Wm. 84,91
Dabs, Wm. 79
Danelly, Patrick 42
Daniel, Aaron 5,7,8,14,17,18,21,22,
    23,26,32,35,40,47,62-64,65(2),
    66,67,68,79,81,82,98-102
  Aaron Jr. 64,70,72,75
  Ann 17
  Benjamin 121
  Jno. 86
  John 7,9,24,33,48,49,53,56,58,61,
    62
  Mathew 66,69
  Moses 64,65
Darby, Jacob 33,44
  Jno. 14,17
  John 76
  Nicholas 1(2)
  Timothy 3,8
  Tymothy 35,40
David, Ann 6
  Az'ah 33
  Azariah 22,23,24(2),25,26,27,48,
    61,63,70,76,77,83,85,89,93,100,
    102
  Benjamin 3,29,46,53,57,66,69(3),
    89,90,93(2),103-112,113,116
  David 70,74
  Elizabeth 125
  Ezariah 16,17
  Henry 119
  Jesse 113
  Jinkin 16
  John 9,16,17,21,22,27,75,83,89(2),
    102,109,110,112,113,120,124,127
  John H. 123
  John Jr. 122,125
  Jon 1
  Jonah 8,48

David Continued
Joseph 127
Joshua 4,5,8,10,27,53,66,67,
72,89,90,120,124,126
Joshua Jr. 124,127
Josiah 5,68,79,83,104,110,
112,113(2),114(2),115,116,
124,126
Mary 127
Mary B. 122
Mathew 69
Moses 20
Sarah 113
Thomas 95
Davis, Andrew 25,59
David 65
Isaac 115
Isham 59
John 37
Dawson, Daniel 117
Dean, Thos. 35,78,79,82,84,85,
87,90,92,98
Debruhl, Edward C. 41,42,62(2),
63,66(2),71,74,79,80
Mary F. 52
Deen, Thomas 82
Deir, John 1
Deleisseline, _____ 78,83,84
Francis G. 92
Delport, Joseph 66
Dempsey, Athel 99
Dewitt, Harris 112,113
John 79,115,120
John Jr. 112
William 115
Dibbley, John Ellis 36
Dickson, Thos. 36(2)
Dilling, Henry 63,89
Joshua 79
Dilport, _____ 81
Joseph 63,78,84,86(2),87,92,
105
Dixon, Jesse 9
Dobbins, Hugh 11-14
Dodsworth, Ralph 73,75(2),76,
77,86,89,90
Donaldson, John 127,128
Dosson, Solomon 100
Doughlas, Elizabeth 27
Jesse 23,45,70,81,83
John 63
Nathaniel 27
Doughty, John 45
Douglas, Daniel 128
Duncan 128
John 116,120
Douglass, _____ 76
Jesse 18,40,53,56,59,75,98,
105
John 20,76
Downer, _____ 41
Thos. 30,57,58,60,61,64
Downs, Joseph 37
Driggers, Elizabeth 97
Joseph 21
Leasy 21
Mary 35,97
Nancy 21
Naomi 123
William 42,52

Dubose, Lucretia 128
Simon 128(2)
Vernon 128
Dudley, David 9,11,12,35,47,50,53,
54,55,96,97
George 128
Due, Christian 58
James 3(2),8,12(2),14,15,23,27,
40,43,47,50,53,54,58,108,109
John 27,45,47(2),54
John R.124
Dunbar, _____ 81
Daniel 125
James 76
Dunham, John 123
Dunn, John 128
Dunnam, John Peter 123
William 125
Dunstan, Richard 60,82
Dwiggins, _____ 74
John 71,73,75
Dyer, _____ 77
John 8,15,17,20,21,22,48(2),56,
63,65,70,74,80,82,85,88,89,93,
98,100,104,110,112,114
Joseph U. 114

Easterling, Bennett 27
Henry 38,45,55,61,123
James 22,25,66,67,72,89,125(2)
Joel 73,121
John 108
Peter 93
Shad. 48
Shadk. 85
Shadrach 24,61,117,118,123
William 20,21,23,25,27,34,38,44,
45,46,51,54,56,58,67,69,72,75,
79,83,90,97,98,101,104,106,107,
108,109,113
Edens, _____ 17
John 16,19,24,89
Mary 49
Phillip 19,64
Richd. 12,16,29,49,57,59,78,86,
91
Wm. 18,29,59,64
Edmondson, _____ 13
Edwards, Able 16
Edward 22,25,98,115,120,121
John 71,120
Mary 116
Ellerbe, _____ 22
Ellerbee, Thomas 20-33
Ellibe, William 113
Elliott, Ann(e) 81,84,88,91,100
William 74(2),80,99,101
Ellis, Isom 11
Ellison, Ezekiah 115,116
Hezekiah 99,114,118
Joseph 3,21,27,63,72,110
Oliver 118
Thomas 67,69
Elizer, Eleazer 62
Emanuel, Simon 128
England, Joseph 122
Ervin, James R. 126(2)
Samuel 114(2),115
Esterling, Henry 46
Jas. 8

Evans, _____ 44,73,77,78,80
  Ann 112
  Arter 60
  Benjamin 61,103,104,105
  Elizabeth 80,88,90,112
  Elizth. 87,96,98,102,103,105
  Enoch 41,48,56,66,68
  Daniel 69
  David 50,51,67
  George 67,69,80,83,86,87,92,
    95,96,98,102,103,105,108
  Jesse 43
  Jno. 56
  John 1,48,67,69,86,89,93,94,
    96,112,125
  John Jr. 29,44
  John A. 124,125
  Josiah 21,22,25,38,40,42,46
    (2),52,57,78,87,96(2),98,
    107,111
  Josiah Jr. 121,124
  Mary 126
  Richard 48
  Samuel 9,26,29,36(2),56,68
  Thomas 1-8,10,11,13,15,17-22,
    24,25,27-29,31,33-42,45,46-
    48-53,55-57,64,66,69,70,71,
    75,76,77,79-80,81,83,84,85,
    88,90,91,92,95,96,98,99,
    100-104,106,107,108,110-112-
    116,119-120
  Thomas A. 125
  William 2,3,8,29,40-43,55,56,
    60,65,70,76-78,80,81,96,102-
    105,112,126
Evers, Samuel 41

Faircloath, Luvesey 45
Faircloth, Lucres 46
Falconer, _____ 43,91
  James 66,69(2),70,75
  William 13,27,48
Falkner, James 29,36
  Mary 36,39,49,54
  William 68
Farless, Elisha 55
Farnace, Willm. 35
Fart, Jonathan 88
Faulkner, Edward 100
  James 83,100
  Wm. 6
Fazar, Charles 69
Feagan, Edward 40,63,72,101
  John 57
Feagin, Burgess 14
  Edward 5,88,104,108,111,112,
    113,119
  James 76,81,88,90,106,108,
    113,114,117,118,119
  Richardson 119
  William 119
  William G. 117,119
Fearson, Bently 101-103
  James 101-103
  John 101-103
  William 101
Felts, Frederick 47
Ferguson, George 120
  James B. 120
Fernice, Wm. 15

Ferrel(1), Peter 60
Ferrell, Samuel 41
Fields, _____ 95
  Eliz. 16
  James 115,122,123
  Saml. 66,67,70
  Will 15
  William 21,22(2),40,49,53,56,59,
    62,63,65,70,73(2),74,75(2),76,
    81,86,93,97,99(2),100,102,104,
    105(3),113-121,109,125
Firhitts, Jno. 37
Fitts, John 14,16
Fletcher, Joshua 126,128
Flowers, Hardy 68
Folk, Frederick 42
Ford, Moses 49
Foris, James 119
Forness, James 114
  Wm. 22,85,114
Forniss, _____ 124
  James 77,86,87,102-105,114,115,
    122,125
  William 21,43,46,56,63,75,84,103,
    114
  William J. 127
Fort, Moses 35(2),56,96
Fortt, Moses 18,38
Foster, Ambrose 3
Frazer, Charles 22,29,49,56,59
  John 48,52
  William 25,46,80
Frazier, Ann 8
  James 111
  Jno. 9
  John 7,8,33
  Wm. 45,81
Frazor, Charles 67
  Isaac 73
Freeborn, _____ 39
  Jas. 10
  Joseph 19
Freeman, Archibald 36
  Josiah 36
  Martha 50-51
Fuller, Hamlet 118,125
  Jas. 83
  John 31
  Jonathan 110
  Joseph 8,33,68,73,118
  Lucy 109
  Shadrack 8,64,76,81,101,109
Furnace, William 40
Furnall, Wm. 45
Furness, _____ 82
  James 112
Furnis, William 3
Furniss, James 94
  William 42,82,90

Gaddy, Thomas 118
Gainer, Wm. 24
Gallaway, Wm. 116
George, John 38,39,41,43,46,56
German, _____ 95
  William 66,67,73,75,91
Gerring, Daniel 8
Gibes, Hugh 34
Gibson, Andrew 16,39,40,41,44,45,
    49,52

135

Gibson Continued
  Edward 69
  Levy 18
Gift, _____ 74
  Jonathan 58(2),60,71,81,83,92,
    95
Gilespie, James 1,3,15,29,37
Gillespie, Francis 119-120
  James 18,44,48,56,58,59,62,75,
    79,85,86,87,90,98,99(3),101,
    105-108,119,123,127
Gilispie, James 3,8,18
Gin, Edward 73
Ginn, Mashack 9,63
  Stephen 66
Gipson, Andrew 16
Godfrey, _____ 13,77
  T. 86
  Thomas 10,15,22,24,27,48-56,
    66,69,71,83(2),84,92,93,96,
    99,102,103,105(2),108,113,
    114,115,117
Goins, Jesse 43
Goodwin, Britt 9,12,16,74
  Brittain 16,78,81,86,94
  Britton 23(2),26
  Demsy 5
  Lewis 9
  William 62,63
  Wm. Davis 76
Gordon, Elizabeth 29
  James 44,56
  Mary 2,12(2),26,109
  Wm. 2,3,8,12(2),14,15,16,18,
    26,29,51,56
Gourley, John C. 118,122
  Joseph 118(3),122
Graham, David 74,80
  John 128
  Mary 125
Grant, William 122
Graves, James 18
Gray, James 117
  Levy 71,96,118
  Robert 46
Green, _____ 19,38,95
  Edward 69
  Jacob 6,22,29,59
  Richard 22,29,56,66,67,68
Gregg, Alexander 110
Greyer, George 105
Grice, Wm. 90,93(2),118
Grier, Wm. 89
Griffen, Francis 34,38,40
  William 40
Griner, James 121,123
  Mary 123
Grooms, Colsom 118
  Rachel 118
  Sarah 118
Gross, _____ 18
  Solomon 20
Growter, David 25,27,29,30,40,
    44,53,55,57,58
Gum, Thos. 12

Hagan, Colson 123
  Malachi 123
Haggins, David 68
  Polson 68

Hagins, Isham 61
Hall, Abraham 92
  Peter 92
  Thos. 31
Haines, John 83
Ham, Charles 112
Hamer, _____ 118,125
Hammer, John 115
Hammond, Thomas 15
Hancock, Thos. 23
Handford, Enoch 1,22
Handon, Benjamin 117
Hardick, William 48,57
Hardwick, Wm. 3,4,27,52
Harmon, Thomas 7
Harper, James A. 122
  John 100
  Lewis 88
  Mary 100
Harringdine, Thomas 5,34
Harrington, Henry Wm. 44
Harris, Arthur 105
  George 34
  Jas. 22
  Mary 105
  Obediah 119
Harry, _____ 82,87
  David 61,72,82(2),87,104,105,125
  David H. 125
  Enoch 22,24,25,27,30,44,46,63,78,
    80,94,102,104
  Mary 125
  Sarah 102
  Susannah 104
  Thos. 8,18,22,25,98
Hart, Darby Smith 5,7,8
  James 105
Harvey, Thomas 15
Harwell, Landey 92
Haskew, Jesse 123
  John 122,123,124
Hasque, Moses 118
  Zacchariah 118
Haws, Doctor Oliver 122
Hayes, Ebenezer 71,73
Haygin, Isham 72
Hayse, Amey 126
Heagan, Peter 34,40,54,55
Heagin, Peter 50
Heazans, Peter 50
Hedgecock, Sarah 26
Hedleston, William 122
Henagan, Barnabas 85,119,128
  E.L. 128
  Elhanan 128
  Elizabeth 121
Henaghan, Barnebass 8
Henderson, Alexander 118
Hendly, Jesse 111
Henegan, Barnabas 121
Henigan, Barnabas 66,75
Henigham, Barnibas 15
Hennagan, Barnabas 20,22,29,53,57,
    68,97
  John 121
Hennegan, _____ 90
  Peter 89
Henneghan, Barnabas 18
Henneghin, Barnebas 12
Henry, Benj. 92

Henry Continued
  Susannah 91
  Thomas 12,84,91,94
Henson, Elijah 85
Herndon, Benj. 122
  John 121,122
  William 122
Heringdine, _____ 64,70
Herring, Daniel 29,57,59
Herringden, Thos. 53
Herringdine, Thomas 8,15,24,36,
  37,44,60(2),64,65
Herrington, Henry William 40,70
Heustiss, Agness 23
Hewett, Jas. 128
Hewson, Rebechah 82
Hickmon, Wm. 24,43,81
Hickoboy, Thomas 12
Hicks, Benj. 9,12,15,16,18,19,
  21,22(2),24,26,35,40,45,53,
  54(2),65,70,72-79,82,96-99,
  105-107
  Col. 1,46,50,71,73
  Daniel 46
  Geo. 1-7,9-23,25,28,30-31,33-
  46,51,53-57,89,94,96,99,101,
  113,114
  George 61,85,87
  J. 33
  James 6,20,22,34
  Sarah 46
Hill, Henry 22,24,59,74,93
  James B. 127
  Mary H. 127
Hills, Henry 13
Hillson, _____ 17,33
  Elias 46,64
  Henry 12
  John 3,15,48
  Jon 8
  Silas 106
Hindley, Darkes 28
  Dicey 28
  Judah 28
  Selah 28
Hinds, Dawson 127
  Francis 126
  Jane 127
  Orison 84
Hinson, Elijah 87,89
Hodges, _____ 17,75,82,92
  Abel 74,77,80,86
  Edmond 100,110(2)
  Elizabeth 125
  George 88,110,114(2),116,118,
  (2)
  Isam 6-8,12,13,15,17,22,28,
  85,87
  Isham 19,20,27(2),30-32,34,
  35,38-40,44-46,48-50,52-55,
  57,58,60(4),61,63-67,69,71,
  79,80,84,90,95,100(2),102-
  104
  Isom 62,110(2),111,112
  James 1(2),2,10,15,16,21,27,
  40,42-45,51,56,100
  Jesse 40
  Joab 100
  John 17,34,115
  Leon 115

Hodges Continued
  Mark 100
  Martha 104
  Mary 110(2),112
  Philemon 27(2),29,73
  Philip 20,47
  Rachel 27
  Robert 59,68
  Sion 66,69(2),92,123
  Thomas 24,28,53,56,64,83,87,99,
  118,120
  Welcom(e) 3-5,18,19,22,24,28,30,
  34,52,57,67,73,75,79,85,90(2),
  110,114
  Wm. 5,34,44,65
  Willis 44,71
  Wilson 15-17
Hoges, Thomas 85
Holecome, Jno. 56
Holcomb, John 14,52,63
Holloway, James 112
  Mark 11,12
Holmes, _____ 54
  Lewis 18,22,29,32,53,63
Holt, Francis 84,92
Hothorn, John 14
Howard, James 34
  Richard 83
  Shadrock 73
Hubard, John 8
  John Carraway 8
  Peter 14
Hubbard, _____ 111
  Agness 59
  John 25,48,53,59,68,73,111
  Peter 22,24,25,53,59,69,83,89,
  107(2)
Hubbart, Jn. 33
Hubbert, Peter 66
Hucabe, Thomas 48
Huckabe, Thos. 22
Huckabee, Thomas 33,83,93,94,117
Huckaboy, Thos. 3
Huckerby, Thomas 66,67,68
Huckobie, Thomas 56
Hudges, James 70
Hues, John 101
  Solomon 100
Huggins, Burch 122
  Burrel 10,66,112
  Burrell 116,119,122
  Burwell 22,29,53,56,69(2),93(2)
  Burwill 86
  James 119
Hughs, Amr(?) 37
  Solomon 82
Humphress, Samuel 67
Humphreys, Nath. 63
  Samuel 94(2)
Hunter, Robert 74
Husbands, John 2,10,14,15,16,18,19
Huse, John 29,48,63
Huson, John 98,105
  Rebeccah 98
  Rebekah 105
  William 43,98,105
Hustes, Mathew 120

Insley, Job 22,29
Irby, Catherine 128

Irby Continued
  Charles 93,113-116,120,124
  James 124
  John 128
  Mrs. _____ 2,12,13

Jackson, Edward 6,8,20,41
  Jos. 83
James, Benjamin 33-34
  Capt. 78
  James 7,42,43
  J.J. 63,78
  Jessie 61,62,66,67,72(2),78,
    80(2),86-89,90-92
  John 100,107
  John Jones 22,27,46,57,64,66,
    67,72,75,76,78,79,80,81,83
    (2),85,87,96(2),98,106-108,
    115
  Mary 103,105
  Philip 43,44
  Richd. 34
  Sarah 26,47,70,112
  Thomas 79
  Thomas A. 82,93(2),115
  Thomas Alexander 110,112
  William 26,27,103,105
Jenkins, John 24,25,26
  Sarah 25
Jinkins, Jno 23
  Rubin 8
John, Alcy 22,29,34
  Alex 66
  Aley 69,100
  Aly Jesse 82
  Daniel 124
  Eli 57,96
  Elizabeth 124
  Jess (Jesse) 7,14,35,40,50,55
    (2),82,93(2),95
  John L. 89
  John Little 29
  Jonathon 8,19,29(2),40,47,53,
    57,59,60,72
  Thomas 56,61,77,80,96,106,124
  William 115
Johnes, John 8
Johns, Jesse 1,59,115
Johnson, James 12,20,21,42
  John 66,120
  Mordica 64
  Robert 121
Jones, _____ 37
  Abel 119,122
  Edward 49,50,57,71,89,96,99
  Edw. W. 122
  Elias 119
  James 43,70,117,121
  Jesse 23
  John 9,12(2),19,22,25,42,52,
    96
  Joseph 34,63,72,74,89,93,119
  Joshua 22
  Mary 15,51,57,65,71,96,99
  Mrs. _____ 1
  Thomas 9
  William 111,116,122(2),127
Jordan, _____ 17,34,49
  Mary 108
  Wm. 8,11(2),12,24,58,60,61,97

Jorge, John 45

Keaton, Kader 3,9
Keel, James 114(2),115
Kenedy, Francis 37,108
Kennedy, _____ 74,80
  David 69,77,109
  Francis 21,40(2),41,56,79,84,88,
    109
  John 77
  William 50
Kerby, David 86,114
  Elizabeth Frizel 114,115,116
Kershaw, Ely 39,50
  Jno. 91
  Joseph 26
Kiby, Charles 52
Killensworth, Jno. 85
  John 113
Killingsworth, John 115
  Wm. 49
Kimbrough, John 78,80,37
King, _____ 70,71,76-78,84,86,
    88,89,91,92,94
  Charles 36
  David 93,110
  Eli 24,61
  Miles 66,98,99,113
Kirby, Archibald 94
  Charles 52
  David 114
  Sarah 35
Knight, _____ 64
  Aaron 1,2,5,15,23,48,52,64,97,
    119,120
  Achilles 119,120
  Akillis 63
  Elizabeth 119
  Elizabeth Rye 120
  John 8,9
  Moris 48
  Moses 21,39,40,41,44,49,51,97
  Nathaniel 48,68,97
  Stephen 54
  Thomas 114
Kolb, Abl. 5
  Benj. 49
  Josiah 27(2)
  Martin 11
  Peter 11
  Sarah 16
  Widow 27

Lamb, Alexander 119,120,124
Lamdon, _____ 17
Leadenham, Stafford 95
Leavenworth, Henry 106,107
  Nathan 3,10,14,25
Lee, David 22,24,25,26,37,44,50,55,
    57
  Jno. 56,57
  John 3,9,15,22,29,48,63
  Mary 81
  Mason 127
Leggett, Wm. 4,22,24,48,57,59
  Wm.Jr. 79,83,90
Legitt, James 117
Lesonby, Joshua 12
Lester, William 24,59,79,124
Lewis, Edward 49

Lewis Continued
Joshua 116,121
Louisa 116,121
Lide, _____ 95
Ann 124
Charles Irby 124
Elizabeth 122
Hugh 112
James 112
Jno. 36
John 47,79(2),83,85,89,93,94,
103,107,108,115,119,121,122
Mahetable 114
Mehetibel 38,76
Robert 19,31,70,93,102,108,
115(2),120
Thomas 1(2),10,19,31,105,106,
108,119,120,121,124
William 15
Lisenby, Solomon 30,76
Lisonbe, John 97
Lisonby, John 12,97,98
Jno. 37
Joshua 51,56
Solomon 37,52,53
Stephen 79,84,94
Lissenby, Solomon 24,28
Lister, Elias 88,109
Jos. 83,88,89,101
Joseph 72,109
Wm. 93
Little, Jas. 11
John 59
Littlejohn, John 22,56,67,72,76
Lockeler, Joseph 128
Long, Short 3,8,53
Lourie, Sam 33
Lowrie, Samuel 10
Lucas, Joshua 37,49
Wm. 89,90
Luke, Daniel 96(2)
David 37,48
Enoch 40,56,83
John 122
Owen 51
Reece 69
Sarah 101
Wm. 48,64,100
Lundman, _____ 34
Lyons, Guthridge 49,76
Lytle, James 12

McBride, Francis 125
Malcom 124
McCall see McColl
McCall, _____ 90
David 61
Duncan 61,79,84,85
George 65
Lockran 76,84,90
McCallum, Evander 60
McCarley, James 56
McCartee, James 29
McCartey, John 60
McCaskell, Finley 46
McClain, Angeush 11
McClaren, Lockran 83
Lockran Jr. 83
McClarin, Daniel 111
Hugh 111

McClarin Continued
John 111(2)
Lachlan 111(2)
McClarrin, Danl. 93(2)
Lackrin, Jr. 93
McClelland, John 87,88
McClendal, Stephen 68
McClendall, Stephen 19
McClendol, Stephen 53
McClendon, Stephen 81
McClenon, Stephen 76
McCloud, Turtle 100
McColl, Catherine 120,127
David 85,115,119
Duncan 93(2),111,116,120,125,126
Hugh 119
Lachlin 92,116,120
John 103,120,124,126,127(2)
John S. 127
Solomon 103,118
McColloch, Jno. Jr. 127
McCollum, John 126(2)
McCormick, Rebecca 3,4
McDaniel, Alexander 116,122,124,
126,127
James 113,117,120,127,128
John 20,42,95,116,122(2)
Joseph 113,119,121,127
Mary 12
Thomas 128
McDearmed, Danl. 115
Donald 127
McDermid, Donald 93(2),127
McDonald, Andrew 99
Edey 99
James 120,121
John 114
McDowel, Wm. 16
McFarlan, _____ 95
McFarlane, Rebecca 128,129
McFarlin, Rebecca 128
McGee, James 40,53,59,79,83,88,89,
110,118
McGill, John 63,89,90,95
McIntire, Archd. 89
Archibald 111
Charles 117
Danl. 56,84,111
Isham 72
John 61
McIntyre, Charles 127
Danl. 116,119,120
McIntosh, Gen. 9
Ells 9
John 55,59,73
McIver, Evander 70,87,120
McKay, Daniel 116
John 117,121,125,128
McKnatt, Mackay 32
McLannan, Daniel 117
McLaurin, Daniel 127
Duncan 115,123,124,127
Hugh 115,119,120,121
John 115,119,120,125,127
John L. 128
John S. 127
Lauchlin 115,116,119,120
Neal 115
McLendon, Stephen 29
McLennan, Daniel 117

McLennon, _____ 118
McLerin, Hugh, Jr. 73
McLoud, Norman 29
McLucas, John 115
McNatt, _____ 90
McNat(t), James 5,6,50,51,90,92
  Joel 3,15,17,33,40,48,49,54,
    65,66,69(2),85,92
  Jn. 56
  Jno. 8
  John 22,64,85,89,96
  Mackey 1,3,5,8,9,18,21,22,27
    (2),29,35,37,53,57,65,70,
    72,74,77-80,84-87,89,90,100,
    102,103,110,113,114
McNeal, Jno. 117
  Neal 68
McPherson, _____ 91,92
  Duncan 57,59,66,69(2),70,71,
    84,87,95
  Jno. 61
  John 27,40,59,63
  Murdock 40,55
McQueen, Mary 128,129
  James 116
  Rebecca 129
  William 128,129
McRa, Alex 76
  Charles 40
  Charles, Jr. 79
  Christopher 61,83
  Duncan 11,31,35,46,49(2),52,
    55,56,61,67,80,84,89
  John 61,83
  Malcom 93
  Philip 76,89
  Philip, Jr. 90
  Rhodrick 83,90
McRae, Alexander 120,126
  Alexander Gilbert 117,120
  Charles 115,117,118,120,121,
    125,126,128(2)
  Christopher 125
  Daniel 121,127
  Duncan 86,121
  Gilbert 118
  James 126
  Malcom 120(2)
  Margaret 125
  Roderick 118,120,125,126
McRea, Daniel 81
McTier, Robt. 128
McTyre, Elizabeth 116
  Danl. 79
  Robt. 6,50,55
  Saraar 6
  William 116

Mackintyre, Daniel 16
Macy, Henry 119
  Joseph 119
Mahony, Patrick 95
Makay, Daniel 94
Malone, Lewis 98,112
Mandevel, _____ 32
Manderville, Cornelius 20,26(2),
    38,43,56,58,68,77,79,96,99,
    101,102,107,110,114
  David 26,58,77,79,84,86,90,
    96-99,101,102,104,110-114,

Manderville Continued
  David Continued, 120,124
  David C. 55,59
  Davin 43
Manship, Aaron 108(2),124
  Charles 124,125,126
  John 59
  Sarah 108(2)
Marler, James 118
Marine, Jonathon 40,48,75,79,89
Marshall, _____ 87
  Adam 23,24,26,82
Masine, Jonathan 72
Mason, _____ 13,17,40,42,45
  Charles 42,43,46
  Elizabeth 71,103
  Jas. 56
  John 66,69,103
  Joseph 8,12,37,48,50,103
  Michael 42,60,75,77
  Thomas D. 125
Mathews, George 114
Matthews, Joel 114
Mauris (Morris?), William 72
Maxwell, Joseph 117
May, John 121
  Matthew 121
  Paul 121
  Pleasant H. 127
  Wm. 121
Mayes, John 20,47
Mcrae, Daniel 116
Meekin, _____ 76
Meekins, Jonathan 68,81(2),93,115
    (2),118
Megee, Celia 123
  Dicey 123
  Elizabeth 123
  Hartwell 123
  James 114,123
  John 122,123
  Margaret 125
  Selah 122
Melone, Lewis 115
Mendenhall, Betty 117
  John 117
Merchison, Edward 117
Merine, Jona'n. 85
  Jonathan Jr. 120
Michael, Wm. 120
Mickins, Jonathan 93
Miles, Francis 120,121
  Jesse 121
  James 119
  John 121,123
Miller, Abner 86,93(2),102,115(2)
  Sarah 115,126
Mills, Brown 39
  Wm. Henry 19,33,38
Mims, _____ 71
Mitchel(l), Goodwin 122
  Jno. 25,37,57
  John 30,36,37,47,58,60,62
  Lewis 113
  Smith E. 44
  William 125
Mixon, Buen 31
  Merida 123
  William 52,53(2),56,61,86

140

Quick Continued
  Levi 117,126
  Levi Jr. 126
  Quillar 16
  Solomon 49,84,92,117
  Thomas 6,77,117
  Thomas Jr. 122

Rabon, James 59
Rankins, Duncan 125
Ratcliff, Wm. 9,23,24,38,39,41
Ratliff, Clothier 58,60,61
  William 45,77
Raybon, Abraham 69(2)
Rayborn, Abraham 66
Rayburn, Ann 96
Rayfield, Thomas 83
Red, Joseph 9,12
Reed, James 36,47,52,55,63,72,
  102
  John 103
  Rob 6
  Robert 35
Reid, James 28,30,61
  Nancy 61
  Will 3
Rials, Jesse 119
Rice, John 122
Rigdon, Ephraim 45
Robertson, D. 2,87
  Deliesseline 84
  Drury 4,11,13,15,18,19(2),20,
    21,28(2),32,35,39,41,41-43,
    45,46,57,58,61,63,68,71,79,
    88,90-93,95,96,98,100,103,
    105(2),107,109,110,113,115,
    117(2),120-122,126
  Jepthah 125,126
  Leggett 128
  Legitt 126
  Luke 19,117,121
  Thomas 122
  Wm. 33,41,66,70,71,97,100,102
Roe, Edward 35,53,72,82,106(2),
  114,117
  John 114
  Joseph 52,72,82(2),106(2)
Rogers, Benj. 83,86,88,90(2),
  95,98,99,101,102,106,107,
  110,112
  John 113(2),119,120,122(2)
  N. 96
  Nicholas 113
Roll(?), Edwd. 97
Rolo, Elizth 3
Roper, Jeremiah 78
Rothmahler, Eras. 86
Rous, Cornelius 22
  John 22
Rowe, Edward 63
  Joseph 63
Ryals, Jesse 111
Rye, Solomon 119

Sanders, Elizabeth 35,36,38,43
Saunders, Nathaniel 16,50
Scipper, John 117
Scizm, _____ 70
Scott, _____ 74
  Thomas G. 26,45,46

Scott Continued
  Wm. 11
Scotts, Winny 7
Seally, Thomas 92
Seals, William 119
Sealy, Thomas 24
Self, Parish 66
Seizm, Stephen 82
Seneath, _____ 64,70
Sewat, Benj. 123
Shackelford, John 86,88,89,95
Shanks, George 110
Shepherd, William 39,52
Sheras, Alex 18
Shitefield, Geo. B. 125
Shoemake, Sampson 31,33
Silivan, Daniel 31,61
Sims, Edmund 87
Sister, Joseph 61
  William 22
Skipper, Silas 84
Slay, Isha 106
  Mary 106
  Thomas 106
  Wm. 106
Smart, James 1,9,17,70,75,77
Smith, _____ 26,45,68,78,80,81
  Alexander 23(2),24,26,27,30,38,48,
    51,56,59,60,62,65(2),68,123
  Andrew 92,94
  Backter 97
  Bartee 79
  Baxter 72,98
  Charles M. 126
  Edward 5,7,14,19,20,22,23(2),24,
    26,27,39,42,45,50-52,62,70,84,
    98
  Frederick 20,98
  Geo. 29,56,57,63,72,83,120
  Harbert 78
  Herbert 60,67,93
  Hubbard 107
  James 64,85,121
  John 123,125
  Millington 97,98
  Peter 6,25,27,45,46,60,62
  Peter Jr. 27(2),29
  Samuel 55
  Wm. 18,24,62,76,118,123
Smithhart, Darby 51,52(2)
  Jno. 63
  Jno. Jr. 66
  John 61,62,68,73,76
Snead, Daniel 91
  Israel 84,85,86,90
  Iarael 77
  Samuel 95
Snoden, Aaron 29,45,54,57,60,63,
  69,80,100
Snowden, _____ 17,33,76,77,80,101
  Aaron 68,73(2),81,82,87,89,90,91,
    100
Soloman, _____ 20,70
  Levi 62,66(2),71
Sowles, Gideon 51
Sparks, Danl. 2,4,9,15,17-19,20,31,
  33,36-38,43
  Daniel 3,6,19,20,22,23,38,41-43,
    45-52,55,59,75,83
  Martha 42,46

Sparks Continued
  Samuel 7,8,11(2),12(2),18,27,
    29-35,41,43,45,48,51-43,55,
    57,60,66,68,70,71,83,122
Spears, James 3,8,15,29,33,48,
    53,57,63,68,73,86,104,115
Spedger, Wm. 21
Speed, John 2
Spencer, Elijah 127
Spiller, James 74
Sproles(?), Gideon 50
Stackey, Nathan 117
Stafford, Esther 29
  Jarvis 63,68,73,79,90,108
  Rabell 91
  Revel 95
  Zerababel 25,26,28
Standard, Wm. 18,24,25,33
Stanley, Lands 58
Stanton, Geo. 23,63,72
  Richd. 23
Stapleton, William 123
Steagel, Bolton 121
Steed, Griffin 120
Stenson, Richard 26
Stephens, Ann 7,15,66,69,71,74,
    81,121
  Francis 100
  Hubard 3(2),7,8
  Hubbert 64
  James 88
  Jesse 72
  John 60
  John W. 78
  Margaret 71
  Thomas 7,9,13,15,17,66,69,72,
    74,78,121
Stevens, _____ 43
  Ann 67,95,112
  Hubart 18
  Hubbard 23,45
  Hubbart 20,47,52,55(2)
  Jesse 40,61
  John 33,36
  John Washington 61,62
  Pearce 20,112
  Silas 51
  Thos. 15,30,39,44-46,52,67
Steward see Stewart
Steward, Charles 100
  Charles Anslee 49
  Charles Augustus 43
  David 8,12,56,64,75,83,97,115
  Grady(?) 93
  Hardy 17,53
  Jno. 11
  John 8
  L.E. 128
  Wm. 61,72
Stewart, Charles A. 37,38,39
  Chs. F. 125
  David 44,89,106,111,116,119,
    121
  Hardy 79,84
Stinson, _____ 66
  Richard 21,26,27,43,45,47(2),
    58,60(2),62,65(2),74,77,79,
    80,81(2)
Stocker, John Jones G. 9
Strickland, Jacob 127

Strother, Charles 113,115(2)
  Charles S. 127
  Geo. 15,16
  Geo. Jr. 119
  Lucy 115
  William 62,89,99,115
Stroud, Elizabeth 27,46
  Isam 9,22,46,56,69
  Isham 66
  Jno. 56
  John 8,61,72
Stubbs, Alexander 126
  Benjamin 126
  David 124
  James 8,33(2),35,48,53,57,64,79,
    84,121,126(2)
  Jno. 19,34,51,98
  Jno. Jr. 8
  John 6,9,15-17,33,56,58,117,118,
    124,126
  Lewis 24,30,35,66,76,108,109,111,
    113,121
  Lewis E. 128
  Mary 98
  Peter 116
  Silas 124,126
  Thomas 68,76,90,105,116,122,123
  William 11,24,32,45,47,48,64,66,
    67,83,93,116
Stucky, Nathan 114,117
Studivent, Lucretia 62
Sturges, William 117
Stuty, Isaiah 58
Sullivan, Danel 85
Summerlin, Isaac 29,79
  Thos. 48
  Thos. Jr. 22,29,35
Summertine, Thos. 8
Summons, Detinue P. 15
Sumrall, Isaac 67,72
  Thomas 68(2)
  Thomas Jr. 68
Sutckey, Nathan 120
Sutton, John 22,29,48
Sweat, Ephraim 125
  Gilbert 123
  Solomon 123
Swinton, Alex 34
Syllivan, John 68

Tarlton, Abner 125
Taylor, _____ 20,40,42,95
  Arch. 87
  Archibald 88,92,94,95
  Capt. 43
  Joseph 68
Teague, John 29,68,73
Terral(1), _____ 80
  Edward 66,67,71,87,88,89
  Samu. 66,68(2),70(2),73,78,89,
    100,101,103
  William 102(2),105
Terrel(1), Dunston 62
  Edward 56
  Jno. 9
  John 114(2),121,122,124,127
  Lewis 127
  Martha 127
  Samuel 23,40,48,50,60,62,98,114
Terril(1), Ann 6

Watson Continued
  Mary 125
Way, John 116
  Peter 79
  William 117,119
Wear, James 77
Weatherly, Isaac 73,89,106,110,
    111,117
  Isaiah 104
  Leaven 68
  Leavin 73
  Thos. 68,76,81,90,106,111,117,
    119,120
Webb, Isaac 120
Webber, George 111
Webster, James 114,118
Welch, Daniel 1,49,50
  Henry 78,80
  James 72,76,78,80,115,120
  Mary 84,116
Welsh, James 93,105
West, Charles 92,95
Wetherley, Isaac 19,68
Whickear, H. 127
White, John 62,63(2)
Whitefield, George B. 126(2),
  William 88(2),103,106,108,109,
    111,112,118,120,121
Whitfield, George B. 125
  Mathew 5-8,12,14,17,25,47,54,
    57,58,60,62
  William 8(2),14,18,32,35,36,
    38,49,52,55(2),86,87
Whitehead, Arthur T. 124
Whirfield, Mathew 30
Whittingham, Garret 32
Whittington, Aphraim 73
  Barnet 6
  Bartholomew 11,20,38(2),41,
    48,83
  Burrel(l) 32,56,61,86,90
  Elizabeth 60,115,116
  Ephraim 6,56,63,68,79(2),80,
    85,86,87
  F. 59
  Francis 110,114(2),115,116,
    118(2),123
  Jarrett 38,81
  Jarrot 6
  Jno. 13
  John 2,3,127
  Mary 48
  Nathan 116
  Nathaniel 118,127
  Noah 122
  Penelope 81
  Richard 6,8,14,23,24,67
  Susannah 60
  William 98,102
Wickfield, George B. 123
Wiggins, Baker 115,116
Wilcuts, Thomas 117
Wilds, _____ 64,87
  George 7,63(2),72,75,89,90,
    93(2),112
  Jesse 7,8,23,40,43,48,51,56
    (2),57,60,62(2),76,77
  John M. 113
  Joshua 67
  Saml. 8,9,12,17,63,115

Wilds Continued
  Saml. Jr. 88,112,113
Wilks, John 65
Williams, _____ 73,74,77,80,95
  Ann 128
  Benjamin 34,66-68,71,73,78,79,92,
    93,96,107,113,119,120,128
  Berry 99
  Brummit 91
  Burgess 5,7,15,34,35,37,39
  Edward 100
  John 89(2)
  John Jefferson 128
  Joseph 120
  Mary 117
  Thos. 13,18,27,32,40,55,74
  Wm. 76,81(2),117
Williamson, Willis 43,53,59,68
Willing, Henry 68
Willis, Eli 124,126
  John 63
  Mathew 70
  Nancy 126
Willison, John 99
Willson, John 24
Wilson, James P. 14
  John 1,2,7,10,14,18,19,21,22,25,
    35,38,45,47,50,51,53,61,63,66-
    68,73,83,87,89,90,97-99,102,
    105-109,115
  Robert 68
  Wm. 22
Windfield, _____ 78,83,84
  Joel 17,18,21,23,28,43(2),49,51,
    52,54,87,88,94,95,107,110,111,
    113
  John 115
  Mary Marler 113
Windham, Jno. 18
  John 24,25,27,33,58,66,110(2),
    112,114
  Rachel 114,127
Winds, Samuel 127
  Thomas 127
Winfield, _____ 66
Wise, Drury 59
  Elinor 59
  James 31,45,47,51
  Joshua 67,71
  Mary 23
Wodkins, Isaiah 61
Wood, Isham 127
Woodley, Nancy 124
Woodward, Elisha 90,92,106,107
Woodruff, Simion 3,42
Wright, Benjamin 26
  Carney 1,3,6,8,10,12,14,16,18,20,
    22,23,25-27,32,35,38,42,45,47,
    48,56,58,69,73,98
  Edward 127
  James 116
  John 14,16,41,45,48,51,54
  John Jr. 38,39
  Jonathan 39,54
  Joseph 108,124,126
  Sarah 123
  William 98,108,124

Yeomans, Alfred 124
Yoe, James 67,75